HUMBUGS and HEROES

A Gallery of California Pioneers

By Richard H. Dillon

Bully Waterman (Privately Printed) (1956)

The Anatomy of a Library (Privately Printed) (1957)

Crusoes of Pitcairn Island (Privately Printed) (1957)

Conduct of the Modoc War (Privately Printed) (Editor) (1959)

Embarcadero (1959)

La Panza (Privately Printed) (1960)

The Gila Trail (Editor) (1960)

Shanghaiing Days (1961)

California Trail Herd (Editor) (1961)

The Hatchet Men (1962)

Meriwether Lewis: A Biography (1962)

J. Ross Browne: Confidential Agent in Old California (1965)

The Legend of Grizzly Adams (1966)

Perpetual Motion and Emotion (Privately Printed) (1966)

Fool's Gold (1967)

Wells Fargo Detective (1969)

A Cannoneer in Navajo Country (Editor) (1970)

Humbugs and Heroes (1970)

Burnt-Out Fires (1973)

Exploring the Mother Lode Country (1974)

Siskiyou Trail (1975)

Images of Chinatown (Privately Printed) (1976)

We Have Met The Enemy (1978)

High Steel (1979)

Great Expectations (1980)

Delta Country (1982)

HUMBUGS
and
HEROES

A Gallery of California Pioneers

BY RICHARD DILLON

Yosemite-DiMaggio, Oakland, California
1983

Humbugs and Heroes
Printing History and
Copyright Information

1970 Doubleday & Co.

1983 Yosemite-DiMaggio

Jacket Design by Jim Kingwell

First number below indicates Yosemite-DiMaggio Printing
1 2 3 4 5 6 7 8 9 10

ISBN 0-911819-00-2

Printed in the United States
by Braun-Brumfield, Inc.

*Dedicated
to the memory of
Charles Borden
of Spindrift Point, Marin County,
California*

PREFACE (1983)

It is good to see an old friend back again, especially after many years of absence. I am delighted to find my collective biography of pioneering Californians back in print. Although it was the product of a very substantial press-run by this country's largest trade book publisher, Doubleday, copies of *Humbugs* have remained elusive. As the Western Americana expert, Robert Hawley, proprietor of Ross Valley Books, Albany, California, has so often commented to me, "For a book consistently in demand, *Humbugs and Heroes* is exceptionally difficult to locate."

I would have liked the book to pass through various editions and remain in print for years but, alas, it was one of the lesser gods on Doubleday's enormous totem pole of publications that year (though of more significance than the how-to-raise goldfish manuals), so it utterly vanished after an indecent period of time. It did well enough, however—indeed, it sold out—so that I, at least, did not have to suffer the trauma of seeing copies "dumped" en masse, as is sometimes the fate even of fine books in this puzzling world of publishing, nor view them collecting dust for seeming eons on the remainder tables of Bonanza Inn Book Shop or Books, Inc.

My major regret, a dozen years ago, was that Doubleday's trade books people apparently failed to run across the hall with the manuscript, as I urged them, to alert the institutional (i.e., schools) department to push the title as "additional reading" for history and social science courses in California's schools.

I wrote the work as an adult book, to be sure, but I counted on the appeal of both its content and style to be just right for so-called "Y.A.'s" or young adults, and I was not wrong. However, there was no discernible marketing campaign with classrooms and school libraries as its special targets. Naturally, the book won quite a following among teachers and school librarians and their wards (after all, it was that *rara avis,* history that was fun to read) but, largely, the hard way—by word of mouth recommendation—much as was the case with my earlier (1966) *Legend of Grizzly Adams* for Coward, McCann.

Luckily, reviews in the media which were most often consulted by book-buying teachers and school librarians were as favorable as those in more general journals. True, Doyce Nunis, professor of history at USC, grumbled a bit in his *Library Journal* critique about the "balance," or rather the lack of it, in my choices. But his was a kindly review, over all. "The title is catchy," he wrote, "but misleading. The sub-title [*A Gallery of California Pioneers*] more accurately describes the book's contents. By my evaluation, I find that there are no more than half a dozen humbugs in the whole volume. And there are heroines, as well." I think that this was tongue-in-cheek grumpiness and that Professor Nunis did not really expect to find good guys and bad guys in a strict 50-50 ratio. But he may have been serious in his complaint of another imbalance, the shortage of female and non-WASP heroes. I included "only" five women, two blacks, two Chinese-Americans, one Japanese-American, two Indians and two Mexican-Americans in my sixty-three sketches. Better candidates for blame than myself would be the times themselves, if not the Indian Bureau, Immigration Service, and the Workingman's and Know Nothing Parties, etc., etc., all of which threw up obstacles to success by members of early California's ethnic minorities. Thanks to them and their ilk, the state was short on non-mainstream and non-male pioneers, at least in the shape of mountain men (mountain persons??), governors, soldiers, business moguls, even artists and writers. I did the best that I could to show the variety of people in early California while refusing, just as I would now, to indulge in games of artificial quotas and historical revisionism. These offer us a misleading—no, a false—picture of our history, on a par with the work of those editors of the Soviet Encyclopedia whose job it is to delete references to Party folk gone out of favor with the crowd currently in office.

The human errors of the past cannot be corrected now simply by the do-good hindsight of authors. I was, at the time that I wrote the manuscript in 1969, pretty well in front of others in giving women, *Issei,* blacks, *Mexicanos* and Sino-Americans the credit due them for their roles in building the state.

I stand behind my choices, still. I am proud of them. I have no apologies to make to Clio. Anyway, Dr. Nunis confessed in his review of *Humbugs* that "The general reader will find much to give him pleasure."

As for the American Library Association's *Booklist,* there were no quibbles by its reviewers, my professional peers. (I was then head of the Sutro Library in San Francisco, the history branch of the California State Library, and was only moonlighting as a freelance writer of popular American history.) They considered my choices to be "a strange mixture," but they stated that "The profiles are pithy, humorous and informative and, since they cover a wide range of California history, have more than local appeal." I particularly appreciated the pithiness plug since, modesty aside, I consider the book to be quite well written, not only a useful reference tool but a pleasant reading experience, to boot.

The syndicated Western Books Roundup by the Old Buckaroos, namely Washington D.C. bibliographer-critic Jeff Dykes and his *amigos,* reviewed my sketches in *American Book Collector* and other periodicals. They found them to be "snappy biographies" that not only provided interesting and entertaining reading but also proved "useful as a guide in sorting out California's heroes from its humbugs."

Richard Dillon

CONTENTS

vii

ix

INTRODUCTION

Governor Richard B. Mason should have declared California a disaster area on January 24, 1848. For Jim Marshall's discovery of gold that day in the South Fork of the American River blew open a bottomless Pandora's box whose lid has never since been found, much less closed.

Marshall's discovery loosed upon Mexico's old Pacific Coast province of Alta California a tidal wave of humanity which is still in flood and which, early, washed away a simple pastoral arcady which would have delighted Rousseau as much as it haunted Helen Hunt Jackson and Charles F. Lummis, who arrived on the scene not long after it was gone.

This *tsunami* of immigration was composed largely of common men in an uncommon area and time, but it also boasted a higher proportion of men of heroic mold than is usual in such movements of people. This is because of the curious and unique circumstances of California's rebirth. The settlement of the state immediately after 1848, unlike Arkansas or Indiana, was the result of a world-wide response to a call for adventurous argonauts to exploit an El Dorado, a land of gold. Prominent, too, in the wave of humanity were adventurers of another stripe—the humbugs, the frauds, impostors, and swindlers of all kinds who lusted for California gold. If they could not get gold, they were content with land. And if land was not to be had, they would find a profit in one way or another. Bret Harte sized up the founders of modern California darkly: "The less said about the motives of our pioneers the better; very many were more concerned with getting away from where they were than in going to any particular place."

Many diligent readers of Californiana have spent years trying to determine which of the state's major figures belong to the humbug category and which to the heroic. The volume in hand may serve as a (hopefully) lively source book, helpful in sorting out the many major figures of the state's long legend and short history, but it is not meant as a manual for instant-labelers. It may even add to the confusion but, at least, as an exercise in eclectic collective biography it reduces the number of Californians whose credentials must be examined before admission to a paper pantheon.

Many prominent politicians, military men, and captains—even colonels—of industry have been refused admission to this "haul" of fame even though they are customarily given refuge in history textbooks. This is because they flunk the rather stringent entrance examinations because of low interest-quotient scores. It is not enough to have rounded up great sums of money if the rounder has behaved in a dullish fashion in carrying out his financial coups. To balance the well known, certain little-known personalities—mountain men, artists, writers—have been memorialized. In some cases, this is virtually the first time they have found themselves in the pages of a book of collective biography. It is time they had their day.

Too many Americans, both readers and writers, are obsessed with an *idée fixe* that our historic figures must be either all-good or all-bad. This inflexibility of acceptance is probably the product of so many morality plays, especially Westerns, in our publishing, radio, TV, and movie programming. These are most likely, in turn, the crippled and inbred products of our New England Puritanism. Black and white are favorite colors in this area, with few or no intermediate shadings. Fundamentalists in biography insist not only on labeling absolutely but also in squeezing their subjects into one or the other pigeonholes marked *Good Guys* and *Bad Guys,* no matter how they have to distort, maim, and torture their captives. The people in this book are of all kinds. They are alike in only one respect—they are extra-ordinary. They are not ordinary but something "extra," something *out of the* ordinary.

None of the individuals selected for the pages of this book are supermen or demigods (a secondary definition of heroes, to be sure), but a considerable number do fit the less exclusive definition found in dictionaries—"Men of distinguished courage, either physical or moral." Perhaps a few genuine scoundrels will be found, too, among the humbugs as a kind of leavening. The reader will have to make up his mind as to whether any given subject is hero or humbug, incidentally; there are no obvious distinguishing marks. The profiles must be read throughout and a decision arrived at by the reader in each individual case.

Another shibboleth which deserves discarding is the idea that bad men and naughty women are, *ipso facto,* fascinating. This idea is a perfect humbug itself, for many thugs, road agents, prostitutes, *et al* are ruddy bores. A catalogue of such characters is a guaranteed soporific. Variety is the spice of biography as well as of life. Luckily, the pull of the West, which became irresistible to so many people in the States and all over the world, brought a great medley of types. Some were settled, some were rootless, but all dropped whatever they were doing, even if it was nothing, and headed for the sunset horizon.

The great English historian Thomas Macaulay claimed that the history of a country is best told as a record of the *lives* of its people, not in the form of a ledger of highfalutin trends and movements. A Yankee went him one better. Ralph Waldo Emerson stated flatly that there is no such thing as history, only biography. If such is the case then this book has great utility. If it helps to place in focus sixty-three men and women of the most rugged individuality who helped build California, it may offer a clue to the general course the state has been setting over the years. It is easy to see the various doglegs of the passage but the whole journey is far from being charted.

Many of the persons included in this gallery have never been honored by civic center statuary or road map place names. Yet they are all worthy of recognition, in their individualized ways. Appreciation of some of them for their peculiar contributions will seem long overdue to the reader. So tightly drawn are the drapes of nineteenth-century textbook history that many a good man and woman is fated to pass unnoticed by Clio, the Muse of history. Other figures are seemingly well-known but have been so pedestaled, bronzed, and bespattered with the guano of Main Street's pigeons that they have become only effigies, not real men, in books as well as in public squares. John A. Sutter and John C. Frémont are two examples which virtually hurl themselves to mind.

A large number of the men chronicled here were classed as failures by Victorian standards and would probably suffer a same fate by Dun & Bradstreet. But most of them were either spectacular failures or not really failures at all. The fault in the latter case is due to the parallax or myopia of many historians and biographers, not to the lack of ability in the Californians. Thomas Jefferson died land-poor, a failure by chamber-of-commerce measuring tapes. Meriwether Lewis left an estate of about nine dollars. John Paul Jones's grave was forgotten and lost for a hundred years. Were these men failures?

What makes a person a Californian in terms of this book's selection? Not birth, necessarily, nor even long years of residence in the state, exclusively. The region is so young and has profited so much by immigration to it from what smug Californians might call underdeveloped states that even sojourners who have made a major contribution to California are included. Robert Louis Stevenson was in the state only a short time, but he took it to his heart and has been, in turn, adopted so completely by literate Californians that he must be among those covered. "RLS" is as much of a state historical monument as Calaveras Big Trees or Jack London's Ranch. The criterion for inclusion is not the candidate's birthplace or the chronological totting up of the duration of his stay in the state but rather the effectiveness of the individual in changing California, for the better or worse, by his presence.

The values in this book are different from those of some textbooks and earlier works of collective biography where the mere acquisition of power, property, or prestige was sufficient criterion for inclusion. While not disclaiming the validity of the traditional and prudential virtues and such American attributes as hard work, cleanliness, godliness, and pluck, nor patronizing middle-class mores, there is room here for creative persons of a different bent, compassionate people, and free spirits. The basic drive of none of these individuals, of course, is economic but ethical or artistic. Hence the appearance of Mary Austin, Galen Clark, Andy Furuseth, and Grace Hudson in this volume. Many men and women similar to this quartet, often loners and usually not understood or accepted in their day because they never met a payroll, have made California immeasurably richer by their presence. You can meet them here.

Richard Dillon
Mill Valley
St. Swithin's Day, 1969

Humbug: A person that practices deception; an impostor, a fraud.
(*A New English Dictionary* . . . , i.e., the O.E.D.)

Hero: A man eminent for bravery; a man of the highest class in any respect.
(Dr. Samuel Johnson, *A Dictionary of the English Language*)

HUMBUGS and HEROES

A Gallery of California Pioneers

GRIZZLY ADAMS

(*1812–60*)

On the façade of a government building in Sacramento is carved the well-known maxim of California—"Bring Me Men to Match My Mountains." Massachusetts, in sending Grizzly Adams, might be accused of contributing a man who was more than a match for the whole rugged Sierra. This mystery man, who was known incorrectly for a hundred years as James Capen Adams, was one of those rare men who do what myriads threaten to do—"chuck it all,"—turn one's back on civilization for a life in the wilderness.

Adams had fled the humdrum life of a New England cobbler in 1849. But misfortune dogged his steps in California. He explained his decision to become a hermit in these words: "I was dead broke. The lawyers and judges . . . contrived to rob me of everything I possessed. . . . I was disgusted with my fellow-men and their hypocrisy, their betrayal of confidence, their treachery and fraud." For some reason, Adams hid his identity for the rest of his life. It was a short life for John Adams, alias James Capen Adams (actually his brother's name). Born in Medway, Massachusetts, on October 22, 1812, he died nearby in Charlton on October 25, 1860. But

1

in the eight years he spent in the California mountains he had enough adventure to hold a man for a century. Among all of the mountain men of the West, Grizzly was unique. No one, before or after Adams's time, was able to rival him as a tamer of wild animals. Small wonder he was called the Wild Yankee. His closest friend was a burly grizzly bear, Ben Franklin by name. When he was asked to explain his strange power over wild beasts, he just said that it was because he was the "hardest" animal of the lot.

Adams, making a semipermanent camp in the Sierra, began trapping animals in 1852. He had a bedroll, two fine hunting rifles, a battered wagon, and two oxen. These beasts were so feeble that he claimed he had to lift them by their tails just to get them on their feet. As for the wagon, he said that it would not even hang together until he had soaked it for a week. But, after beginning as a deer hunter and a trapper of small animals, he graduated to the taking of *Ursus horribilis* —the dreaded California grizzly, the most dangerous animal on the continent. And not only did he take them alive, but he tamed them, made friends of them, used them to carry his packs and, from time to time, rode on their backs!

In the process of becoming the greatest wild animal tamer the West has ever known, Grizzly Adams collected considerable scar tissue. One time, he was about to slit a downed bear's throat for good measure, when the touch of the blade revived the beast. The animal, a huge female, leaped upon him and sank her teeth into his flesh. Adams never forgot that painful moment which came so close to being his last: "The exquisite pain left me nothing but an instinctive sense of the necessity for prompt action. We were both down on the ground, together, now. Her teeth and claws were both at work. I was desperately struggling to get my arms free for offensive measures but, growing exhausted with my loss of blood, I was not at first successful. At length, I twisted myself around underneath her and, catching her with my left hand by the great goatee which hung under her mouth, I plunged my knife into her heart with my right and worked it briskly 'round to insure its fatal operation. Her jaws opened, her claws relaxed her hold and, after one or two more spasmodic endeavours to mutilate me, she rolled over and expired." Bloody and temporarily crippled, the boastful Adams still crowed, "I was worth twenty men, yet. . . . I felt like Alexander, sated with victory and wishing another foe worthy of my prowess to engage."

Adams opened a Mountaineer Museum on Clay Street in San Francisco, where his wild animal menagerie of bears, wolves, mountain lions, elk, deer, and other animals soon brought him fame. He went on the stage locally and in 1860 sailed for New York, where he entered a partnership with Phineas T. Barnum in another menagerie.

Adams and Barnum made a great pair. The latter dyed some park-bench pigeons gold and, after showing them to Grizzly, asked him why he had not brought some of these golden California pigeons with his other animals. The Californian fell for the bait beautifully. He sputtered, "Rare birds! Indeed! Why, they are just as common in California as any other pigeon. I could have brought a hundred of them from San Francisco if I had thought of it. They are *so* common there. I have eaten them in pigeon pies hundreds of times and have shot them by the thousands."

When the pigeons' feathers grew out, Adams realized that he had been humbugged by Barnum. He swore revenge. The chance came when his health began to fail as a result of bad head wounds he had received in one of his hand-to-claw combats with a grizzly. He asked for the loan of a new hunting coat of Barnum's, promising to return it when he had done with it. Adams never left his sickbed, once he took to it, except for the short trip to the cemetery. But he gave his wife strict orders to bury him in it, since he was not through with it. The irascible, eccentric mountain man died with a chuckle on his lips, saying, "Won't Barnum open his eyes when he finds I have humbugged him by being buried in his new hunting dress? Barnum agreed to let me have it until I have done with it. I am determined to fix his flint this time. He'll never see that hunting dress again!"

It is difficult to measure the "importance" of Grizzly Adams. He was one of a kind when it came to taming wild animals. He left few traces behind him. He built nothing. But his life is more than just a grand story. He played a role in the creation of an institution which has made living in cities somewhat more bearable. This is no small thing. The institution was the zoo. Adams led the way with his Mountaineer Museum. It was followed by Woodward's Gardens in San Francisco, and the "lineal descendant" today is the Fleishhacker Zoo. New York's great zoological garden in the Bronx owes something to Grizzly Adams too. On June 23, 1860, *Wilke's Spirit of the Times* editorialized in favor of zoological gardens for the public: "We trust the project for the establishment of zoological gardens in Central Park of this metropolis will be prosecuted with vigor. . . . Just look at the collection made by the old Rocky Mountain [sic] hunter, Adams, and then see what might be done with means and science."

MARY AUSTIN

(1868–1934)

An unhappy life, or an unhappy childhood, at least, is reckoned by many to be good for an author. Writing becomes a catharsis, a therapy. It is as meaningful to the writer as it is satisfying to the reader. This may explain the success of Mary Austin, born Mary Hunter in Carlinville, Illinois, in 1868. Her father died when she was ten years old; her favorite sister died that same year; her own marriage was a disaster; her only daughter was mentally retarded. To culminate this series of misfortunes, Mary's mother never paid the slightest attention to her writing success and blamed the child's mental condition on her.

Like Bret Harte and many other California writers (some critics would throw in John Steinbeck and William Saroyan), Mary Austin wrote her best works early in her career. However, rather late in her writing life she returned to her knowing treatment of man's oneness with nature in *The Land of Journey's Ending*. But even the writer herself, when a *grande dame* in New York, finally came to realize that she had put her best work not into the ambitious novels and plays of her "prime," but into the minor classic *The Land of Little Rain* and her other early books about the California desert country.

Mary Austin came to California in 1888, homesteading a drouth-blasted 160 acres of sage and sand at the end of the San Joaquin Valley, where it gives up the ghost below Tejon Pass and the Grapevine area of today's Highway 99. She almost starved in her one-room shack, but she learned about plant and animal lore and the legends and folk tales of the people. Although she had started writing at the age of ten and had become school poet and literary editor at little Blackburn College, her first published work appeared in California's *Overland Monthly* in 1892, thanks to the help of California poet Ina Coolbrith. Mary put her new knowledge into an almost forgotten book which deserves to be remembered. This volume, *The Flock,* preceded her very popular *The Land of Little Rain.* In the latter work she sloughed off all of the derivative and imitative influences which she had picked up in college and in her years of wide reading. For the first time, she wrote directly out of her own character. No one, before her or since, has so surely understood the brooding and aloof spell of the desert or expressed it so well in print. The uncorrupted corners of Southern California fascinated her as much as the jerry-built and tasteless expanse of Los Angeles repelled her. Better than anyone else she saw the relationship between the desert and its people, both red and white. She did so by studying the most minute details of dry-country life, particularly after she moved east of the Sierra Nevada with her husband, Stafford Austin, in 1891. There, in the lonely Owens Valley, Mary Austin could put together the track of a mouse, the rhythm of Indian drums, and the creaking of twenty-mule team harness to capture the secretive moods of the desert. Her desert prose was crisp and clean like its subject and totally unlike the obscure and puzzling style of her "loftier" works done in the East. These latter are now not only dated but virtually unreadable, while her Owens Valley paragraphs remain attractive and even poetic:

"From the height of a horse you look down to clean spaces in a shifty yellow soil, bare to the eye as a newly sanded floor. Then, as soon as ever the hill shadows begin to swell out from the sidelong ranges, come little flakes of whiteness fluttering at the edge of the sand. By dusk, there are tiny drifts in the lee of every strong shrub, rosy-tipped corollas as riotous in the sliding mesa wind as if they were real flakes shaken out of a cloud, not sprung from the ground on wiry three-inch stems. They keep awake all night, and all the air is heavy and musky sweet because of them."

Mary Austin was most at home in such Owens Valley towns as Lone Pine, Bishop, and Independence. There she enjoyed "the smell of sheep and claret in the streets." Her portraits of desert folk are memorable, such as the vignettes of the "proper" townswomen who came in committee to chide her for her impropriety in dancing with the Indians and giving the Oriental cooks of the valley a layer cake on Chinese New Year. Some of her descriptions remain haunting "pictures in the mind" as her account of the Mormon Danite, or Avenging Angel, who had to pay for his part in the Mormon-Indian massacre of emigrants at Mountain Meadows (1857) by unceasing vigilance. The "Saint" had to arrange his bed, cookstove, table, and other cabin furnishings so that he always had his back to a blank wall, to forestall a surprise attack and revenge by some friend or relative of the murdered Arkansans. Once Mary Austin described having to jump down from the Mojave stage to bend over a dying man, victim of a shooting scrape, and to offer a prayer for the fellow who was bound for a secret and unmarked grave. Another time she depicted with photographic clarity the lonely scene at Red Rock Cañon where an itinerant

7

priest was saying mass before a rude altar, his entire congregation being three shepherds kneeling amid their stupid and bewildered sheep.

Completely won over as she was by the desert (and by Carmel, where she pioneered the literary circle there with Jack London and George Sterling), Mary Austin turned her back on California after her estrangement from her husband and the suicide of several friends, including Sterling. She lived in New York and London and was lionized as one of the most popular and important female writers of America. Finally, she returned to the desert she loved, but, unable to bear California's painful memories, chose Santa Fe as her residence. There in the old Spanish capital of New Mexico, the second-oldest city in the United States, she dedicated herself to the preservation of Indian ways and Pueblo arts and crafts until her death in 1934.

LUCKY BALDWIN

(1828–1909)

According to tradition, there was not a single wet eye at the funeral of Elias Jackson (Lucky) Baldwin in 1909, not a solitary sob of grief. If legend is accurate, those present were there for the sole purpose of verifying the happy fact that they were rid of Southern California's most ruthless speculator and most notorious millionaire.

Actually, Lucky Baldwin had friends, but they were far outnumbered by his enemies. By the time of his death he was legendary as a gambler in business and as a libertine in love. The editor of *The California Turf,* pressed to say a kind word about Baldwin, finally came up with the fact that Lucky had never thrown a horse race. Controversial, contradictory, and hated by whole platoons of business rivals, E. J. Baldwin was a California phenomenon. With ten or twenty million dollars in property, he was usually broke. He was chased by women as much, probably, as he chased them. He was so arrogant about these affairs that when a woman filed a complaint against him for his bad conduct, he responded with the plea that any woman who came near him must be considered to have been warned in advance, such was his reputation.

The man who would be classed as California's most rascally promoter and developer was born in Hamilton, Ohio, on April 31, 1828, the son of a preacher. As a child, he demonstrated a taste for mischief. He never lost this appetite. When Elias was six, his father moved the family to Indiana, where the boy enjoyed hard work and rough fare on a farm. The first *real* money he ever made, two hundred dollars, when he was eighteen, came from a bet on his own horse in a South Bend race. He used it to finance a honeymoon, eloping with his girl. But he settled down to hard work to support his wife, supplementing his scanty income with the profits of some shrewd horse trading. Thanks to his "luck" (actually, skill and business acumen), he ran up a nest egg of two thousand dollars from this cob swapping and took his bride to Valparaiso, Indiana, where he set up a grocery store and saloon. It was the first of a series of businesses he would own, usually hotels or groceries, but by 1853 he was bored with this humdrum kind of life and took off for golden California.

The crossing of the plains was uneventful until Baldwin's party passed Salt Lake City; then it was attacked by Indians. Lucky was always convinced that it was a Mormon-instigated raid, with Brigham Young's own brother (!), in disguise, leading the savages. Although Baldwin was already pegged as a gambler, he was actually very thorough in exploring business opportunities. He decided that Hangtown (Placerville) did not offer enough opportunities, so he went on to San Francisco, where he immediately made his mark by buying a hotel, holding it for thirty days and improving it and then selling it for a net gain of five thousand dollars. He profited by the lesson of the fires which destroyed a wooden San Francisco, several times over, and invested in a brickyard. He put his profits into sand-lot real estate, hiring armed men to chase off the squatters who pre-empted them. Adolph Sutro tutored

Baldwin in proper mining speculation and Lucky made big money out of the Comstock strike in Nevada.

In New York, Lucky Baldwin had been impressed by the posh Fifth Avenue Hotel. He determined to give San Francisco a fine hotel and he started it in 1873. In time, the Baldwin Hotel, at Market and Powell Streets, would rival the Palace Hotel itself, and the adjacent Baldwin Theater would welcome such talent as Modjeska, Edwin Booth, Lillian Russell, and John Drew. On his first visit to Southern California, he discovered the San Gabriel Valley and bought six thousand acres, choosing the old Mexican Rancho Santa Anita as his home ranch, or headquarters. In acquiring this great acreage, Baldwin learned a thing or two about business. He offered Harris Newmark, whose firm owned Rancho Santa Anita, $150,000 in cash from a tin box which he carried. Without blinking an eye, the latter refused and asked $175,000. Baldwin shook his head and went away. Eventually, having thought it over, he returned and took $175,000 out of the box. But Newmark said, quietly, that the price was now $200,000. After Lucky protested, he added that, next week, it would be $225,000. Baldwin stomped out of the office but shortly returned, grumbling, to pay the sum.

On the other hand, Baldwin knew how to make the grand gesture too. When the Bank of California tottered during a business recession and lines of depositers thronged the bank to withdraw their funds, Lucky made a noisy entrance, bearing two heavy bags of coins. He had the teller clink them into shiny stacks and announce, loudly, that Lucky Baldwin, president of the Pacific Stock Exchange, had just deposited $40,000 in gold in the bank, which already held his $2,000,000. The run stopped; the lines dwindled. Confidence was restored and the bank was soon back on its financial feet.

At the Centennial Exposition in Philadelphia, Mark Twain

persuaded Lucky to buy a $25,000 Tiffany clock for his hotel and Baldwin also laid in expensive carpeting, furniture, and pianos. The Baldwin Hotel opened in 1877—just in time for a depression. It was one of Baldwin's greatest monuments, but it was never really a paying proposition, as was the Santa Anita Ranch. Although business was slow in his palace of crystal, leather, silver, and mahogany, he did not pull in his horns but, instead, built another hostelry, the Tallac Hotel, at Lake Tahoe. Meanwhile, a wholesale liquor firm attached his hotel safe and his help was on strike for unpaid wages. When the hotel's gas bills got too high, Lucky built his own gas works and cleared five hundred dollars a month from it after supplying his hotel's needs. But he was tight, and he liked to try to stretch his money by getting free legal advice in the hotel bar from prominent attorneys staying in the Baldwin. They went along with him, and when his hotel bills arrived they countered with bills for the same sum for their legal advice.

Luckily, the Santa Anita Ranch made money on its vineyards, orchards, and truck gardens. It produced two thousand pounds of butter a week, alone. Much of the food, wine, and brandy produced went to the Baldwin Hotel. Baldwin gave the Santa Fe Railroad a right of way through his property with the proviso that any passenger train must stop on signal at his station. When a ticket agent once told him that the through train he hoped to ride would not stop at Santa Anita, Lucky began composing a telegram to his major-domo to get two hundred men to work tearing up the Santa Fe tracks on his ranch. The conductor was persuaded to stop and let Lucky alight at Santa Anita.

Baldwin now became one of Southern California's early real estate promoters. He subdivided his property, and the towns of Sierra Madre, Monrovia, and Arcadia began to grow. One line of Lucky's ad copy may suggest the whole catalogue: "Epidemics, diseases, poisonous insects, tornadoes, cyclones, earthquakes and thunderstorms are practically unknown." When a customer balked at paying two hundred dollars an acre for land, Lucky snorted and said, "Hell! We're giving away the land; we're selling the *climate!*"

Because of his business deals and amorous escapades, Baldwin was often the target of lawsuits. But he became a different kind of target in 1883, when a woman whom he had dropped shot him. The Los Angeles *Times* depicted her as the victim of Baldwin's heartlessness. Horace Bell's little *Porcupine* called him "Beast Baldwin" and his home "Baldwin's Harem." But Lucky was completely indifferent to public opinion. He just rode out the lawsuits, which only increased his reputation as a Don Juan.

At racing, Lucky was a great success, his nags even winning the bizarre chariot contests of the Tournament of Roses. But he was land-poor, that is, possessed of a lot of real estate but short of hard cash, and although he had three Derby winners in his stables, he announced in 1889 that he was considering retirement from the turf. He was so hard up that he paid his Mexican ranch hands in orders at his company store, arguing them out of their demands for cash and keeping them in something like peonage. He won the reputation of never paying a debt unaccompanied by a court judgment.

The turn of the century brought bad luck to Baldwin. He was involved, at age sixty-one, in another sordid lawsuit and the sister of the woman involved took a shot at him. She barely clipped a wisp of his hair. On November 23, 1898, the Baldwin Hotel burned. And Lucky had not a penny of insurance on it. He said, "By gad, I'm not licked yet" and tried to set up a saloon and gambling house in gold rush Alaska but failed.

Elias J. Baldwin returned home and, somehow, managed to juggle his debts and mortgages so that he retained possession of his Santa Anita property, working ten hours a day and living on corn bread and milk. He was still kicking and scuffling to maintain his position when death came at eighty-one years, on March 1, 1909. A new rash of lawsuits broke out over his ten-million-dollar estate, all very much in keeping with Lucky Baldwin's stormy career, and before they were settled (Baldwin must have smiled and uttered a "By gad!" in his grave), the ten million dollars had swollen to twenty million dollars and when oil was discovered in the Baldwin Hills, Elias J. Baldwin was turned into a dead Croesus.

It is easy, even today, to sense the baronial style in which Lucky Baldwin lived by simply visiting part of his old estates in the beautiful Los Angeles State and County Arboretum. There in Arcadia, not far from Santa Anita Racetrack, are preserved not only Baldwin's gardens (much enhanced, now), his lagoon, carriage house, gingerbreaded "Queen Anne Cottage" and stable and barn, jammed with rolling stock of another era, but the squawking, strutting descendants of his flock of beautiful peacocks. Baldwin preserved the old adobe house of pioneer Hugo Reid, who held the property earlier, and it is there to see, too. Students of botany and history will learn much from the grounds, exhibits, and library at this vast arboretum—a magnificent "breathing space" for a megalopolitan area which needs to breathe, badly.

HUBERT HOWE BANCROFT

(*1832–1918*)

Without chroniclers to record their exploits, California would have no heroes at all. Thus, historians are the most necessary of all evils. Oddly, the greatest of the state's historians—its latter-day Thucydides—was not a professor but a businessman and amateur historian. He was Hubert Howe Bancroft, a brilliant Ohioan from Granville who was able to read the Bible by the time he was three years old. However, instead of going to college when he grew up, he turned to the business world. After working as a bookseller in Buffalo, he migrated to California, where he tried mining briefly but soon returned to merchandising. In 1858 he founded the bookselling and publishing firm of H. H. Bancroft & Company in San Francisco.

Bancroft's moment of decision came in 1859, when he was about to publish a Pacific Coast guide. He began to buy all of the books which he could find on California and the Far West. Bancroft became an omnivorous and ravenous bibliophile. Before he stopped collecting, many years later, he had sixty thousand volumes. These he sold to the University of California, where, today, they form the nucleus of the Berke-

15

ley campus's Bancroft Library, the greatest collection in the world on the history of the American Far West.

But Bancroft's greatest work was as a writer and editor, rather than as a library builder. A cartoon in a California magazine once showed him with more arms than an Indian god. This was a tribute to his prodigious output of books. His name, eventually, was on the title page of every one of the thirty-nine large volumes of Pacific Coast history which his firm produced. His method was to hire a corps of researchers, editors, and writers to break down the writing of history into a number of fairly simple operations. Some collected old books, manuscripts, pictures; others indexed this material; still others pioneered the modern field of oral history by going out into the field to interview old-timers for Bancroft. By the time he was done, H. H. Bancroft had written (with the help of up to fifty colleagues at a time) an excellent history of America from Panama to Alaska and from the Rockies to Pacific tidewater. He became the Henry Ford of historians, mass producing history with assembly-line techniques. And yet it was surprisingly good history; a body of material which has not yet been equaled.

Apparently, Bancroft planned to rewrite every line of narrative turned out by his hired hands. But the task proved to be too much for even his monumental talents and energies. Perhaps because he had only one or two writers on his payroll who could be considered trained historians or professional authors, Bancroft saw no need to give them credit for the volumes which were really the product of their labors, not his. (Bancroft here confused the rights of publishing with the rights of authorship.) Eventually, several of his colleagues demanded recognition, but Bancroft refused to give them so much as a coauthor's by-line. Criticism of the historian and publisher now changed from gentle cartoons to harsh accusations by Ambrose Bierce and others of the press that Bancroft was exploiting talented people at low wages and, in fact, purloining their brains.

Hubert Bancroft's puritanical upbringing in Ohio had persuaded him that industry—hard work—was *the* great virtue and that sloth was a cardinal sin. As a result, he worked harder at whatever he did than any two or three other ordinary men. His unwillingness to give due credit to his aides at the same time that he made great demands upon them was his one great blind spot. But if he was a hard—and seemingly selfish —taskmaster, he drove himself far harder than anyone in his employ. The urge to write became a compulsion. He once said, "I would strike at once for the highest, brightest, mark before me. . . . History-writing I conceived to be among the highest of human occupations and this should be my choice." And how he worked! Although he complained, "I have tried many occupations and there is no kind of work, I venture to say, so wearing as literary labor," he normally got up at seven, breakfasted at seven-thirty, and worked at a stand-up desk, like Palmerston or Hemingway, from eight to one in the afternoon. After lunch, he exercised or devoted his time to recreation, stealing an hour for work just before tea or dinner. Then, in the evening, he would stand at his high desk for another four hours to close out a working day of a minimum of ten hours of production.

Bancroft's *Works* were well received upon publication but his cavalier dismissal of the efforts of his colleagues soon tarnished his public image. His fame was further tarnished (unjustly) when the Society of California Pioneers drummed him out of the society for daring to tell the plain, unvarnished, and iconoclastic truth about Frémont, Sutter, and the rogues of the Bear Flag Republic. Bancroft, in comfortable retirement in Walnut Creek, shrugged off the yapping of critics and dismissed the Pioneers as "the Society of Incurables." For many years, the Bancroft Library was his monument. Of late, however, the greatness of his writing and editing of between forty and sixty volumes has come to be appreciated. The heart of his thirty-nine volumes of Pacific Coast history consists of eleven works on California. Whatever the credit due his helpers, these eleven volumes are a fantastic monument to a man who essayed the task of writing the detailed history of California in 8800 pages and 4,500,000 words.

PHINEAS BANNING

(1830–85)

Los Angeles was a drowsy cow town marooned on the
coastal plain some twenty miles from tidewater when Phineas
Banning arrived on the scene in 1851. He did not look it
(there was nothing wild-eyed about him), but the young man,
born near Wilmington, Delaware, on August 19, 1830,
was a revolutionary. He soon started to revolutionize transportation in Southern California, to bring the area out of the
dark ages. And, by developing a harbor at Wilmington, California, he forced Los Angeles to face the sea, to end its isolation, and to start on its way to the megalopolis it is today.

Banning, for whom the city in Riverside County is named,
knew that he had to tie Los Angeles to the rest of the state,
the nation, and the world, if the town were ever to develop.
That meant efficient freight, stage and mail lines, telegraph,
railroads, and a seaport. He set out to get them all for L.A.
When he arrived where the Los Angeles-Long Beach Harbor
is now, he found only the great open bight of San Pedro Bay.
The "town" of San Pedro was the corral and boat landing of
the Sepúlvedas and the warehouse of Don Abel (Cara de
Caballo—"Horseface") Stearns. The anchorage was shallow

and unprotected; vessels had to lie far offshore and lighter all passengers and cargo in rowboats. Ashore, rude *carretas* with solid wooden wheels (tree-trunk rounds) shrieked and groaned their way slowly to the pueblo of Los Angeles behind shuffling oxen. The Sepúlvedas ran an uncomfortable stage to the town but mainly as a convenience and were not interested in improving their equipment or service.

Banning went to work as a clerk at San Pedro and in his spare time built a scow which he poled around the mud flats and sand bars, seeking the channel into what was called the Inner Slough, an *estero,* or estuary, which caught his eye. He had the gift of foresight and in his mind's eye the tidal creek behind Rattlesnake (now Terminal) and Dead Man's islands became the heart of a harbor as great as Philadelphia's. San Pedro itself would not do, for it was exposed to the full force of the winter's storms.

Before he could build a harbor and do away with the costly overhead of lightering, which made freight costs so high, he had to improve Los Angeles's land communications. He persuaded his employers to start a modern stage line and occasionally drove the six-horse teams himself. He got local citizens to petition Senator Thomas H. Benton of Missouri to make San Pedro a port of entry so that foreign vessels could call there. The go-getter was soon partner instead of clerk and importing mules and wagons from Mexico to modernize the Southern California freighting business. Not content with serving only Los Angeles and its surrounding ranches, he began a run to the Mormon settlers of San Bernardino and eventually reached across the deserts to Salt Lake City. He ordered fine Concord stagecoaches from New Hampshire. When he learned of plans for Fort Tejon in the Tehachapi Mountains, he proved that a road could be cut to the isolated post by driving a Concord coach there himself, and then hiring a gang of Chinese coolies to build a wagon road.

With two partners, the newly married Banning next bought 2400 acres around the slough. Most Los Angeleños immediately dubbed it "Banning's Hog Wallow," but the short-lived newspaper the *Californian* showed remarkable prescience: "With some expense, the creek can be made as good a harbor as is on the Pacific Coast and in case the Pacific Railroad makes its terminus in this valley, it will be directed to this point and build up a city of considerable importance and enrich the gentlemen who have embarked on this new enterprise."

On his personal 640 acres of "hog wallow," Banning began to build his harbor and town. He called it New San Pedro at first but later changed it to recall his Delaware home town of Wilmington. Although the canal was still too shallow for seagoing vessels, Banning employed lighters and began to take some business away from San Pedro, which was six miles farther from Los Angeles. He had men rake away at the sand bar closing the channel's mouth, predicting correctly that the ebb tides would become his ally in deepening it. He laid out streets, planted shrubs and trees, especially the now-ubiquitous eucalyptus, and sank wells for a water supply. When these proved insufficient for the growing population, he built a nine-mile flume from the San Gabriel River. Fishing began to grow as an industry and some curing was done at Wilmington. Briefly there was a boom in abalone when the shellfish's beautiful nacreous shell became a fad, an ornament which just *had* to be in every natural history cabinet or knickknack shelf in the East.

Banning was delighted in November 1859 when the first ocean-going vessel unloaded directly to the shore at Wilmington. People began to call him Port Admiral Banning, now,

21

with a mixture of respect and jest. He tried out a "steam wagon" for freighting, a predecessor of both the truck and the tractor, but it was an underpowered failure. When the telegraph line being built southward from San Francisco lagged, he persuaded the company to send wire to Wilmington and build northward, too. The line opened October 8, 1860. Meanwhile, Banning had been forwarding the U.S. mail to Los Angeles, without any remuneration from the Government at all.

A strong abolitionist and Unionist in a region teeming with secessionists, Banning was a key figure in keeping Southern California tied to the North. He gave speeches, led Fourth-of-July celebrations, accepted a brigadier generalcy in the California Militia. Now he had *three* titles—General, Port Admiral, and "Duke of Wilmington," as his critics called him. When the Los Angeles paper had to be closed by the military as disloyal, Banning started one in Wilmington which was true-blue in its sentiments. Largely due to his efforts, Los Angeles County finally "went Union" in the 1864 elections. When Banning dabbled in politics, he was elected state senator and introduced a bill to build a railroad between Los Angeles and the Pacific. He had only one major failure on his record: his Pioneer Oil Company was not a commercial success. It was ahead of its time and his wells produced more salt water than petroleum. The time was not ripe for Southern California's oil boom. Still, his reputation soared. The *Arizona Miner* stated: "General Banning is one of those irrepressible, large-minded, free-hearted men whose very presence is life and success. Whatever he turns his mind to is bound to triumph. Southern California boasts no citizen who has done so much to advance its interests." General James S. Rusling in his popular book *Across America* intoned an amen: "A man of large and liberal ideas, with great native force of character and powers of endurance, he was invaluable to

Southern California and Arizona, and both of these sections owe him a debt of gratitude which they cannot repay."

Banning made enemies as a matter of course, and the "tidelands grabber" replied to many of them in a letter to the editor of 1873: "If there is one man in this county except the Hon. B. D. Wilson and myself who has ever made the least exertions to have our harbor improved, I am entirely ignorant of his existence. . . . The great object of my life has been to assist in getting a good harbor for this county, in which I have steadfastly persisted and am determined to continue in until the great object has been accomplished."

The port admiral was a director of the Los Angeles and San Pedro Railroad, and he saw to it that rails were laid by September 1868 and a locomotive on them by December. He kept his Wilmington shops busy turning out rolling stock—freight, passenger, and baggage cars—and the line opened on October 29, 1869.

The Army Engineers now recommended a breakwater to link Rattlesnake and Dead Man's islands; Congress voted money in 1871 and in 1872. Next, Wilmington was declared a port of entry, and a deputy customs collector was appointed. The channel was dredged and in 1874 Banning saw 350 steamers and 94 sailing ships call at his port.

Now Banning worked harder than ever to tie his harbor and short-line railroad to the Southern Pacific, which was building its way southward from San Francisco and heading for the Colorado River. There was a rub. The S.P. did not plan to go out of its way to touch Los Angeles. Phineas Banning knew that the power of the railroad's moguls, the Big Four, was too much for the Texas Pacific, the only other hope. So he had to watch the Southern Pacific collect $600,-000, a sixty-acre station site, and the county's stock in the Los Angeles and San Pedro Railroad in exchange for running fifty miles of track to L.A. On September 5, 1876, with the completion of the Southern Pacific, Banning's "wallow" was tied to the East Coast by a through railway. Victory seemed complete. Or was it?

Nevada's Senator John P. Jones tried to lure railroad speculation to Shoo Fly (now Santa Monica), where he built a pier 1700 feet out into the Pacific from the cliffs. He swore that he would ruin shoal-water Wilmington with his deep-draft wharf. But the S.P., which now owned Banning's Los Angeles and San Pedro short line, shrugged Jones off, and by 1877 his pier was all but abandoned. The story went around that it was about to collapse because its piles were riddled by teredos, or shipworms. It would have to be torn down. Localites were puzzled at the difficulty of the sweating laborers in dismantling Jones's folly. Finally, they had to saw the pilings off at the water level. Down it came, and with it went local property values. Santa Monica's population dropped to some 350 people by 1879.

Then came the switcheroo. The S.P. was the buyer of Jones's seaside ghost town! (Theodore Judah or Adolph Sutro could have told the Santa Monicans that Collis P. Huntington had more switches than a thousand miles of S.P. track.) Shortly after Banning's death on March 10, 1885, it became clear that Collis had really changed his mind about Shoo Fly. He was going to build a million-dollar pier there and he expected to get congressional money for breakwaters in order to build a port from scratch, on Southern Pacific-owned land at the base of the Palisades. Huntington was miffed because he did not have a complete monopoly at San Pedro. The Terminal Railroad paralleled his own down to the wharf Banning had built, letting in competition. This would not be allowed at Santa Monica. Huntington's railrogue partner, Charles Crocker, tipped his hand when he threatened the

24

City Council of Los Angeles that, if the S.P. did not have its way, "I will make the grass to grow in the streets of your city." The City Council did not display much spunk, but when Huntington pressured the Chamber of Commerce to support Santa Monica and abandon its "hopeless" advocacy of San Pedro because he had "some little influence in Washington," he bungled. When he revealed that eighty-three members of the chamber were with him, a poll showed that San Pedro partisans outnumbered supporters of Santa Monica by 328 to 131. The press began to rally behind the chamber; the Santa Fe Railroad threw in its support; and soon the people were writing letters to their congressmen—and not in praise of C. P. Huntington.

Luckily, at the critical juncture, Los Angeles inherited a San Franciscan who was more than a worthy successor to Phineas Banning in the fight for a so-called "free harbor." He was U. S. Senator Stephen M. White. Thanks to him, Banning was vindicated; Huntington was licked for once; and Charlie Crocker was proved a liar, for no wild oats grow in the middle of the streets and freeways of Los Angeles.

BLACK BART

(c1832–?)

Black Bart was born Charles E. Boles, probably in Norfolk, England, circa 1832, and was brought to the Alexandria Bay area near the St. Lawrence River's Thousand Islands when he was about two years of age. Boles came to California twice during the Gold Rush but returned to the Midwest, married, and enlisted in the Union Army in 1862 in Decatur, Illinois. He was, apparently, a good soldier and was seriously wounded in the Battle of Dallas, Georgia, in 1864. Returning to duty from the hospital, he was promoted all the way to first sergeant of his company and was commissioned a second lieutenant but never mustered in that rank, probably because of the ending of the Civil War.

Boles abandoned his family and went to work in the mines of Idaho and Montana but by 1874 had shifted his attention to California. He set about prospecting the green treasure boxes of Wells, Fargo, which almost every stagecoach carried, and found them far more remunerative than panning for gold in a cold Sierra stream. In the eight years following 1875 the mysterious lone bandit struck twenty-nine times at Concord coaches from Shasta, in the north, to Fort Ross on the

Sonoma coast, but mainly in the Mother Lode region of the Sierra Nevada foothills. Only once did he fail to get away with the lockbox. He probably netted only about eighteen thousand dollars in all of his holdups of Wells, Fargo express shipments, but his almost unerring success was both embarrassing and unnerving to the company. The Number One order given Wells, Fargo's chief of detectives, James B. Hume, was to put the lone robber out of business. This would not be easy. The bandit wore a sack mask; he never fired a shot. (Later, Hume found that Bart never even loaded the shotgun he waved so menacingly.) He slipped away into the brush and seemed to leave no tracks. Thus Bart remained a mystery during his career in crime until Hume unmasked him by patiently studying his *modus operandi* and the clues which he dropped from time to time.

Bart's first victim was driver John Shine, on July 26, 1875. On Funk Hill, between Copperopolis and the Stanislaus River, he dashed into the dusty road from a dense tangle of brush and boulders. Although he was polite, saying, "Please throw down the box," when Shine hesitated a deep voice roared from out of the flour-sack mask, "If he dares to shoot, give him a solid volley, boys!" The driver looked at the hillside and through the manzanita and other brush saw at least a half-dozen rifle barrels pointed his way. Suddenly he became as peaceable as an Anabaptist and threw the box down. After the bandit had looted it and gone his way, on foot, Shine went back to get the emptied box. He experienced a shock as he found the rifles of the highwayman's confederates once again leveled at him from the chaparral. When nothing happened after some little time, he gingerly approached the brush and found the guns to be sticks fastened in place as a ruse by the lone road agent.

Later the bandit began to leave poetry at the scenes of his

crimes, signing it "Black Bart, the Po8." The first time, he left but one stanza; the second time, at the site of his fifth robbery (July 1878), the poet laureate of California banditry left three stirring stanzas:

> Here I lay me down to sleep
> To await the coming morrow
> Perhaps success, perhaps defeat
> And everlasting sorrow
>
> I've labored long and hard for bred
> For honor and for riches
> But on my corns too long you've tred
> You fine-haired Sons of Bitches
>
> Let come what will, I'll try it on
> My condition can't be worse
> And if there's money in that box
> 'Tis munny in my purse.

Bart never rode; he preferred shanks' mare. He was, like John Muir or Meriwether Lewis, an absolutely superb walker or "pedestrian" in the nineteenth-century sense. He could cover the most rugged ground with ease, even though he began his California career at age forty or so and was almost fifty when Hume put a stop to it. He carried a blanket roll, tools to pry open locks, and a shotgun which he broke at the breech to fit into his roll. He liked nothing better than to give a posse the slip on foot, even though the lawmen were well mounted.

Between robberies Black Bart alternated between roaming the hinterland, bumming meals or doing manual labor, and settling down in the role of a gentleman in San Francisco.

(He even liked to dine in a restaurant which was a favorite hangout for detectives and policemen.)

Bart's luck finally ran out on Sunday, November 3, 1883. Ironically, incredibly, it did so almost on the very spot on Funk Hill where he had held up his first stage more than eight years earlier. He was hammering open the lockbox which he had taken from the driver when he was interrupted by that gentleman, and a young hunter, taking potshots at him with a shared Henry rifle. Bart held onto his loot and disappeared into the chaparral, but he left behind about a long ton of clues. Jim Hume found these to include: a derby hat, a sack of crackers, a package of sugar, a belt, a razor, a pair of field glasses, shirt cuffs, and empty flour sacks. In a knotted handkerchief was a quantity of buckshot. Sheriff Ben K. Thorn found a laundry mark—F.X.O.7—on the kerchief and passed it on to Wells, Fargo's chief of detectives. Jim Hume had already hired Harry Morse, ex-sheriff of Alameda County, to do nothing but nab Bart. Morse spent eight days checking laundries and laundry agencies in Frisco before he found what he wanted. A tobacconist on Post Street identified the mark as belonging to one of his customers who used his laundry drop and pickup service. The man was a mining engineer, Charles E. Bolton. Morse got the tobacco store man to introduce him to Bolton and, identifying himself as a fellow mining man, got his new acquaintance to accompany him to Jim Hume's office.

Hume questioned him, convinced himself he had his man, and called a police officer to arrest him. Hume, Morse, and the officer searched Boles/Bolton's room and found plenty of incriminating evidence including laundry items marked F.X.O.7. But when Bart was booked and the desk sergeant asked his name, he snapped out a brand-new alias, "T. Z. Spalding." Hume had him identified by victims of his robberies and Bart began to do some deep thinking. The last holdup occurred on November 3, 1883. Bart pleaded guilty (to the one holdup only) on the sixteenth. On the twenty-first, only eighteen days after the robbery, Black Bart entered the gates of San Quentin and changed his name again, this time to 11046.

Boles was a model prisoner who acted as druggist for the penitentiary doctor. Thanks to lots of time off for good behavior, he was a free man again on January 21, 1888. When he left San Quentin, a reporter asked him if he intended to return to stage robbery. His answer was a vehement "No!" Bart still had his wry sense of humor; when another reporter asked if he was going to write any more poetry, the ex-con answered, "Young man, didn't you hear me say I would commit no more crimes?"

After his release, Bart hung about San Francisco and then drifted south to Visalia. He then disappeared, leaving a valise in his lodgings. Whenever a stage was held up, suspicion would be fixed on Bart. But Hume and his chief aide, Jonathan Thacker, were convinced that he had retired from his old career. Thacker, in fact, was quoted as saying in 1897, "He was straight as a string. Finally, he made a bee line for Vancouver and boarded the steamer *Empress of China* for Japan. He is in that country now."

Black Bart simply vanished from the face of the earth. There was an apocryphal story that an unnamed New York paper carried his obituary in 1917, but no authentic reports of his last years, or of his death, have ever come to light. Rumors had him everywhere, of course—California, Colorado, Kansas, and Mexico as well as Nippon. Possibly he spent the remainder of his life tramping through the beautiful Japanese countryside, like an exiled John Muir, demon-

strating the truth of Jim Hume's estimate of him as a hiker—
"He is a person of great endurance, a thorough mountaineer,
a remarkable walker, and claims that he cannot be excelled
in making quick transits over mountains and grades."

DELILAH L. BEASLEY

(1871–1934)

It was Delilah Leontium Beasley's misfortune to be born fifty years before her time. In the 1960's, both black and white Americans have become cognizant of the long-neglected role of Negroes in American history. But in post-World War I California, Miss Beasley's voice was the traditional one crying, unheard, in the wilderness, when she told their story in the taming and building of the West.

Born in Cincinnati in 1871, Delilah Beasley began a pioneering career (for one of her sex and race) in journalism when she was only twelve years old. She submitted short articles to a Cleveland paper. By the time she was fifteen, Miss Beasley was contributing a regular column to the Cincinnati *Inquirer*. But journalism did not satisfy her; she became interested in history and, particularly, in the history of her own race—a subject which she found to be practically unwritten, as yet. She determined to do something about the lack personally.

The newspaperwoman's study of the Afro-American role in the story of the United Stated lasted almost twenty years. She began her research by reading as widely and deeply as possible for a full decade, doing much of it in the private libraries of friends in Springfield, Ohio. These same friends persuaded her to go to California when her interests, more and more, led her to investigate the early years of the Far Western frontier. She followed their advice and moved to California, where she continued her newspaper career, writing for the Oakland *Tribune* as well as other papers and magazines, at the same time that she rededicated herself to research.

When Miss Beasley migrated to the Pacific Coast, she also became active in politics and the nascent civil rights movement. For twenty-five years she labored in this field and was rewarded not only by seeing the general lot of the California Negro improved but by getting civil rights legislation enacted in 1933 by the California legislature. Still, her great contribution to California's story is as a self-taught historian.

Originally, Miss Beasley had planned only to write a series of lectures which she hoped to deliver to interested audiences. But when she read her first one, titled "My City of Inspiration —San Francisco," to Reverend David R. Wallace, of Oakland, Father Wallace was so enthusiastic that she complied with his urging to devote a whole book to the subject of the West's pioneer blacks. It took her—to the very *day*—exactly eight years and six months from the time she started writing until she sent the manuscript off to the publisher. During that time, she ransacked the State Archives for data and prowled the bookstacks of the Bancroft Library on the University of California campus. She anticipated the oral history program of American universities by ranging all over California to interview old pioneers, going (in her own words) "wherever a railroad or horse and buggy could go." She pored over brittle files of ancient newspapers, explored land records and other documents, and plunged into the terra incognita of assembly and senate journals and legal reports and statutes in the University of California's Boalt Hall of Law. Many Californians helped her, including such well-known scholars as Theodore H. Hittell, Charles E. Chapman, and Herbert Priestly.

The result of her long and diligent efforts was a 317-page book titled *The Negro Trail Blazers of California,* published in Los Angeles in 1919 by the Times-Mirror Press. It was an important volume, if an imperfect one. (Delilah Beasley was an amateur historian, and, like all amateurs, she made some mistakes.) But it was neglected and became quite scarce in the years following its publication. Not until 1968 was it reprinted under the sponsorship of the California Historical Society and the San Francisco Negro Historical and Cultural Society.

On her last visit to the aging dean of California historians, Theodore H. Hittell, Miss Beasley read him a portion of her manuscript. Hittell, pacing the floor of his library, exclaimed to her, "Oh, that I could live to see your book published! Every Negro in the United States ought to buy a copy and more than one white person will buy one." Charlotte A. Bass, managing editor of the *California Eagle,* the major Los Angeles Negro newspaper, contributed a brief foreword to Miss Beasley's book in which she echoed Hittell's sentiments, venturing, "It is hoped that the appreciation of her people for these earnest efforts for the uplift and general enlightenment will place this book in a conspicuous place in the home of every Negro and that, as a work of literary and historical value, it will occupy its place upon the shelf in every public library." This, alas, was too much to expect in 1919 and only now are Delilah Beasley and her book coming to be appreciated.

Toward the end of her period of research and writing, Delilah Beasley fell seriously ill. She was grateful for the kindness of her many friends, who took care of her, sent her money, and—in her words—"never allowed her, for one moment, to entertain a thought that she would not get well nor complete the book. . . . They stood by in many dark hours and threw around the author a mantle of love that would not let her sink. . . . May God never let me be unmindful or ungrateful of my friends."

Delilah Beasley's task was difficult. Not only had California's second-class citizens been hard put to play major roles in history, but even when they did, there had been no one to chronicle their achievements. But she dug the names and the facts from the great mass of historical records, finding that San Francisco's leading merchant before the Gold Rush, for example, had been a Danish West Indian Negro, William Leidesdorff; that John C. Frémont was accompanied to California in 1844 by a Negro freedman, Jacob Dodson; that many 49ers were blacks and that some of them became very successful and prominent mine owners, like Moses Rodgers of the Hornitos area. Black Americans, she found, were involved in the Bear Flag Revolt, the Pony Express, and the wars to which California sent her sons.

Even in a free state like California, colored men and women in the nineteenth century could not take advantage of the Homestead Act; could not give testimony in court (till 1863); and were often prohibited by bigoted conductors from even riding in San Francisco streetcars, until Mammy Pleasant sued the transport company and won damages. Because Delilah Beasley was the first to record the long-ignored story of California's Negro pioneers, who contributed so much to the state despite overwhelming obstacles and handicaps, she should be both honored and remembered. In rescuing so many of these "invisible men" from oblivion, she missed a few of course, but only one great Negro of California, probably, does not appear in her book. Had someone else written the volume, Delilah Beasley, herself, would be honored in the pages of *The Negro Trail Blazers of California.*

JIM BECKWOURTH

(*1798–1867*)

The first white child to cross the Sierra Nevada into California by Beckwourth Pass, northwest of Reno, did so during the summer of 1851. She was destined to become famous, much later, under a different name. The ten-year-old girl, Josephine D. Smith, a niece of Mormon prophet Joseph Smith, eventually took the name Ina D. Coolbrith and went on to become California's Poet Laureate. Little Ina rode through the 5210-foot pass in front of the weather-beaten hunter, trapper, and squaw man who had discovered it, Jim Beckwourth. Her hero, whose saddle horse she shared, differed from such other mountain men as Jim Bridger, Grizzly Adams, or Caleb Greenwood in only one major respect—he was a Negro.

The dark, muscular mulatto had his long hair braided Indian-style over his shoulders. He wore beaded buckskins and moccasins and he scorned a hat. Pendant from a thread of sinew around his neck hung a bullet, with a large oblong bead on each side of it, his talisman, his amulet as a chief of the Crow Indians. Jim was as good as any mountain man in most areas and probably exceeded them all—except perhaps

Jim (Old Gabe) Bridger—in one, lying. As a teller of tall tales, Beckwourth was hard to beat. The story of his adventurous life might have slipped into oblivion had he not run into a man at Rich Bar, on the Feather River, in the winter of 1854–55, a man who was well acquainted with book learning and who was a pretty fair-to-middlin' writer, to boot. This was T. D. Bonner, a wandering journalist of whom virtually nothing is known except that he was the Squire in Dame Shirley's classic account of the Gold Rush, the *Shirley Letters.* The newspaperman whiled away the rainy and snowy winter by pouring liquor into Jim while the latter decanted tales of his adventurous life. Dame Shirley described the bibulous oral historian and his equally sloshed subject thus: "The more they drank, the more Indians Jim would recall having slain, his eloquence increasing in inverse ratio to the diminishing rum supply, and, at last, he would slap the Squire on the knee and chortle, 'Paint her up, Bonner! Paint her up!' And Bonner painted her up for the joy of posterity."

According to T. D. Bonner, Beckwourth's "only pleasurable excitement was found in facing danger." This is not quite true (as witness the many squaws he befriended), but 'twas close enough to fact—if that word can be used at all in connection with the reminiscences of one who liked to draw the longbow. Like all mountaineers, he had difficulty in separating fact from fiction and was never known to forbear improving upon a good yarn. Francis Parkman, author of *The Oregon Trail,* tried to put down Beckwourth, stuffily, but it was his caste (New England gentleman) getting in the way of his calling (historian) when he dismissed the mulatto as a ruffian whose narrative was largely false. Bernard De Voto and others have found that, in many cases, Beckwourth's tales (when they do not concern himself) stand up well, even though his *wild* yarns, such as fighting General Ashley and then saving his life not once but three times, are sometimes figments of his imagination. His undependability was almost absolute only when he discussed the favorite character of all —himself. But, if not the veriest kind of academic history, Beckwourth's biography as written down by Bonner was dependable mythology or folk history, like Grizzly Adams's tales of the hunt.

James P. Beckwourth was born in Fredericksburg, Virginia, on April 26, 1798. He was sent to school in St. Louis, then was apprenticed to a blacksmith in that Missouri city. In 1823, he ran away and joined the Rocky Mountain Fur Company brigade of General William H. Ashley, Lieutenant Governor of Missouri, probably as a smith. But he soon metamorphosed into a mountain man when he was tutored by the likes of Moses (Black) Harris. The latter, despite his nickname, was not a fellow-Negro; he had suffered a flashback from his rifle and bore a powder-blackened visage. By 1826, Jim was adopted by the Crows into their tribe, which occupied the beautiful country of the Yellowstone, Powder, Bighorn, and Rosebud rivers. The Crows were friendly to "whites" (which, to them, included Negro Jim Beckwourth) because they were natural allies against the deadly Blackfeet, their mutual enemy. Beckwourth became a warrior of the tribe and then a chief, called Medicine Calf (Nan-kup-bah-pah in Crow) and doubled as American Fur Company trader to the Crow nation, receiving (so he claimed) three thousand dollars a year for his services while resident with the tribe.

Beckwourth returned to St. Louis and civilization in time to take part in the Seminole War. Bill Sublette recommended him to General Edwin Gaines, who was recruiting volunteers in Missouri for the Florida campaign. Beckwourth was, frankly, tired of Indian fighting, but Gaines promised him lots of renown and Sublette painted an idyllic picture of

Florida, so he decided to enlist as a kind of scout. He re-cruited some unemployed mountain men and joined Colonel Zachary Taylor for the Christmas 1837 Battle of Okeechobee. Taylor puffed this battle so that his "victory" helped him get not only a general's rank but the Presidency of the United States. Beckwourth's brief description of the conflict was probably accurate; the battle was most likely about as much a victory as any other Florida engagement for the Army. Taylor's 1600-man army met the Seminoles and their Negro allies in a live-oak woods on the north shore of Lake Okeechobee. The fight raged for four hours before a bayonet charge routed the Indians. They left about ten dead on the field and Zack Taylor had more than hundred dead or wounded, but he somehow managed a victory of the affair in reporting it to Washington. After further service as a dispatch rider, Beckwourth grew tired of Florida and quit the peninsula. "It seemed to me," he told Bonner, "a country dear even at the price of the powder that would be required to blow the Indians out of it, and certainly a poor field to work in for *renown.*"

Beckwourth returned to the Rockies, working for Bill Sublette and Luis Vásquez near Denver as a trader to some of the very Indians (Cheyennes) he had fought as a Crow warrior-chief. He then tried the Santa Fe trade briefly before moving on for a look-see at California, arriving in Los Angeles in 1844.

In Southern California, the revolutionaries against Governor Micheltorena got Beckwourth to join a company of riflemen composed largely of fellow-Yanquis, although he refused its command. The Negro was one of the men who persuaded Colonel Sutter's followers to switch sides or, at least, to abandon their chief. Thus he was instrumental in the victory of the rebels and the toppling of the governor. When the Mexican War broke out, Beckwourth and some friends drove off 1800 Californio horses as their contribution to the U.S. war effort and herded them all the way from Los Angeles to Bent's Fort on the Arkansas River. Jim joined General Stephen W. Kearny on his march to Santa Fe and again performed as a dispatch rider, this time on the 913-mile stretch between the New Mexican capital and Fort Leavenworth. According to Jim, it was his job to inform General Sterling Price of the uprising and massacre of Americans in Taos in which Governor Bent was killed. Certainly, he marched in the punitive expedition against the Mexicans and Indians.

Returning to California, Beckwourth set up a clothing business in a tent in Sonora in 1849. When he grew bored, he moved to Murderer's Bar, on the American River, and settled down for a while with his old friend, Jean Baptiste Charbonneau, Sacajawea's baby on the Lewis and Clark Expedition of 1804–6. During the following spring, Jim prospected and mined and during his rambles discovered a fine route from the Nevada desert to Marysville via Beckwourth Pass. He got the citizens of that city to back his project of an improved (toll) road through the gap, but shortly after he guided the first emigrants through it and before he had collected more than a couple hundred dollars of the money due him, Marysville burned to the ground, taking most of his backers' resources. Out of pocket some $1600, Jim set up a trading post and inn in Beckwourth Valley in 1852.

In 1854 and 1855 he was in the Feather River gold camps, and around 1856 he was run out of California by the vigilantes for stealing horses. Jim went on to New Mexico and Missouri, then to Denver by 1859, where he kept a store. Later, he operated a ranch south of the city. In 1864, he tried to act as a scout for Colonel John Chivington during the latter's dastardly raid on the peaceable Sand Creek Cheyennes, but he was too old to be of much use. When tribe after tribe arose in war during the last days of the Civil War, the Government sent Beckwourth to keep the Crows peaceful. On this mission, in 1867, the Negro mountain man died among his adopted people in their tribal land of Absaroka.

Beckwourth's claim to fame is not just that he was a prototype of the so-called "reckless breed of men," the Rocky Mountain fur trappers. His accomplishment was earning his way into the select company of mountain men in the first place. With one exception (Ed Rose), no other Negro made the grade. Jim's force of character (it would have been called sheer "guts" then) was such that he became a full-fledged member of the Rocky Mountain fraternity when his fellow-blacks of slaveholding America were having a very hard time in even becoming freedmen. Beckwourth was not the first of a long line of Negro plainsmen or trappers, but he did show the way for many free blacks who went West and became miners, cowboys, or cavalry troopers. He broke the trail.

JOHN BIDWELL

(1819–1900)

When California author George R. Stewart chose six men whose careers typified what we have come to call "the good life," he threw John Bidwell in with such better-known figures of history as Prince Henry the Navigator and Heinrich Schliemann, the archeologist who uncovered Troy. Bidwell's life can perhaps be taken as disproof of the old adage that "good guys finish last." This so-called Prince of Pioneers, moral and ethical to the point of primness (some of his enemies called him "Sister Bidwell"), had a life which was as rich in both personal accomplishment and public prestige as it was in material things. Bidwell possessed certain positive traits which set him apart from most of his fellow-pioneers. He was active, honest, responsible, courageous (but never foolhardy), ambitious, stable, and, above all, prudent. With all these virtues, he was no paragon. What did Bidwell lack? An artistic and aesthetic sense; vision, humor, emotion, the zest for living of men like John Sutter.

Although John Bidwell participated in several "lost causes" in politics, especially prohibitionism, he was anything but a fanatic. In fact, although he espoused unpopular movements, he was not very dynamic as a rebel or crusader because of self-discipline and a dispassionate nature. Still, he managed to outlast most of his peers, even giants like Sam Brannan and John Sutter, whose rough-and-tumble tactics could not prevent their being swept aside by fate. Compared to Sutter's somewhat raffish career, his life was a little on the dull side because of his strictness and excessive prudence. He was, in fact, the epitome of the Protestant ethic in nineteenth-century California, as well as the Horatio Alger success story personified.

Bidwell was born on August 5, 1819, to farm folk in the westernmost tip of upstate New York only four miles from Lake Erie and the Pennsylvania border. His parents were hard-working, disciplined, and religious, and they left their marks on the boy during his childhood. He differed from them mainly, as he matured, in his craving for book learning. Three months of school each year, when winter limited the number of farm chores, was not sufficient for young John. When he was sixteen, he walked from the family's new home in southwest Ohio to Kingsville—three hundred miles away—because he had heard that it boasted a good academy. There he enjoyed his most intensive stint of education, a year and a half in science, then called natural philosophy. When he returned home, he was not only tolerably well educated but, now a man of eighteen, ready to set out on his own. Bidwell started hiking westward, teaching as he went, in order to earn money.

John Bidwell almost settled down on 160 acres in Missouri but did not contest the action of a claim jumper. Instead, he quietly moved on. What might seem to have been a lack of common courage was, more likely, a case of discretion. After all, not only was he a peaceable and gentlemanly young fellow, he was underage and in no position to take the matter to court. As is often the case, this seeming stroke of bad luck turned into the greatest good fortune for Bidwell. Not tied down to the land, he had time to listen to the words of one of the Robidoux clan about legendary California, just as John Sutter had listened to Carlos Beaubien, a few years earlier in New Mexico. Even the oak-solid, no-nonsense Bidwell found himself strangely excited by the promise of El Dorado. He helped to organize a Western Emigration Society, which came to number five hundred men—on paper. When Bidwell reached the rendezvous on the prairie in 1841, however, he found only a handful of pioneers and a dozen or so wagons. All of the others had suffered acute attacks of cold feet.

In later years, the wagon train came to be called the Bidwell-Bartleson Party, but this was after fame came to John Bidwell. In truth, he was just one of the boys in 1841, a member of John Bartleson's party. Bidwell told the story of his overland emigration in a book titled *Echoes of the Past.* Like his life, itself, the crossing of the plains was rich enough in incident, and yet, compared to others, it lacked drama. He and his comrades reached California, alas, not at New Helvetia but at the Mount Diablo Ranch of Dr. John Marsh, a miser who insisted upon payment for the passports he secured in order to release the Yankees from a Mexican *calabozo.* Bidwell was glad to see the last of Marsh, "one of the most selfish of mortals," and took himself to New Helvetia to seek employment by John Sutter.

There was an immediate and lasting rapport between Sutter and Bidwell, although they were opposites—Sutter being erratic, swashbuckling, and irresponsible, where Bidwell was strait-laced and as dependable as the sun. The latter became the Swiss's right-hand man, his major-domo and bookkeeper. When Sutter wanted his Fort Ross and Bodega properties liquidated, he sent Bidwell there. So thorough was the young man that he sent Sutter not only the lumber and portable

45

property which he expected but even apple cider and dried fruit from the unmovable orchard.

When Sutter went to war in 1845 in Governor Micheltorena's behalf, Bidwell marched as his aide-de-camp. He thereby suffered the same defeat and humiliation at the hands of the victorious rebels as did his employer. But he bounced back in the same fashion as the man he emulated in part. Imitating Sutter, he learned how to handle the Indians firmly but fairly and to speak their tongues. He became a naturalized Mexican citizen and secured a grant of land, like Sutter. Unfortunately, he chose a low-lying tract which was not as healthy as most California land grants and he finally had to buy property, Rancho Chico, from other American settlers after his rather routine Mexican War service. (Perhaps his modest role in the conflict was due to his awareness of the bald land-grabbing motivation of the fight: "If there ever was an unjust war in this world, it was that war," he later commented. "It was an unjustifiable war.") Bidwell's Chico Ranch was well watered, higher, and more rolling acreage than his earlier tract. He left Sutter's employ, entirely amicably, in order to fend for himself. Luck was with him when gold was discovered in 1848. His property was off the major routes to the mines and was not ground into a wasteland, like Sutter's, by the stampeding boots of thousands of greedy miners. He was much more patient and successful, too, than Sutter as a gold miner and took from the Feather River thousands of dollars which he poured into his ranch. At twenty-two thousand acres his rancho was as big as a township back East.

Bidwell soon demonstrated that he had an even greener thumb than Sutter. He turned his vast grant into a model farm. He sowed wheat and dug irrigation ditches and built a flour mill, just as his mentor had done, but he also rode all the way to Mission San Luís Rey in Southern California to purchase choice vines and fruit trees. He raised cattle, horses, sheep, chickens, and hogs, put in corn, oats, barley, peaches, pears, and apples, experimented with figs, quinces, sugar cane, and sorghum, English walnuts and almonds, pioneered in the manufacture of olive oil, and introduced casaba melons to California. He was all business. He looked forward, not back. He had no romantic nostalgia for the old days. He tore down his fine old adobe house when his handsome (and pretentious) scroll-saw Gothic mansion was completed.

With prominence and wealth his, power came to Bidwell because of his interest in public affairs. He was not content with his presidency of the State Agricultural Society and was elected a member of the state Senate during the first legislature. He was a member of the committee which created the great California State Library. In 1850, with Judge Henry Schoolcraft, he escorted a block of gold-bearing quartz to Washington as California's contribution to the building of the Washington Monument. There he tried to get California admitted to the Union. In 1855 he was a Democratic candidate for the state Senate but lost. Four years later, he chaired a Railroad Convention in San Francisco and in 1860 founded the town of Chico. A strong Union man during the breakup of the Democratic Party in the ante-bellum decade, he was the only California delegate at the national convention to oppose pro-Southern Senator William Gwin and cast his lone vote for Douglas—and the Union. When the Civil War came, Southern sentiment was so strong in the Sacramento Valley that Bidwell was told to get out of Chico although he was the *grand seigneur* of the area. He stayed put and accepted Governor Stanford's appointment to the command of the 5th Brigade of California Militia, with the rank of brigadier general.

In 1864, still keeping up his model farm and princely estate, Bidwell went East as a delegate to the Union Party convention. He met General Grant, whom he admired, and shortly he was elected to Congress. His record, like that of most very junior congressmen, was not impressive, but he helped save the Department of Agriculture when purse-pinchers in the Congress would have killed it, and he fought against taxes on wines (in spite of his temperance leanings) because of the damage such legislation would do to California agriculture. He also met his future wife, strong-minded Annie Kennedy, and he made a tour of Europe. Bidwell married in 1868, when he was forty-eight and Annie was twenty-nine. He changed after his marriage. His wife did not dominate him, but she was a great influence upon him. He gave up tobacco chewing and smoking and became not only a churchgoing Presbyterian but an active prohibitionist.

Visitors to Bidwell's estate were many and included scientists like Asa Gray and Sir Joseph Hooker, and public figures like John Muir, General William T. Sherman, and President Rutherford B. Hayes. But neither General Bidwell nor his equally dignified and formal Annie succumbed to snobbery.

Bidwell was absolutely incorruptible and leery of any compromise which resembled a deal. One awed newspaper correspondent described the gubernatorial candidate who was "too good a man to be Governor"—"If he could not receive a nomination in the most honorable manner, he did not desire it, nor would accept of it if any bargain were made. . . ." As a result of his rigid moral posture, Bidwell was never very successful in big-time politics. He ran for governor on the Peoples Independent Party ticket and taxed the imagination of his mud-slinging opponents, but finally they came up with accusations that he was a hypocritical land monopolist. Bidwell lost but stuck with politics, a strange mixture of liberalism and conservatism. While he opposed graft, land monopoly, and trusts, he was anti-Catholic, anti-immigration, and far too accommodating to the anti-Chinese zealots of his day. Yet he proposed women's suffrage and the Australian ballot. His attitude on civil liberties was enlightened for his day; he was sympathetic toward and protective of the Indians and, doubtless, would have extended this paternalism toward the Negroes of the West. (Yet some of the Me-choop-da Indians of his Chico *ranchería* gave him the name of "The Man with the Whip.")

Curiously, the only party which could find room for a man of Bidwell's rugged individualism was the Prohibition Party. He ran for governor on its ticket in 1890 and, two years later, was its candidate for President of the United States. It was no one-plank party. He was interested in party principles other than prohibition—including income tax, arbitration, and government regulation of public utilities. He meant his hopeless race to be a gesture of protest and dissent, and was gratified when he received 264,133 votes for President, the largest number ever cast for a Prohibition Party candidate.

In his seventies Bidwell gave up politics but remained as active as ever, devoting himself to the fields and gardens of a lifelong agriculturalist. He was busily at work, cutting cottonwood logs with a crosscut saw, on April 3, 1900, when death called.

The puritanical Bidwell was, typically, fond of climbing and disliked walking on level ground. He was California's greatest impractical politician, a man of strict principle and character who made his fellow-candidates shake their heads in disbelief, but who would have made Diogenes's quest easy, had that searcher ventured along the reaches of Chico Creek.

AMBROSE BIERCE

(*1842–1914?*)

Born at Horse Cove Creek, Ohio (June 24, 1842), of poor and eccentric parents who gave all twelve children Christian names beginning with the letter "A," Ambrose Gwinnett Bierce found nothing eccentric about his childhood and hated its humdrum routine. So much so that it made him, as an adult, the most famous cynic in the West, if not in the whole country. The Civil War offered him his first escape, and although he was involved in bloody fighting, was seriously wounded, and was captured, the war years were glorious ones for Brevet Major Bierce and, in retrospect, seemed the best years of his life. His wartime experiences later provided him with themes for his best short stories, such as the oft-reprinted "Occurrence at Owl Creek Bridge," which probably influenced Stephen Crane and *The Red Badge of Courage.* Later in life, he made pilgrimages to such battlefields as Shiloh and Gettysburg. All of his life, Bierce remained fascinated with violence, death, and terror, as is documented by the gruesome pages of his fiction.

After the war, Bierce came to California and worked in the San Francisco Sub-Treasury while submitting articles to the

San Francisco News-Letter. His caustic wit soon won him the editorship of the journal, but he arrested his soaring local reputation as a littérateur by marrying Mollie Day and sailing to London. When he returned, late in 1875, he was made associate editor of the *Argonaut.* A profitless Black Hills gold-hunting expedition interrupted his career, and when he came back to California, *Argonaut* editor-publisher Frank Pixley declined to hire him again. Bierce never forgot such "slights." He had the sensitivity of a prima donna and he began to call his ex-boss "Frank Pigsley of the Hogonaut." He wrote a poem to him which included these lines—"Must I hear you call the roll, Of all the vices that infest your soul?"

The *Wasp* took him on, but Bierce's real break came when William Randolph Hearst hired him for the San Francisco *Examiner.* The two were strange allies, but Hearst gave him a free hand, so, although Bierce frequently quit in anger, he always returned to his *Examiner* column. His fame as an acid wit soon transcended the West and invaded the East. Bierce became the Pacific littoral's literary dictator, making and breaking reputations with his criticism. His most famous literary review was probably his shortest—"The covers of this book are too far apart." At the same time that he excelled in personal journalism, he was a so-so poet, a good short story writer (of horror and war tales), and a mediocre critic. He was so blunt that he sometimes had to scuffle with his readers and was commonly believed to pack a six-gun when he took a *paseo* on Frisco's streets.

Wise Willy Hearst saw Bierce's satire as a weapon against the Southern Pacific Railroad's domination of California. So he sent him to Washington to fight C. P. Huntington and his fellow-railrogues. They were trying to escape payment of principal or interest on their immense government loans, via a funding bill in Congress. Huntington did not take Bierce seriously when the latter proclaimed, "To hate rascality is my religion." Sure that every man had his price, he asked, "How much does he want?" Bierce's answer was: "My price is about seventy-two million dollars. If, when he is ready to pay, I happen to be out of town, he may hand it to my friend, the Treasurer of the United States." Although he broke down from overwork, Bierce and his allies defeated the old cutthroat and his pet bill.

The satire of the "Town Crier" and the "Prattler," Bierce's favorite noms de plume, won him the nickname of Bitter Bierce. But he was not a gloomy person. He had a serene—even smug—personality because of his great ego. Although touchy with oft-injured dignity, he was happy enough most of the time. Van Wyck Brooks noted that his Olympian poise saved him from *personal* bitterness, no matter how savage his satire.

Bierce loved to debunk the assorted humbugs and hypocrites of public life. In two lines he summed up the career of well-hated William Sharon—"Served in the Senate, for our sins, his time; Each word a folly and each vote a crime." He described a shrill French journalist as "suffering from an unhealed wound. It is his mouth." An untiring critic of the S.P., he not only called Stanford "Stealand Landford" and "£eland $tanford," he pounced upon every denting of a switch engine's cowcatcher in the local yards as if it were the derailing of the Overland Limited. He warned his readers that buying an S.P. ticket was like entering a suicide lottery, and he argued that Stanford's trains were so slow that, in addition to the danger of wreck, the passenger before arriving at his destination would be "exposed to the perils of senility." He was no easier on missionaries and reformers, whom he described as men who would beat a dog with a crucifix. In his most important and lasting book, *The Devil's Dictionary,*

Bierce defined the African tsetse fly as an insect "whose bite is commonly regarded as Nature's most efficacious remedy for insomnia, though some patients prefer that of the American novelist." His definition of a publisher has never been bettered, of course—"A person who drinks champagne out of the skulls of authors."

Although the handsome and dignified cynic preserved his military bearing into his seventies and, likewise, his stamina for long hikes and rugged canoe trips, he suffered badly from asthma and moved constantly in hope of relieving it. Finally he left California and made his home in Washington, D.C., for a decade. When he returned to California, he was weary, aimless, and reactionary, but still refused to compromise with the "frothing mad" world he saw around him, peopled by knaves and fools. He decided in 1913 to visit Mexico although it was in the spasms of revolution. He told the New Orleans press that he intended to visit the rest of Latin America after Mexico, but in a letter to his niece he wrote, "If you hear of my being stood up against a Mexican stone wall and shot to rags, please know that I think that a pretty good way to depart this life."

Ambrose Bierce disappeared in Mexico, suddenly and utterly. He was never seen again and the details of his death are absolutely unknown. There were a half-dozen theories advanced, of course, but he was probably shot to death by Villistas and buried in an unmarked grave. The public continued to harvest a bumper crop of rumors for several seasons —that he was in hiding, somewhere; that he had committed suicide in the Grand Canyon; that he was on Lord Kitchener's Royal Army staff. There are San Franciscans today who insist that he was party to a suicide pact with his friends George Sterling and Jack London, although he had dropped Sterling (his friend of longest standing) and he loathed London.

A grab bag of contradictions, Ambrose Bierce was alternately churlish and genial, kindly and unforgiving, brilliant and hackneyed in his work. His hard carapace hid an internal softness. He distrusted everyone, and especially his friends, whom he drove away in dozens. Bierce was an antireligious Puritan, a prude who liked his liquor and his ladies. In command of a battering ram of a pen, with which he assaulted the Establishment, he was as contemptuous of bohemians—because of their studied nonconformity—as he was of Bible-thumpers and do-gooders. He detested socialists, lumping them with bomb-throwing anarchists, yet in 1894 proposed a sort of New Deal to cure America's socioeconomic ills. It included abolition of private ownership of land; prohibition of the importation of cheap labor; checking the control of property by the dead; creation of jobs by the state in time of want; limitations of private fortunes by scaled taxation; and abolition of competitive wage systems.

Bierce was not an absolutely first-rate writer. (He was, incidentally, no second-rate or secondhand Poe, either. He may have borrowed a wee bit of the Baltimorean's macabre touch, but he was largely *sui generis*.) The Westerner wasted too much of his talent on local, temporary, and unworthy targets. He could not create flesh and blood characters for his stories. Unlike Mark Twain, he could seldom laugh at himself, only at others. When his vanity demanded that he edit his collected works, it would not allow him to discard *anything* and the set is a jumble of good and bad writing. He was ambitious but confessed to his poet-friend George Sterling, "I've a preference for being the first man in the village, rather than the second man in Rome." And this has been his fate. He is, easily, one of California's best writers but fails to measure up, nationally, to the front rank of Hawthornes and Twains. Yet he was much more than California's uncommon scold. He was a Jonathan

Swift in miniature, a witty muckraker, and the prototype for a long line of social critics and satirists whose ranks include the East's H. L. Mencken, the West's Arthur McEwen, and, in more recent times, San Francisco's Lucius Beebe, Art Hoppe, and Charles McCabe. Curiously, there are even poetical links between Bierce and the present, too. His favorite pupil was George Sterling, and it was the latter who "discovered" Robinson Jeffers, who inspired Brother Antoninus of today.

Bierce's bitterness and disappointments gave him his strength as iconoclast and critic, yet weakened him as an artist. Mary Austin saw this and said, "I judged him to be a man secretly embittered by failure to achieve direct creation, to which he never confessed; a man of immense provocative power, always secretly—perhaps even to himself—seeking to make good in some other's gift [for] what he had missed."

SAM BRANNAN

(1819–89)

Someone once wrote that the motto on Sam Brannan's coat of arms, were he entitled to an escutcheon, would ideally have been "Easy Come, Easy Go." For a brief time, Sam had the true Midas touch, turning virtually everything he fondled and fingered lovingly into profit and compound interest. His fans will claim that he, and not James Lick, was the state's first millionaire. Hardly anyone will deny that he was the first millionaire in California to turn pauper.

Brannan has been called "The First Forty-Niner" because he was so early on the scene. He beat most of his eventual merchant-rivals by reaching San Francisco (then called Yerba Buena) in 1846, shepherding a colony of Mormons on the *Brooklyn*. Like Brigham Young himself, Brannan hoped to escort the Latter Day Saints to an asylum far beyond the reach of the Yankees, whose principal diversion seemed to be the persecution of the sect. He failed. By the time the *Brooklyn* rounded Fort Point, entered Yerba Buena Cove, and dropped her hook in the mud off Rincon Hill, nascent San Francisco was in American, not Mexican, hands. Historians say that Brannan's first, bitter words in San Francisco came as he saw the flagstaff of the Customs House in Portsmouth Square, "There's that damned flag, again!" Purists insist, however, that Sam actually growled, "There's that damned rag, again!"

Long before Sam Brannan became a full-fledged fallen-away Mormon, his intransigence toward gentiles began to break down. This was partly because he was brought to trial by members of his shipboard flock for alleged misuse of church funds. (Some of these passengers were also tried themselves and convicted of "licentious and wicked conduct" during the long voyage.) Sam made history by being acquitted in the first jury trial in California. Hardly was he vindicated when he was in the thick of things. He preached the first non-Roman Catholic sermon in the territory if you ignore the Russians at Fort Ross and such devout British sojourners as Francis Drake's Chaplain Fletcher. He established a flour mill, set up a printing press, and brought out California's first newspaper, the *California Star*. In 1847, he tried to get Brigham Young to move Zion from Salt Lake City to San Francisco but failed to budge that stubborn man's mind. Again, Brannan wavered in his faith. It toppled completely next year and the enterprising Saint became an apostate. In a way, Jim Marshall was responsible, via his discovery of gold in Sutter's Mill at Coloma. It was Sam Brannan who spread the word of the strike throughout San Francisco, shouting it to the winds of Portsmouth Square—"Gold! Gold from the American River!" Probably, Sam wanted to draw some customers to his trading post in Sutter's Fort. Certainly, he was one of the first to see the superiority of mining miners' pockets and pouches, rather than shoveling gravel in icy Sierra streams for a living.

There were few, if any, flies on Sam Brannan. The pious entrepreneur insisted that L.D.S. miners working at Mormon Bar give their tithe to the church. In the meantime, he would hold it for them. When Brigham Young sent an apostle or two to pick up the receipts, Brannan sent them back to Utah empty-handed. He told them flatly, "You go back and tell Brigham that I'll give up the Lord's money when he sends me a receipt signed by the Lord, and no sooner." Rumor has long had it that Young's reaction was to dispatch a couple of his Danite avenging angels to persuade Sam but that Sam met them en route with his own hardcases and turned them back. To the surprise of no one, including himself, Sam Brannan was now cast out of the Latter Day Saints Church.

The firebrand civic leader, in 1849, led a preview of the Vigilance Committee movement, rescuing the city from the clutches of the Regulators, or Hounds, a loosely knit Mafia headed by Sam Roberts. These toughs balanced their criminality with nativist bigotry. They liked to beat up Chinese and, especially, Chilenos. When Alcalde T. M. Leavenworth was able to do nothing after a vicious attack on the Chileans, Brannan organized a paramilitary force to police the city. He broke up the gang, tried and banished Roberts and his cohorts, and brought peace to San Francisco.

The makeshift organization of 1849 fell apart, but it served as a model for the First Vigilance Committee in 1851, of which Sam Brannan was elected president. Once again, the Augean mews were cleaned. It was now said that Brannan was a millionaire. Perhaps he was, for he owned something like one-fifth of San Francisco and, thanks to his flimflamming John Sutter and his son, about one-fourth of Sacramento. About this time, however, his luck began to cool. He sailed to Hawaii with a jolly crew of filibusters on the clipper *Game Cock* and nearly talked King Kamehameha into ceding the Sandwich Islands to him. In the nick of time, the king's *haole* ministers talked some sense into His Royal Highness. Had his machinations worked, Sam's Hawaii coup would have made his Sutter bilk seem almost like a favor in comparison.

When Brannan and his cohorts left Hawaii, they were busted. Sam had spent some $125,000 on real estate and then had sold out for only $45,000, a sum which he could run through in jig time. Loafers on the Embarcadero jeered and called to him as he arrived on the *Golden Rule*—"Well, have you taken the Islands? Who's the king? Is it you, Sam?"

Brannan did not give up. He tried to make Calistoga into the Saratoga of the Far West, but the town fell considerably short of the mark. He drifted on to other projects and began to drink a drop too much. His wife left him. Before the end, he was stony broke, reduced to staying in two-bit flophouses when he visited San Francisco for the last time, where, only a few years before, the Palace Hotel would have been his cup of tea.

On May 14, 1889, Sam Brannan died in Escondido, near San Diego, almost entirely forgotten. The traditional tale is that he was buried in unhallowed ground. Actually, Sam's body lay in an undertaker's vault for sixteen months until a ninety-five-dollar embalming bill was paid by his nephew, Alex Badlam, Jr., who had the remains interred in Mount Hope Cemetery. The grave then was neglected, true enough, for thirty years. After that period of time, a friend of Sam and his family replaced the rude redwood stake, which made do as headboard, with a gravestone. (Like Sam himself, Mrs. Brannan and her son and two daughters all died in poverty, or right next door to it.)

In recent years, nostalgia has done its work and Calistoga has tried to bring Sam "home" to the Saratoga of the Napa Valley, where he belongs, now that he is safely dead. But San Diego County citizens are not about to give up the mortal remains of the colorful swashbuckler, one of the most prominent citizens and pioneers the area ever chose to forget, eighty years ago.

J. ROSS BROWNE

(*1821–75*)

Over the years, San Francisco has been called, by Texan-sized braggarts, "the City no coward ever set out for, and no weakling ever reached." The truth, of course, is that cowards, weaklings, and crooks were never rare abaft of the Golden Gate. The Gold Rush of '49 was both paralleled and .superseded by a great Graft Rush, although native sons are loath to admit its existence.

Within a bare five years of James Marshall's gold discovery, the federal Government was so disturbed by reports of a carnival of corruption on the Pacific Coast that the Secretary of the Treasury was instructed to send a secret agent to San Francisco. He was to make a confidential investigation of the charges that the '49ers had turned from the lodes and placers of the Sierra to mine, instead, the public treasury. The secret agent was to be authorized, too, to take appropriate measures to stop the systematized looting if it were, indeed, a fact.

Secretary Robert J. Walker's task was not an easy one, especially in the District. He had to find a competent man who was, at the same time, that *rara avis,* an honest man. The secretary searched from Foggy Bottom to Credibility Gap without success. Then, in the nick of time, he found his man, returning from a tour of Europe. He was an Irishman, John Ross Browne, born on February 11, 1821, at Beggar's Bush, near Dublin. Browne was a best-selling author who had served as Walker's secretary after being a police reporter. He was already familiar with California, too, having served as recording secretary of the California Constitutional Convention of 1849 in Monterey.

J. Ross Browne's first action in San Francisco was to recommend that the Customs House's expenses be cut by $136,000 a year! And, he assured the Government, this could be done without the slightest detriment to service. He found some twenty-odd inspectors doing literally nothing aside from claiming and cashing their checks. The Customs House work force had doubled since 1853 but was doing only two-thirds as much work. When he recommended that the offices of deputy naval officer and deputy surveyor—fifteen-thousand-dollar-a-year sinecures—be abolished, he reported, "I am prepared to prove, if necessary, that they are not actually employed upon their official duties one hour a day during the entire year." The rent for the building, two thousand dollars a month, he termed a gross fraud upon the Government. Customs House heads rolled as a result of Browne's investigations, up to and including that of Collector of Customs Richard P. Hammond himself.

Browne next examined the Appraiser's Office and the United States Marine Hospital. At first, he thought that he found traces of honesty, but soon determined that the appraiser was a usurer and that the hospital was paying just double the market price for the beef it fed its beached sailors. When he moved on to the Mint he found it a Tammany Hall, a hangout for idlers and political job seekers. Rent with scandal, it was not even able to meet the demands of the city for coinage, much less that of the entire West. In the fall of 1855, Browne discovered that Assayer Agoston Haraszthy, later the founding father of California's wine industry, had formed a private gold refining firm with Mint Superintendent Lewis Birdsall in as blatant a case of conflict of interests as California has ever seen. Both were fired, upon Browne's recommendation, when they blamed considerable losses of gold at the Mint upon the updraft of the building's chimneys.

J. Ross Browne found most of California's so-called ports to be lifeless, and he recommended layoffs of customs officials at Benicia, Sacramento, Stockton, and elsewhere. Santa Barbara he found so dead that he reported its population was "almost exclusively composed of native Californians whose only business, so far as I have been able to discover, is gambling and horse racing."

Investigating the Indian reservations of California, Browne found the agents' policy to be, apparently, that of expending Government money to feed white men and to starve Indians. "In the brief period of six years," he stated, "they have been nearly destroyed by the generosity of Government. What neglect, starvation and disease have not done, has been achieved by the cooperation of the white settlers in the great work of extermination."

The blood blisters of the many toes stepped on by Browne, the hard-nosed Diogenes, eventually stretched all the way to Washington itself. His days became numbered. Browne realized that he was committing political suicide by his ruthless insistence upon honesty in governmental affairs, but he continued his crusade. In the 1860's, his roving commission was deftly retrieved, but he had made enough of an impression to be named Minister to China by President Andrew Johnson in 1868. But here, too, his obstinate honesty was his undoing. When he expressed ideas almost opposite of those of his predecessor, Anson Burlingame, he was recalled.

Browne retired to Oakland, California, and returned to his writing career. Some critics have designated him a precursor of Mark Twain in American humor; certainly his witty articles and books were very popular a century ago. He died, suddenly, on December 9, 1875, after being taken ill on a ferryboat in San Francisco Bay. But before he died, he left a last testimonial in which he surveyed his career as a secret agent with a neat blend of humor and bitterness:

"During a period of three years, the agent made his reports, piling up proof upon proof and covering acres of valuable paper with protests and remonstrances against the policy pursued, racking his brains to do his duty faithfully, subjecting himself to newspaper abuse for neglecting it, because no beneficial result was perceptible, and making enemies as a matter of course.

"Reader, if you ever aspire to official honors, let the fate of that unfortunate agent be a warning to you. He did exactly what he was instructed to do, which was exactly what he was not wanted to do. In order to save time and expense, as well as further loss of money in the various branches of public service upon which he had reported, other agents were sent out to ascertain if he had told the truth; and when they were forced to admit that he had, there was a great deal of trouble in the wigwam of the Great Chief. Not only did poor Yorick incur the hostility of powerful senatorial influences, but, by persevering in his error and insisting that he had told the truth, the whole truth and nothing but the truth, he eventually lost the respect and confidence of the powers that be, together with his official head.

"I knew him well. He was a fellow of infinite jest. There was something so exquisitely comic in the idea of taking official instructions literally, and carrying them into effect, that he could not resist it."

LUTHER BURBANK

(*1849–1926*)

California's all-time botanical wizard was born (March 7, 1849) in New England, but his ancestry was not that of a Boston Brahmin but a more typical American hodgepodge of French, Dutch and Scots as well as English strains. From his mother he acquired a sensitivity and a love of plants and flowers while still a youngster (his father's thirteenth child in three marriages) in his birthplace, Lancaster, Massachusetts. Luther became supersensitive, in fact, and was known to break into tears if someone either praised him or criticized him to his face, but he later overcame this insecurity.

After grammar school, young Burbank attended the Lancaster Academy and, in a sense, "attended" the Lancaster Public Library. In his case, the sometimes rather too grandiose designation of America's modest public libraries as "the people's university" was apt. For there, in the library, the turning point of Burbank's career occurred in his teens. He took from the bookshelves a copy of Charles Darwin's *Variation of Animals and Plants under Domestication*. He went on to the more famous *Origin of Species* and determined to become a plant breeder. The first volume which he bought for his own private book collection was the same *Variation of Animals and Plants* and the second was Darwin's *Cross and Self-Fertilization in the Vegetable Kingdom.*

Luther Burbank improved upon his natural farm boy's knowledge of the so-called vegetable kingdom by going into the business of market gardening about the time that he began to read Charles Darwin. With the help of a little money from the estate of his father, who had just died, Luther Burbank bought seventeen acres near Lunenburg and began to grow vegetables there to supply the markets of the nearby city of Fitchburg. Burbank had such a green thumb that he not only grew far better vegetables than did his competitors but he got them to market before they could even harvest their crops. He began his plant experiments at this time, too. The first of his many new creations was the Burbank potato.

After four years of market gardening, Burbank decided to sell out and head for California, where three elder brothers had preceded him. By the time his accounts were settled, he was almost broke, so he sold all of his rights to his new potato to a seedsman of Marblehead, Massachusetts, for $150. His travel costs to the Pacific Coast were $140, so Burbank's total capital in 1875 was $10—plus, luckily, ten of his Burbank potatoes which the buyer had allowed him to keep in order that he might get a fresh start in the Far West. The trip to California took nine days, during which Luther sat up in a day coach, living out of a lunch basket or hamper which his mother had packed for him, and catching what sleep he could in his seat. He had decided upon Santa Rosa, the seat of Sonoma County, north of San Francisco, as his destination.

Burbank was not disappointed in the town. He described it in letters home as Nature's chosen spot above all others on earth. He pronounced the climate to be perfect and spent large quantities of ink describing the sweet air, the soft sunshine, the mountains, and the oak-dotted valleys. Small wonder that Luther Burbank scarcely budged from Santa Rosa during the next fifty years of his exacting work.

This half century in the gardens and greenhouses of Santa Rosa and Sebastopol was a time of great fame, of years in which his discoveries were so exaggerated, in fact, by the press (mainly Sunday supplement hacks) that a reaction developed and some ill-advised debunkers labeled the horticultural genius a faker.

Burbank's motives were not at all in the area of pure science; scarcely research "for its own sake." He wanted to apply his findings in order to produce more delicious fruits and more beautiful flowers. He was not completely accepted by scientists, possibly because he was something of a poet, with a dash of Thoreau and Muir in his nature, and very much a common man. As he experimented with thousands of different plants and literally hundreds of thousands of specimens, he chose to "waste" little time in building up a huge mass of written data. He preferred to be out in his fields of flowers rather than hunched over a ledger in a laboratory. The Smithsonian Institution tried to salvage the scientific data which he collected (only to discard), put him on salary, and sent him an assistant to compile proper records. But the project did not work out well. Burbank was basically a loner and the arrangement was ended, by mutual agreement, after five years.

Burbank imported many plants which were new to California both to test their economic potential and to use them in his real forte—hybridization. He not only hybridized closely related plants in order to produce new varieties but also mated very dissimilar plants and successfully avoided the mulish sterility which so often resulted from overtinkering with Nature's laws of genetics and botany. It was as if some sixth sense told Burbank the limits which Nature would tolerate. He was not always sure that his new form would be a useful plant; he wanted to "perturb" his specimens enough so that he could secure as wide a variation as possible, just to see what might result. He crossed some plants in order to multiply desirable traits and others in hopes of reducing or even eliminating entirely bad characteristics.

Burbank's recognition of desirable characteristics in his modifications of plants was perhaps his true genius; he knew —instinctively?—which seedlings or cuttings to select to be saved and which to discard. What made this gift so remarkable in Burbank among plant breeders was that the new traits or characteristics which he brought into being were often almost imperceptible in the early stages—a firmer-fleshed fruit; a slightly enhanced fragrance in a flower. To speed up the process (for he could not wait for a seedling to grow into a fruit-bearing tree), Burbank mastered the art of grafting. He would graft up to sixty different new seedling varieties on a tree, and one herculean plum tree in his gardens carried six hundred of his plum grafts!

The magician of greenhouse and garden did his best work with plums and prunes, berries and lilies, developing dozens of new varieties. But he also created new roses, poppies, clematises, etc., as well as corn and other vegetables. He is best remembered in California (if not for the Burbank potato) for his magnificent Shasta daisy and for his spineless cactus. He intended the latter to supply feed for stock in the arid cattle ranges of the Southwest. He selected three very hardy northern cacti and crossed them with three southern types. The experiment worked, and Burbank got the big, plump, and spineless beaver tail which he desired, but it was not a complete success. Alas, the smooth crossbred cactus tends to revert back to the spiny condition of its countless ancestors.

Luther Burbank's particular pride and, perhaps, his "monument" is his Shasta daisy. This was the result of a multiple crossing of American and European species of field daisies and then the crossing of their progeny with a Japanese variety. In the Shasta daisy, he not only created a larger, showier flower (up to eight inches in diameter), he transformed a troublesome weed into a flower of great beauty. Perhaps it all began when a gardener of Burbank's said to him as he puttered about a flower bed, "White is white and all these daisies are white." Burbank disagreed, insisting that not one of the daisies bore a truly white flower. But he saw that one was closer to true white than all the others, though none of the gardeners or visitors could see the difference until a San Francisco artist verified Burbank's belief. He decided to use it in his experiments. It was a common weed in the Eastern United States, called an oxeye or oxeye daisy. A pest on New England roadsides, it was unknown in California until Burbank brought it west as a kind of souvenir of his childhood. He crossed it with a European oxeye (so-called, although actually a different species) whose appearance suffered by its coarse, weedy look and unsightly leaves on the flower stalks but which was large and robust. The new hybrids which he created still lacked the crystal whiteness of petals which he sought. But a man who could create a spineless cactus, a white blackberry, and a stoneless plum could not be licked. He found a Japanese daisy (Chrysanthemum nipponicum) which was a coarse and scraggly-leafed plant but which bore an inconspicuous bloom of almost pure white. The first results of Burbank's pollenizing were disappointing. But among a host of seedlings he found *one* tiny plant with not only larger flowers than the others but one whose rays, or petals, were of quartz-crystal whiteness. Four ancestral strains from three continents finally produced thousands of seedlings in six years of experimentation. He selected and destroyed, selected and destroyed, until—by Darwin's survival of the fittest—he had the pure white daisy of which he had long dreamed. Most plant experimenters would have expected that the breeding of an inferior Japanese daisy, for whiteness, would have meant a reduction in the size of the flower in the resultant hybrid. But Burbank was wiser; he realized the immense variation possible by what he called the "conflict of hereditary tendencies" in the crossing of two such dissimilar strains. He gambled on this and he won.

The Shasta daisy is a fitting monument to Luther Burbank, far better than cold stone statuary. It is such a perfect plant that even its creator was astounded. It is a mammoth among daisies, with crystal-white blossoms often four to six inches in diameter. Graceful, abundant in blooms, its stem is unencumbered by unsightly leaves, the tall flower is hardy enough to thrive in almost any soil. Moreover, where its ancestors do not bloom until the second year, the Shasta daisy—with typical California *élan* and zest—blossoms in its first season and is a prolific bloomer almost throughout the entire year.

Luther Burbank's scientific contributions—eight hundred new strains of plants—may seem unimportant. He split no atoms, to be sure, and sent no early astronauts into space. He simply stimulated plant breeding in California *and* devoted a lifetime to making the state more beautiful via its gardens when more hardheaded folk were busily destroying its beauty with industry, commerce, and speculation.

FONG CHING (alias LITTLE PETE)

(1864?–97)

The only Chinatown homicide which is considered a San Francisco "classic" by the rather grisly little school of true-crime aficionados is the murder of the quarter's political boss in a barber chair (shades of Chicago and L.A.!) in 1897. Stories of tong-war killings were usually tucked back with the tide tables in the daily press in the Gay '90's, but when Little Pete "got his," he was given the whole front page of the San Francisco *Call.*

Like most inhabitants of the Oriental district, Little Pete was something of a mystery man to the press and the (Caucasian) public, although he was considerably less self-effacing than most of his fellow-Chinese. But we know that he was born circa 1864 in Kow Gong, about ten miles out of Canton, and that he migrated to the City of the Golden Hills when he was ten. Unlike most of his peers, he studied—and mastered —the English language while he worked as an errand boy in a Sacramento Street shoe factory. (According to tradition, he was ultimately so cultured that he not only became a patron of the theater but actually wrote Chinese operas himself, which were performed in the Jackson Street theater.)

When still only a youth, Fong Ching joined the Sam Yup Company and became that society's interpreter. He was, shortly, the most completely Americanized of all the Chinese in San Francisco, though he retained his queue. He was well liked by most of the whites who came to know him. Fong Ching, seemingly, was a good candidate for the role of the man who would break down the psychological Chinese Wall hemming in the minority group, but it did not work out that way. Fong Ching was interested in *personal* integration into American society, but he was quite content with the separateness of the Chinese community—this kind of *apartheid* made it all the easier to take over. The Americanized Chinese had learned the local political ropes. He saw how a political-criminal alliance could exist and prosper in San Francisco, and he copied it, adding purely Oriental detail and decoration, as it were. His combination of Oriental sagacity and Yankee know-how made him the wealthiest and most powerful individual in the city-within-a-city. His brief but brilliant success story has never been rivaled on Dupont Gai, as the Chinese called Dupont Street, now Grant Avenue. Once he overcame the handicap of his youth in a society where, traditionally, the elder's word was law, Fong Ching found Chinatown his to rule.

By saving his earnings and borrowing some money, Fong Ching was able to establish a shoe-manufacturing business. To fool what was becoming a "union town," most hostile to coolie labor, he gave his shoes the brand name of F. C. Peters. (The F. C., presumably, was for Fong Ching.) He hired white bookkeepers and salesmen to front for him, too. He could not fool all San Franciscans, of course, but those in the know took it as a good joke and dubbed him Little Pete from his Peters trademark. Meantime, he was running slots (illegal immigrants) and singsong girls, or prostitutes, into the city, conducting several lucrative gambling dens, and attracting tough *boo how doy,* highbinders, or hatchet men, to his tong, or private army.

Chinatown's fighting tongs, unlike the family associations and commercial "companies," were paramilitary organizations so tightly disciplined that they made meetings of the Mafia resemble shipfitters' picnics. These hatchet men patrolled his protection racket and kept the profits flowing into Pete's lockboxes. When rival tongs grew jealous or fearful of Little Pete, his hatchet men took care of them. But when his pet bodyguard, Lee Chuck, put five slugs into a would-be assassin, he bungled his getaway and was arrested. The boss of Chinatown then compounded his goon's error by attempting to bribe the arresting officers into perjuring themselves at the trial. As a result, after three trials and the expenditure of seventy-five thousand dollars in bribes, Pete found himself drawing a prison term too.

On September 7, 1887, the judge sentenced Little Pete to five years in Folsom Penitentiary after scolding him for trying to bribe and suborn his way to freedom. Pete listened stoically to both the sentence and the sermon, but he was not repentant. However, he was determined to be more careful in the future. Shortly after he was released, he was back on top of Chinatown again, running lotteries, gambling hells, and singsong houses, forging revenue stamps for opium shipments, and pulling off a real coup during the Midwinter Fair of 1893. He openly imported 257 Chinese (mostly women) to staff the fair's Chinese Pavilion. Just how many were slave girls is open to debate, but customs officials found that all but thirty-seven of the total had melted away by June of 1894.

By now, Little Pete was so Americanized that he became a great fan of the bangtails. He loved horse racing and, like any Chinese, adored betting. But since he was also a good

Yankee businessman, he arranged to come up winners most of the time. He would bet up to six thousand dollars a day and seldom lost. In March 1896 track officials got the word on his "system" from a confessing jockey. Pete had bought up five—some reports said ten—of the key jockeys at the Bay District track and fixed the races, win, place, and show. He, literally, couldn't lose. Little Pete and the jocks he had corrupted were barred from the local tracks, of course.

Pete had plenty of rivals. That was why he was as careful as Jesse James as to whom he showed his back. He also took the precaution of investing $132 in a bulletproof vest of fine steel mesh, or chain mail, weighing thirty-five pounds. He used watchdogs; he replaced his personal hatchet man with a pistol-packing white bodyguard, Ed Murray, first, then C. H. Hunter. On January 23, 1897, however, Little Pete—quite literally—made the mistake of his life. He let his tong men off for the day, since it was the Chinese New Year's season. Then he sent Hunter down the street to the New Western Hotel to pick up a copy of the *Sporting World* for him, so that he might study the latest racing results. Hunter warned his employer to be on his guard, but Pete just laughed, saying, "That's all right, I'll take care of myself. I'll go downstairs and get shaved while you're gone."

Perhaps Hunter brushed past two young men, dressed in black and wearing black fedoras, who were lounging against the wall of a nearby building. Once he was gone, they straightened up and each extracted a pistol from inside his blouse. For the first time in months, perhaps in all the years since his release from Folsom, Little Pete was unprotected. The two strangers performed like well-rehearsed actors. One went inside the barbershop at 819 Washington Street near Waverly Place while the other stopped, blocking the door. It was 9:10 P.M. Pete's bodyguard was fumbling for change or perhaps scanning the racing news a few blocks away as a roar of sound, smoke, and the stink of cordite filled the little barbershop where the King of Chinatown was having his forehead neatly shaved and his pigtail washed and braided. A slug in the chest blasted Pete and his chair over backwards and when he hit the floor two more smashed into his skull, killing him instantly. At 9:11, C. H. Hunter was out of a job, two out-of-town hatchet men were richer by the price on Pete's head, three thousand dollars, and the King of Chinatown was gone.

The barbers, naturally, had seen nothing; they swore it on the bones of their ancestors. Police found the murder weapon, a Colt Storekeeper-model pistol, and rounded up witnesses and suspects. A small arsenal was turned up too, including three knives, another Colt .45, a cleaver, and two hatchets. But it was soon evident that Chief Crowley had the wrong men in custody, and they were released. The murder was never solved; it is still on the books. The coroner's jury returned the familiar verdict of homicide at the hands of a "person or persons unknown."

The prime suspect in Little Pete's killing was not arrested. He had too precise an alibi, was in the clear. But, guilty or innocent, the Dupont Gai grapevine brought word to the tong leader known to the white community only by his nickname, Big Jim, that he would have to pay for his rival's death. A marked man, Jim fled to Victoria and then to China for his health. Counterthreats caused a friend of Pete's, Ung Hung, alias The Russian, to hire a very special kind of bodyguard—Tom Douglass, son of a police captain in Crowley's force.

Because he had handed out quite a bit of charity and had hired a number of Chinese for his shoe factory, Little Pete was whitewashed à la Bonnie and Clyde, in death. The *Chinese Recorder,* for example, insisted that his good qualities more than counterbalanced the evil parts of his nature. Chief Crowley did not agree. He said of Little Pete, "He was at the bottom of every blackmailing scheme and held absolute power over the highbinders of Chinatown." Saint or devil, Little Pete was now a great celebrity. His funeral on January 26, 1898, was one of the grandest spectacles—and one of the most disgusting—in San Francisco history. First came the ritualistic cooking of meats, the burning of candles and punks in front of the bloodied barbershop. Then, in clouds of incense, marchers got under way in a procession, bearing floral tributes and accompanied by a brass band, a black hearse and six horses in jet trappings, although the Chinese mourning color was white, not black. But far more disturbing aspects of Pete's Sino-American ambivalence were to come. Even before the wailing incantations of priests in silk and brocade reached the Chinese Cemetery far out in the Richmond District, before the clangor of gongs invaded the holy ground of the so-called Celestials, a horde of curiosity-seekers was there.

Luckily for us, the *Wave* had assigned its top reporter to the funeral story. He was a pretty fair Pepys, Frank Norris. The future novelist was intrigued by the Oriental ceremony but appalled by the misconduct of the whites in the crowd. He painted a word picture of the tumult, which would have been a fit subject for Hogarth: "A reckless, conscienceless mob of about two thousand, mostly women, crowded into the Chinese Cemetery. There was but one policeman to control them and they took advantage of the fact. The women thronged about the raised platform and looted everything they could lay their hands on—Chinese bowls, punk, tissue paper ornaments, even the cooked chickens and bottles of gin. . . . A mob of red-faced, pushing, women thronged about the coffin and interrupted everything that went on. There was confusion and cries in Cantonese and English; a mounted policeman appeared and was railed at. . . . Then the civilized Americans, some thousands of them, descended on the raised platform where the funeral meats were placed. . . . Four men seized a roast pig by either leg and made off with it; were pursued by the mounted police and made to return the loot. Then the crowd found amusement in throwing bowlfuls of gin at each other. The roast chickens were hurled back and forth. . . .

"Still it remained upon the spot; this thing, the crowd, this shameless mob that was mostly women. There was nothing more to happen; the ceremony was over, but still these people stayed and stayed. This was the last impression one received of Little Pete's funeral—a crowd of men and women, standing in a huge circle, stupidly staring at the remains of a roasted pig."

GALEN CLARK

(*1814–1910*)

Were it not for John Muir's thousand-mile walk from Indiana to the Gulf of Mexico, which led to his migration to the Pacific Coast, the patron saint of California conservation today might be Galen Clark instead of the Scotsman from Wisconsin. There might well be a Clark Woods at the base of San Francisco's Mount Tamalpais and perhaps even a commemorative stamp bearing Clark's bearded features rather than Muir's equally hirsute visage. For the truth is, Galen Clark anticipated John Muir in the role of protector of Yosemite and the Sierra. However, in both the short and the long runs, Clark was eclipsed by the more talented Muir and found himself pushed, first, into the background and, finally, almost into oblivion. Since he was a quiet, modest, and retiring man, he made no protest and was memorialized after his death only by a school in Merced and a mountain and range in Yosemite's back country which bear his name.

Rescue from this undeserved state of near-oblivion waited until 1964. That year, the Sierra Club published a biography of the pioneer conservationist which was titled *Galen Clark, Yosemite Guardian*. It was authored by the nearest thing we have to a resident historian in Yosemite, Shirley Sargent of Flying Spur, a homestead just beyond the national park's western boundary. Miss Sargent is a woman with a spiritual kinship to the grizzled mountain man who, unlike most of his contemporaries, sought not profit, but preservation in the wilderness.

Galen Clark preceded John Muir to Yosemite by a good dozen years. In a very real sense, Muir built upon philosophical foundations laid by Clark to protect Yosemite Valley— the Indians' Ahwahnee (Valley of the Grizzlies)—from the inroads of promoters and developers and sight-seers who would have despoiled the mountain paradise even a hundred years ago. Other pioneers saw Yosemite, with eyes blinded by selfishness, as a place to run sheep or cattle, or in which to saw logs, or—in the case of James M. Hutchings—a locality to improve (!) into a tourist attraction. Clark had the wisdom and the humanity to realize that alpine California was as near perfect as possible an example of God's handiwork and something which should not be tampered with by man. He became a sort of silent partner to the more flamboyant Muir, but he was no less dedicated than the latter in standing watch over the valley and its surrounding high country.

One or two of Galen Clark's books are of permanent interest, although only one is familiar at all to Californians. His *Indians of Yosemite* (1904) does not contain the gifts of expression which came naturally to the more poetic Muir, but it is a journeyman-like book, testimony to the influence upon Clark of his home town (Dublin, New Hampshire) library, one of the first three public libraries in the United States. But Clark's career has little to do with literature. His defensive stance was the first effective act in the long story of Yosemite National Park. The second act was dominated entirely by John Muir. We are still seeing the third act, and the drama seems to be taking a turn toward tragedy. Seasonal overpopulation and overexploitation have taken their toll in Yosemite Valley. Clark would never have dreamed in his worst nightmare that his beautiful vale would ever be turned into a summer slum, clogged with traffic and choked with smog. The park by 1969 was suffering far more from what rangers call "human erosion" than from all the sharp little hoofs of the baaing sheep which Clark and Muir hated so much.

Clark's claim upon our attention and respect is a genuine one. He saw the threat to our landscape even before Muir, and he began the protection of our outdoors, and Yosemite in particular. It is this tradition, born of Clark's efforts, which had kept the valley from an even bleaker condition than its present humiliated state. Were Lake Tahoe only a little closer to Half Dome, it might not now be afflicted with the degradation of the South Shore, where a high-rise casino can block the lakescape and neon lights cheat the visitor of the full glory of a Sierra sunset.

Galen Clark was born on March 28, 1814, in a cabin on a Quebec farm. He grew up in a family in which hunger and poverty were commonplace. At times, he and his brothers and sisters were forced to live on boiled basswood leaves and were grateful for them and the pinch of salt that made them almost palatable. In his early life, he revealed not a whit of the single-minded, stubborn devotion to the preservation of the wilderness which would be his sole claim to greatness. His goals were limited. He apprenticed to a chairmaker and did well at the craft until the sawdust tortured his weak lungs. Then Clark tried farming, moving west to Missouri for a spell, but he seemed to be a congenital debtor. Like Thoreau and other men of principle and vision in this country, he harkened to that different drum roll and was out of step with a community dominated by business. He was labeled a failure, correctly so by business standards.

The failed farmer and chairmaker did not reach California until he was forty-one years old and presumably dying of pneumonia. Perhaps he did die. Certainly Galen Clark was reborn in California. Although it took the state a decade to recognize and reward his services, he enjoyed a personal metamorphosis not only in health but in outlook and importance from the day he arrived in the Far West in 1853. California's virulent gold fever had seized him when he saw an exhibit of nuggets from famed El Dorado when he visited New York's Crystal Palace that year. As with so many other Americans, ill health figured almost as importantly in his decision to go west as did gold lust. Far from the agues, fevers, and poxes of the East and Midwest, he hunted for gold in Mariposa County in 1854 and, luckily, had no luck at all. His frail constitution was not up to a life of pickaxing and shoveling recalcitrant gravel from icy streams. When he joined surveying and prospecting parties as hunter and packer, his health began to improve.

Although he was still not strong, when Clark heard of the fabled Yosemite, or Yohamite, Valley, he was determined to see it. He joined sixteen Mariposa miners in August of 1855 and visited the magnificent chasm via the little-used (today) Chowchilla Mountain route. Like so many visitors, Clark was all but struck dumb by the awesomeness of the canyon which he viewed from Inspiration Point. He tried to describe the scene, but, although he claimed that in the mountain air "the brain breathes as well as the lungs," he failed miserably when he chose an affected elegance of style which resulted in flourishes of overblown and empty Victorian phrase—" a wonderful sanctuary . . . a sanctum sanctorum of Nature's vast mountain temple."

But Clark knew that he had found the place in which to test his doctor's prediction—that he would probably die but that he might recover in a mountain climate. He wrote that he moved to the meadows of the Wawona area of Yosemite in order to take his chances of dying or growing better, chances which he thought were about even. He filed a land claim to 160 acres on the South Fork of the Merced River for grazing and agricultural pursuits. Since his family was still in the East, he lived virtually alone at first, although, like Grizzly Adams, he made friends with the local Indians. Soon, travelers began to stop at Clark's Station or Clark's Ranch, a rude log cabin but one with bookshelves inside. He spent most of his time either exploring or hunting for food. He discovered the Mariposa Grove of Big Trees, or sequoias. These redwoods became an early attraction for the hardy tourists who began to visit Yosemite. Clark was able to subsist by supplying them with comfortable bunks and good meals of venison, trout, and wild strawberries. He also acted as guide and repaired trails on his own hook. He built a second cabin, in Mariposa Grove, and travelers nicknamed it Galen's Hospice.

By 1864, Clark was alarmed at the changes in the valley and afraid that it might be overrun with people. With others, like Frederick Law Olmsted and Jessie Benton Frémont, he worked for the creation of a forest preserve at Yosemite. Senator John Conness's bill was passed and the federal government granted the land to the State of California for "public use, resort and recreation, inalienable for all time." Congress ordered the Governor of California to appoint a Board of Commissioners to oversee the Yosemite Grant, and President Abraham Lincoln signed the bill into law on June 30, 1864. One of the eight first commissioners was Galen Clark. He fought fires, kept an eye out for intruders, and in 1866 was named by the board full-time guardian of Yosemite Valley and Big Tree Grove. He worked hard to keep out stock, maintain bridges and trails, battle forest fires, prohibit the cutting down of trees and the putting up of advertising signboards. He had to be especially tactful with the early settlers, who were allowed by the state to remain for the time being. When James Hutchings preferred an open fight, he and the others were evicted. They then, blindly, used their political influence in the state capital to defeat appropriation bills so that, among other things, there was no money in the Treasury to pay Clark's modest salary. He kept working, anyhow. By the time John Muir arrived in Yosemite in April 1868, the valley and its environs were reasonably safe, thanks to Galen Clark. The two men became friends, and Muir later described his tutor in things Sierran as "the best mountaineer I ever met."

Muir and Clark were opposites, in many ways. The former was merry and extroverted; Clark was kindly, shy, and gifted with a very quiet humor. His writing was pedestrian. But they got along well. Clark needed Muir's support. The transcontinental railroad's completion raised the number of visitors from 623 in 1868 to 1122 in the following year.

Never a good businessman, Clark still, via a partnership, managed to hang onto his inn and his interest in the new toll road. He remarried, not very happily, in 1874 (his first wife was dead) and moved to the valley floor, where he was appointed special deputy sheriff. He took his job of guardianship very seriously and angered friends when he opposed the building of a chapel in Yosemite Valley. But who would argue, today, with his reasoning? "It seems to me like sacrilege to build a church within the portals of this, the grandest of all God's temples. It is like building a toy church within the walls of St. Peter's Cathedral."

A change in administration ended Clark's tenure as guardian in 1881. The new board offered him the subguardian's post, but he declined. He became pretty much of a full-time guide for tourists in the valley, but James M. Hutchings, the development-oriented pioneer of Yosemite, who was Clark's successor as guardian, was ousted in a quarrel and the commission fell on evil days. A political appointee who was also a Southern Pacific Railroad employee was finally fired in 1889, and Clark was restored to the post which he had filled so well. He cleaned up the neglected valley just in time for the creation of Yosemite National Park, surrounding the still state-owned Yosemite Valley, in 1890. U.S. cavalry patrolled the larger park, and John Muir organized the Sierra Club as an auxiliary force to increase the amount of protection available.

At the age of seventy-five, Clark began to spend his winters in sunny Summerland, in Santa Barbara County. But he continued to patrol his beloved Yosemite during the less rigorous seasons of the year, inspecting trails and delivering mail. By 1899, no longer official guardian, he was disenchanted with the State of California's stingy mishandling of Yosemite Valley and Mariposa Grove. Reversing his earlier position, he urged that the grant be handed back to the U. S. Government. This was done in 1905.

Clark visited Yosemite for the last time in 1909. He planned on going back to the mountains from the Southern California coast, as usual, the following year, but he did not make it. Galen Clark died in his sleep on March 24, 1910, just four days before his ninety-sixth birthday. He had severed his official connection with the park in 1890, when he was a lively seventy-six. At that time the Yosemite commissioners had drawn up a handsomely inscribed document praising him for "his faithful and eminent services as Guardian, his constant efforts to preserve, protect and enhance the beauties of Yosemite."

Surely there is a lesson for us in the life of Galen Clark. He came to California (to die), a middle-aged tubercular. He then devoted more years than many people are granted in a lifetime—fifty-five years—to his vision, the preservation of the most beautiful valley in the world for the people who, left alone, might have ruined it utterly through carelessness and greed.

LILLIE COIT

(1842–1929)

Entrance requirements for this volume are not extraordinarily high, as the mere inclusion of madman Emperor Norton will suggest. Even so, there are those to whom Lillie Hitchcock Coit's credentials would be somewhat suspect. Her role, like that of Norton I, was that of public character, civic mascot. At first, she represented only the "bhoys" of the volunteer fire companies but eventually came to be a city-wide mascot in San Francisco like Emperor Norton, and two photographs of Lillie were buried in the cornerstone of the new (1872) City Hall. Too, there is no denying that she was a more attractive city pet than the grimy lunatic shambling his way from free lunch to free lunch, so, perhaps, it is fitting that she be granted equal time and space.

Unconvinced readers are reminded, too, that Lillie Hitchcock's unconventional behavior contributed something to the liberation of women, the feminist movement, which brought us votes for women, ugly fashions, girls riding cable-car running boards, and equality of lung cancer, among other social boons. Because Lillie dared to be different, and got away with it, other ladies in the West screwed up their courage and became individuals too.

The handsome, prominent, and social—but not snobbish—Lillie was the daughter of Dr. Charles M. Hitchcock and a Southern belle, Martha Taliaferro Hunter, one of the "F.F.V." (First Families of Virginia.) As a child in San Francisco, circa 1851, Lillie became a fire buff because of the lack of amusements for children in the raw city. She imitated the local boys, trapping rats under the boardwalks and chasing fires, but preferred the latter as a permanent avocation. During the 1860's she attended daylight fires as an honorary member of Knickerbocker Engine Company No. 5 and saluted their night calls by keeping a light burning in her window until the horses hauled the engine back to the firehouse. Each year on the company's birthday, Lillie would appear at the banquet dressed in a red fireman's shirt atop a black silk dress. Around her waist was a huge-buckled fireman's belt, and she carried her shiny black fire helmet in one hand. Often she rode the engine in parades, and she sometimes treated the tired and dirty men to supper after a difficult fight with a blaze. She always wore her gold "5" pin, day or night. (She was buried wearing it.) She took to signing her name "Lillie Hitchcock 5" and, after she married Benjamin Howard Coit, "Lillie Hitchcock Coit 5."

The Civil War forced the belle of San Francisco and her very pro-Confederate mother to move to France, but Lillie returned in 1863 and resumed her role as the fire company favorite. She was occasionally eccentric, as when her dyed hair annoyed her husband. She shaved her head completely and wore, alternately, not all at once, a red, a black, and a blond wig. Dr. Hitchcock separated her from off-beat Frisco by building a country retreat for her in the Napa Valley. She lived there even after she and Coit separated, entertaining at Larkmead the literary lights who passed that way, including Robert Louis Stevenson and Joaquin Miller. But the pull of San Francisco was strong and she returned to live in a Palace Hotel suite.

In 1904 an insane acquaintance (a Confederate veteran) shot to death one of Lillie's callers in her Palace Hotel sitting room, before her eyes. Although the man was confined, Mrs. Coit was so shocked that she moved to Europe and feared to return until the murderer died, in 1924. She was eighty-one and already a legend. She died in July 1929, leaving one-third of her estate to add to the beauty of the city. An observation tower was commissioned by the city government to crown Telegraph Hill, and it opened in 1934. Accused, mistakenly, of being suggested by a fire-hose nozzle, the silo-like tower has not won the hearts of either citizens or *turistas,* but it is a landmark and is of some use in getting one's bearings on foggy nights.

GEORGE H. DERBY

(1823–61)

San Diego enjoys the honor of having been, for a time, the home town of the West's first humorist, the fun-loving prankster of the U. S. Army, Lieutenant George Horatio Derby. Although he was born in Dedham (April 3, 1823), Derby was nothing like the dour and taciturn Massachusetts man of legend. California's most eccentric and funny pioneer was both a literary wit and a practical joker. His biographer, George R. Stewart, feels that he deserves to be remembered not so much as the writer of two humorous books, *Phoenixiana* and *The Squibob Papers,* which such men as William M. Thackeray, Teddy Roosevelt, and William Dean Howells admired, as for his joyous, nonconformist personality, which brightened the harsh reality of life on a distant frontier. The books are now dated, of course, with many of their nuances and topical references dulled by the relentless passage of time, but they were once very popular, *Phoenixiana* going through twenty editions by 1890.

Even before he entered West Point, George Derby was writing, although not under his noms de plume of John Phoenix and Squibob. For example, he lauded the Puritan founders of New England when he was in his teens—"They planted corn and built houses, they killed the Indians, hung the Quakers and Baptists, burned the witches alive, and were very happy and comfortable, indeed." Somehow the bright but uninhibited and indisciplinable Derby survived the U. S. Military Academy and became a lieutenant in the Corps of Topographical Engineers, where his sketching ability lent itself to cartography. In the Mexican War he was sent to scout one flank of the enemy force while Lieutenant Robert E. Lee reconnoitered the other. Derby upstaged Lee by bringing back not only verbal observations and notes but two drawings of the enemy lines pin-pointing their artillery batteries. He joined a charge led by the fiery dragoon William S. Harney, and had his horse shot out from under him and later was wounded in the hip.

How did Derby get to California after he recovered? The story is that Secretary of War Jefferson Davis exiled him there, for impertinence. When Davis asked him to survey Alabama's Tombigbee River, to see how far up it ran, Derby reported that, after making much study and even interviewing settlers in Alabama and Mississippi, he had, at last, come to the conclusion that it did not run up, at all, but down. The second part of the tale, at least, *is* true. Ordered to dam the often flooding San Diego River in California, he did so but built the dam parallel to the stream rather than across it!

In California, Derby first served on a reconnaissance of the gold country with General Bennett Riley, then he established Camp Far West (near modern Wheatland) and explored both the Sacramento and San Joaquin valleys. Ordered to the Colorado River, he determined that sailing craft could not ascend the shoaly mouth to Fort Yuma but that shallow-draft stern-wheelers would be able to do so. Between expeditions, Derby's reputation began to grow as a California humorist. Mark Twain attributed to him the oft-repeated story of the Fort Yuma soldier who died and was not one day in hell before he was telegraphing for his blankets. Derby may have invented the hoary old crack, too, about the (Fort Yuma) hens which laid hard-boiled eggs. In a mock lecture on astronomy which was one of Thackeray's Derby favorites, the lieutenant likened the planet Mercury, which receives more than six times as much heat from the sun as does the earth, to Fort Yuma, adding, "The difficulty of communication with Mercury will probably prevent its ever being selected as a military post, though it possesses many advantages for that purpose, being extremely inaccessible, inconvenient and, doubtless, singularly uncomfortable."

In San Francisco, Lieutenant Derby joined a group of wags and wits which hung about Barry & Patten's Saloon. Once, when he saw a passing wagon with the words EAGLE BAKERY lettered on its side, he rushed out, halted the driver, and demanded a baked bird. When Don Julio Carillo wished to join the Masons, Derby convinced him that being branded was part of initiation. He simulated the branding of a blind-folded, flinching Carillo by heating an iron red-hot and singeing a scrap of cowhide next to Don Julio's own epidermis. Owen Wister inserted in his novel, *The Virginian* the prank which Derby played at a Sonoma ball—switching babies and blankets so that their mothers hauled home the wrong infants when the dance broke up.

Derby was next posted to San Diego, where, as he wrote:

> All night long in this sweet little village
> You hear the soft note of the pistol
> With the pleasant screak of the victom
> Whose been shot, perhaps in his gizzard.

Lieutenant Derby really did build his dam alongside the San Diego River but not as a joke. He was as competent an engineer as he was a cartographer or surveyor. He did it to shift the river back into its old bed, since it was cutting a new course which dropped its silt into San Diego Harbor. Next he "fixed" a duel by replacing the lead slugs in the pistols with balls of tallow darkened with charcoal. The winner was furious when his projectile merely splattered on the forehead of his enemy. It was Derby, too, who presumably invented for the first time one of the classic practical jokes of all time. Traveling with two strangers in a carriage, he successfully advised each one, privately (and, need it be said, incorrectly), that the other was stone deaf.

Besides building the sidewise dam, Derby did a little moonlighting in San Diego, surveying and buying some lots. He and Mary Coons married in 1854 and settled happily into a little square pine box of a house. He kept his good spirits although afflicted with eye trouble and assigned to the sodden Pacific Northwest to survey military roads in Oregon and Washington Territory. He reported, "It rains incessantly twenty-six hours a day for seventeen months of the year. . . . It commenced raining pretty heavily on the third of last November and continued up to the fifteenth of May, when it set in for a long storm which isn't fairly over yet."

In the fall of 1856 Derby took his family East, where he contributed to New York's *Knickerbocker* during several years of depressing illness, including partial blindness. He died on May 15, 1861, and his passing went virtually unnoticed; Fort Sumter had surrendered a month earlier. But an old friend, Mrs. C. M. Hitchcock, summed up his life well: "What other men would sacrifice for ambition, for love, for the attainment of fortune or personal aggrandizement, he would sacrifice for fun—his best friend would have no more chance of escape than his worst enemy." Editor L. G. Clark of the *Knicker-bocker* added, however, "There was not a particle of the struggling witticist, or imitative 'funny man' about him. He was a man of genius."

San Diego was the scene of Derby's greatest exploit, perhaps *the* Great Jest of California history. In August 1853, editor John Judson ("Boston") Ames of the San Diego *Herald,* a rock-solid Democratic sheet, left town for San Francisco and an election conference with Party bosses. He was confident that San Diego County would again go Democratic, as it had in the last election. He left in charge of the paper his friend, Lieutenant George H. Derby. *Herald* readers noticed a change in tone when a sprightly notice appeared in Ames's August 20 number: "Next week, with the Divine assistance, a new hand will be applied to the bellows of this establishment and an intensely interesting issue will possibly be the result. The paper will be published on Wednesday evening and, to avoid confusion, the crowd will please form in the Plaza, passing four abreast by the City Hall and the *Herald* office." In the columns of this next issue, where Ames had urged his fellow-citizens to vote for Democrat John Bigler for governor, Derby exhorted his readers to vote for the Whig candidate, William Waldo! After pleading the Whig cause in the Democratic paper, he then turned to local news: "There have been no births, no marriages, no arrivals, no dispatches, no earthquakes, nothing but the usual number of drinks taken and an occasional 'small chunk of a fight.' "

San Francisco echoed San Diego's laughter while Ames tried to explain the editorial switch to Party bigwigs. (For San Diego County went Whig!) Before the huge, six-foot-six editor (who had once killed a man with his fists) could return, Derby published—before the fact—an account of his arrival at the *Herald* office: "The sixth and last round is described by the pressmen and compositors . . . We held Boston down over the press by our nose (which we had inserted between his teeth for that purpose) and while our hair was employed in holding one of his hands, we held the other in our left and . . . shouted to him, 'Say Waldo!'"

JOHN C. FRÉMONT

(*1813–90*)

John Frémont's middle initial was C., for Charles, but it might just as well have stood for *Controversy,* for he was in the thick of it much of his life. No Californian, even John Sutter, has been the target of so much abuse at the same time that he has been showered with praise from other quarters. A recent children's biography of Frémont was subtitled "Soldier, Explorer, Statesman." Yet his accomplishments as a soldier were negligible and those as a statesman nil. It is as an explorer that Frémont deserves to be remembered by Californians, Westerners, and Americans in general, *and* as a kind of *agent provocateur*—an agent of America's Manifest Destiny.

With some whopping exceptions, Frémont performed creditably as the leader of exploring expeditions. The great debacle of his life was his fourth expedition (1848), in which he virtually abandoned his men in the Rockies after a reckless attempt to cross the range in the snows of midwinter. Less well known is the reason for the hatred still felt for him today in California on the part of the descendants of the state's original Spanish and Mexican families. Along with his aide,

Christopher (Kit) Carson, he is held responsible for the murder of three peaceable Mexican-Californians near San Rafael during the Mexican War.

Frémont was a fair-to-middling amateur scientist, too, and a better-than-average writer—unless the story of his wife's editing and rewriting every line of his narratives is a true one. In any case, his reports, which were turned into popular books, were responsible for a revival of interest in the Far West and animated many Easterners toward migration when news of the Gold Rush began to spread. Frémont's books also so captivated farm boy Cincinnatus Hiner Miller that he ran away from home for a life of adventure (and bad poetry) under the nom de plume of Joaquin Miller.

John C. Frémont was born in Savannah, Georgia (January 21, 1813), to John C. Frémont, Sr., a French émigré, and his wife Anne (Whiting). His parents were nonconformists, traveling like gypsies and sleeping in tents or Indian cabins as often as in small inns while M. Frémont painted his frescoes, gave his French lessons, or upholstered chairs. Young Charles's mother was widowed when he was but five years old, so, as the oldest boy (he had a younger brother and sister), he was forced to grow up fast and become the man of the family. At first, he was steered toward the law but showed such intelligence and precocious appetite for Greek and Latin that his mother's advisers diverted him toward the ministry. But John's love of life overran not only his interest in the classics but his new favorites, mathematics and astronomy, as well. He became careless about attendance and was expelled in 1831 from Charleston College for "habitual irregularity and incorrigible negligence."

Frémont could not remain idle long. Beneath his surface charm and ambition lay the drive of a fired-up steam engine. His friend, Joel Poinsett, ex-Minister to Mexico, secured him a post as teacher of mathematics aboard the sloop of war *Natchez* when the vessel sailed on a South American cruise. When he returned, he served as an assistant in the survey of the railroad route between Charleston and Cincinnati. At this point, Charleston College was persuaded to give him a five-year-delayed bachelor of arts degree before he began his work as an assistant in the 1836–37 survey of the North Carolina mountains from which the Cherokees had been removed. Poinsett, now Secretary of War, obtained the perfect appointment for him next—a second lieutenancy in the U. S. Corps of Topographical Engineers. He was to accompany Jean Nicollet on a surveying and mapping expedition to the headwaters of the Mississippi and Missouri rivers.

In 1841, Frémont married Jessie Benton and came under the protecting wing of her father, Senator Thomas H. Benton of Missouri, one of the most powerful men in Washington. Benton, like Frémont, was interested in continuing the work done by Meriwether Lewis in exploring and mapping the Far West. To secure the claims of the United States to the area and to chart routes to the Pacific, Benton got a series of expeditions under way, with his son-in-law in command. The first took him only to the Rockies. The second, in 1843, he led all the way to Oregon, making Washington uneasy because he took a howitzer along without authority. Jessie alerted him before orders for his recall reached him and he took off, into the wilds, just in the nick of time.

Frémont said he wanted the cannon for protection against the Indians. There were those who thought he was a potential filibuster who intended to use it against Mexican troops. Despite his deviousness, his vanity, and his ambition, Frémont made many friends, especially among the hard-bitten frontiersmen with whom he associated. He attracted a very strong personal loyalty from Kit Carson and other *yanqui* mountain men, as well as from *métis* (Canadian half-breeds) like Basil Lajeunesse, and Indians, particularly the Delawares who formed his Praetorian Guard. Beneath the self-serving ambition of Frémont lurked an integrity which was not lost upon these guides and scouts. Thanks to them, an unearned title —the "Pathfinder"—was bestowed upon Frémont. His outstanding biographer, Allan Nevins, is correct in suggesting a substitute—the "Pathmarker."

Via South Pass and Great Salt Lake, Frémont reached Oregon safely but did not press westward for the short distance to the sea but, instead, began a southward march toward Mexican territory. At first, he skirted along the eastern edge of the Sierra Nevada, but, at about the latitude of Reno, he crossed the mountains in the dead of winter, a most foolhardy gesture which succeeded but which probably led to his over-confidence in the Rockies during his fourth expedition. In March, he led his tattered and pinch-gutted men into Sutter's Fort, where the Swiss treated them like Christmas guests. Refitted, remounted, and fattened up, thanks to the kindly Captain Sutter, Frémont's expeditionaries marched southward in California, then hooked eastward for home via Salt Lake. (His reports on the great saline basin were so encouraging that Brigham Young decided to found his Deseret there, rather than farther westward, perhaps in California.)

Frémont's return from California and Oregon was a triumph. John Greenleaf Whittier saluted his courage—in crossing the Sierra in winter—with verse:

> Still upward turned, with anxious strain
> Their leader's sleepless eye,
> Where splinters of the mountain chain
> Stood black against the sky.

97

A third expedition was planned for the energetic explorer to lead. This one would survey the Rocky Mountain headwaters of the Arkansas and Rio Grande rivers, the Salt Lake basin, and the Cascade and Sierra ranges. Later Frémont suggested that he was given secret orders to follow should war break out between Mexico and the United States, as was often rumored. On December 9, 1845, Frémont was once again at Sutter's Fort, this time abusing his host's hospitality and repaying kindness with coldness and disdain—because Sutter wore the uniform of the Republic of Mexico. In March, Don José Castro, ranking military officer in Alta California, ordered the trespasser out of the territory. Instead of complying, Frémont dug in atop Gabilán Peak near San Juan Bautista. Mexican cavalry reconnoitered the mountain in strength but did not attack and the Americans retreated, "growlingly," to Sutter's Fort and thence to Oregon.

Unknown to Frémont, a messenger was on his trail. When Lieutenant Archibald Gillespie reached him, encamped near Klamath Lake, Oregon, the Marine lieutenant brought him instructions which remain secret to this day. They were oral, not written, and neither man was inclined, later, to be specific about them. But Frémont acted as if they gave him a free hand in California during the next few months.

Circumstances—and coincidence—almost thwarted Frémont. The Klamath Indians, ironically, chose the very night of Gillespie's arrival for their attack on the Pathfinder's camp. So distracted was Frémont by his dreams of *gloire* that, for once, he failed to post a guard. The entire camp was asleep by midnight. Suddenly, Frémont was awakened by Carson's hoarse shout, "What's the matter over there? What's the fuss about?" The only answer was a groan and Kit, instinctively, rolled out of his blankets and came up fighting. His shout of "Indians!" caused Frémont to scramble to his feet. They found that Lajeunesse had been tomahawked to death and the Iowa half-breed Denny was still writhing in his blankets, bristling with arrows. The Delawares joined the fight and the mountain men—Carson, Alex Godey, Lucien Maxwell, and Dick Owens —soon forced the Klamaths back into the darkness. But they continued their barrage of arrows into the camp, although Frémont hung blankets from cedar limbs to screen his men and impede the shafts. Crane, one of the Delawares, was killed, and another wounded, but dawn finally came and the attackers melted away. Frémont got on their trail, however, ran them down, and killed fourteen braves in revenge for the ambush. This proved to be Frémont's first—and last—victory as a soldier, although he did a lot of maneuvering in the Mexican War and received the final surrender of the enemy in California, through luck. (His Civil War career was hardly a success.)

Back in California, Frémont took over the Bear Flag Republic's tatterdemalion "army" and integrated it into his California Battalion, which he marched to Monterey and then transported to Southern California by ship. The *Californios* briefly regained control of Southern California and defeated General Stephen W. Kearny at San Pascual, but finally Don Andrés Pico surrendered—and to Frémont, rather than his superior. Good luck had ridden with Frémont so far, but now it turned, as it will. He sided with Commodore Robert F. Stockton against Kearny in the quarrel over exactly who was supreme commander in California. Kearny won and Frémont, although he was named Military Governor of California by the commodore, was now subjected to a series of indignities which culminated in his being ordered by Kearny to follow him eastward to the States. At Fort Leavenworth, he was arrested and ordered to report to the Adjutant General in Washington to answer to charges of disobedience of orders and conduct prejudicial to good order and discipline. Frémont hurried to the capital and demanded a court-martial. He got it and, to his surprise and the public's, a verdict of guilty on three of the assorted counts. Public and press sympathy was with Frémont, a hero of the California War, and President James K. Polk, while "approving" the sentence, immediately remitted it and ordered Frémont to return to duty. However, he resigned his commission.

John C. Frémont returned to California to find that the white elephant which he had bought, the Mariposa Ranch in the Sierra foothills, was rich with gold. He hired men to dig for him while he and Jessie resided in Monterey. In December of '49, he was elected one of the incipient state's two senators and returned to Washington. California was admitted to the Union on September 9, 1850, which left Frémont only three weeks of sessions in which to make a mark. He introduced some eighteen bills, largely dealing with California land or education, then returned to the Coast to run for re-election after his short-short term. He failed because of his too antislavery stand, so he toured Europe, led another expedition to survey railroad routes, and settled in the East.

In 1856, Frémont was the choice of the new Republican Party as its first Presidential candidate. But in spite of his high hopes and Whittier's poesy—"Frémont and Victory!"—Buchanan won. Still, a sometime Californian, heading a brand-new party, garnered 1,340,000 votes.

The Frémonts settled on their 43,000-acre Mariposa Ranch, where the colonel engaged in mining and smelting, trying to prove his title beyond a shadow of a doubt and expelling the pestiferous squatters from his lands. The Civil War took him East again to a military command in Missouri, where he soon plunged himself into hot water by taking it upon himself to proclaim all slaves of Missouri rebels to be

1. Occasionally, the camera does lie or, at least, it fibs a bit. Thus, the subject of this portrait would appear to be a refugee from a Popo Agie trappers' rendezvous. Actually, he is the Irish-born surveyor *Jasper O'Farrell*, who, more than anyone else, is responsible for the complicated pattern of streets in San Francisco. *Society of California Pioneers*

2. As mean a man as his slitted eyes suggest was ham-fisted *Harry Love*, commander of the California Rangers. Leading this 1853 band of brawlers, he brought in what he claimed to be the head of the notorious bandit Joaquín Murieta. In any case, Love collected the reward on Joaquín's head, and the latter was placed on exhibit, in pickle. As might be expected of a rough like Harry Love (note the brass butt of the Colt peering out from under his arm in deadly cross-draw position), he died with his boots on. *Fern Sayre*

3. Daft as a Down East loon was Joshua A. Norton, a pathetic ex-businessman bankrupted (even of his senses) by financial reverses in the wholesale rice market. As the self-styled *Emperor Norton,* he was for years the town mascot and buffoon. Only tolerated at first, the gentle Norton eventually won the affection of the greater part of San Francisco's citizens. *California Historical Society, San Francisco*

4. Proof positive of the efficacy of the experiments of "Hatfield the Rainmaker" (*Charles M. Hatfield*) was the response of Sweetwater Reservoir, southeast of San Diego, in January of 1916. Joining forces with the once-impounded waters of equally ruptured Otay Dam, this flood made the city of San Diego into a new Venice, cut off from the rest of the world except by sea. *Richard Pourade—San Diego Union*

5. Demagogue *Denis Kearney* was frightening enough for *Harper's Weekly* cartoonist Thomas Nast to give Boss Tweed and the Tammany gang a rest while he warned the nation about a new menace rising out of the vacant lots of San Francisco. However, the home-grown anarchist's political star set almost as fast as it rose, and Nast did not have to exert himself beyond this portrayal of Kearney—or really "Kearneyism"—on April 10, 1880. *University of San Francisco Library*

6. *Collis P. Huntington,* one of the Big Four of Central Pacific and Southern Pacific Railroad tycoons, was the most thoroughly hated of the foursome. To many Californians of the late nineteenth century, he epitomized the ruthless cupidity of the monopolists of the Gilded Age. However, his enemy, Adolph Sutro, put in a good word for him, stating that Huntington had never been known to steal a red-hot safe. *Southern Pacific Company*

7. *Grizzly Adams* (known for decades as James Capen Adams although he was really John Adams) was the most courageous eccentric ever to decorate the chronicles of California. He made John Muir look like a city slicker and a crowd pleaser. Adams preferred Indians to fellow-whites as company, animals to Indians, and wild animals—especially grizzly bears—to tame animals. He was a genuine Sierra Nevada hermit whose gift for dominating the fierce grizzlies was never equaled. *University of San Francisco Library*

8. *J. Ross Browne* was a gifted writer and artist, as this self-portrait suggests, whose outstanding claim to fame, however, would seem to be his abject honesty. In an era when knavery was triumphant all over the West, poor Brownie went zealously about his duties as secret agent of the federal government, pointing his finger at squalid little deals until an embarrassed Washington got rid of him. Even today historians hardly know what to make of him. *Sutro Library*

9. Perhaps, as the shutter snapped, *Helen Hunt Jackson* was secretly amused by the fact that the first great outpouring of public sympathy for the plight of California's Indians came not as a result of the compassionate crusade of men like J. Ross Browne, Don Benito Wilson, and Joaquin Miller, but because of her tag-end efforts. And, even then, it was not her propagandistic document, *A Century of Dishonor*, which did the trick but her perennial potboiler, the romantic novel *Ramona. Southern California Auto Club—Westways*

10. The man who started it all—*modern* California, as opposed to the cattle kingdom on the Pacific with which the original Mexican-Californians were content—was *John A. Sutter.* A Swiss grandee of California, "Don Augusto" created a New Switzerland in a howling wilderness and became the most powerful man in California before tumbling into defeat. Today his prodigality is as legendary as his kindness to travelers, and, curiously, both hold up under the examination of historians. *California State Division of Beaches and Parks*

11. As charming as any of the pretty Pomo Indian belles who posed for her brush was artist *Grace Carpenter Hudson.* Here, with obvious delight, she catches up on her correspondence in her Ukiah home, Sun House, after having scanned and jettisoned the San Francisco *Examiner. California Historical Society*

12. California's Negroes—and, for that matter, the state's other citizens of whatever color—should band together to honor *Delilah L. Beasley*, first historian of black Americans out West, by naming a school or a library for her. Even among Californians of her own race, the talented and dedicated researcher and writer is little known. *University of San Francisco Library*

13. Even dynamic *Adolph Sutro*, builder of the Comstock Lode's Sutro Tunnel, knew enough to take it easy during the heat of the Nevada day. Here he lounges on a porch in Sutro, today one of the Sagebrush State's many ghost towns. *Howell-North Press*

14. The eccentric *James Lick*, unlike his further-gone contemporary, Emperor Norton, was able to hang onto most of his wits as well as his fortune. He restricted his eccentricities to building a flour mill of mahogany near Alviso, to sleeping atop grand pianos, and to planting orchard trees roots up. *Sutro Library*

15. One of the greatest spectacles in California history accompanied the 1856 obsequies for the opportune martyr of the vigilance movement, newspaperman *James King of William*. The funereal parade may even have eclipsed that of Chinatown's murdered tong emperor, Little Pete. *California State Library*

free. This was two years before Lincoln's Emancipation Proclamation. A rift developed between the precipitous Frémont and President Lincoln and the latter finally lost all confidence in him as the Confederates seemed to outfox him at every turn. Frémont resigned his command.

After the Civil War, John C. Frémont gave up the Mariposa Ranch and lived in the East except for his term as Governor of Arizona Territory (1878–81). He returned to California to restore his failing health but died in New York on July 13, 1890. His widow, Jessie, lived on in California until her death in 1902, enjoying a Los Angeles cottage which was given to her by admirers of the general. Perhaps the greatest tribute paid to her erratic but pioneering husband was her own: "From the ashes of his campfires have sprung cities."

ANDREW FURUSETH

(1854–1938)

Abraham Lincoln freed the slaves in 1863. But the Emancipation Proclamation was but a beginning in the long struggle toward full equality of all people under the Stars and Stripes. Sixty years ago and more, an occupational class lagged behind all others (even migrant farm labor) in human rights. It made no difference whether you were a black or a white descendant of a Revolutionary War hero, if you were an American merchant seaman your civil rights were virtually nil. Today, American sailors of the merchant navy are among the most favored of unionized laborers in terms of rights, pay, and working conditions. How did these onetime Constitutional orphans win such a reversal of circumstances? The answer is locked in the curious career of a dirt-poor Norwegian farm boy who would, one day, be called "The Lincoln of the Sea." It is a story which might tax the credulity of the Horatio Algerine school of potboilers.

The hero of the world struggle for sailors' rights was a San Franciscan who was born on March 12, 1854, in Furuseth (or Furusethskua, "Furuseth Cottage"), on the outskirts of Romedal, fifty miles north of Oslo. This son of a peat bog worker, Andreas Nilsen, was named for his birthplace rather than taking his father's name. This was an old Norwegian custom. By the time he was eight years old, Anders Furuseth had to earn his keep in the cold and hard world that was Norway. He was sent to labor on a farm where his master beat him whenever he stopped working even just long enough to get himself a drink of water. It was a brutalized life for the youngster yet one preferable to starving at home with his nine brothers and sisters. There fish and potatoes, dipped in herring sauce, were the staples, along with bread made of wheat flour stretched with shredded tree bark. Somehow Anders had a brief touch of schooling, enough so that he never lost his taste for knowledge and his love of reading. But, after walking to Oslo, he was rejected by the War School and with a military career closed to him he chose the sea.

In 1873 he shipped out, thinking that the sea would give him the freedom which his personality demanded. Instead, he found himself bound into involuntary servitude, his forecastle a prison. As a seaman, he was the *property* of the shipowner and the latter's representative, the captain, as much as a hawser or a ringbolt. He later told Senator Robert La Follette, "I saw men abused, beaten into insensibility. I saw sailors try to escape from brutal masters and from unseaworthy vessels upon which they had been lured to serve. I saw them hunted down and thrown into the ship's hold in chains." Furuseth's turn came during an Indian Ocean voyage. So sick with fever that he could not stand, he was forced to keep working by a bucko mate. Finally, exhausted, he crawled to his bunk and lay there with his sheath knife in his hand, determined to kill the sadistic mate if he so much as touched him. When he recovered, Furuseth was ashamed of his murderous intent and began to think of positive ways to improve the sailor's lot. Lying in his bunk or standing night watch, he thought, brooded, and planned. Whenever possible he had his nose in a book.

For seven years, Furuseth sailed before the mast in windjammers flying the Norwegian, Swedish, German, French, British, and American colors. In August of 1880 he followed the example of many other deepwater sailors and jumped ship in Frisco. He continued to sail but, from now on, considered San Francisco his home port. It was a great seaport but also the world capital of shanghaiing. This was the new American term for the lucrative business of impressment, forcing sailors to sail against their will. Crimps or shanghaiers supplied masters with men upon demand for bonuses called blood money. No questions were asked and landsmen as well as sailormen were thrown aboard outbound ships. Whores and booze were two of the main elements in this form of "labor recruiting" but the land sharks would not stop at drugging, beating, or kidnaping men. Furuseth tried to escape the system, but when he left the sailors' boardinghouse for new digs, he found himself a pariah, blackballed as a "trouble maker" who would not go along meekly with the system. For six weeks he was on the beach, unable to get a berth. At last, he managed to sign on a coastal lumber schooner and then as a Columbia River salmon fisherman. As La Follette said, "He could not abandon his beloved sea calling and he would not submit to slavery."

Furuseth was a loner, no leader in the ordinary sense at all. He kept to himself, hunched over a book, content to be an able-bodied seaman and not even seeking a boatswain's rating. If anyone ever had to have greatness thrust upon him, it was the austere, self-effacing introvert in the lumber-schooner forecastle. But in 1885, sailors' wages were cut to twenty to twenty-five dollars a month and socialists of the International Workingmen's Association organized the Coast Seamens Union and got them to strike. The union grew from 450 men to

2200 of the 3000 coasting sailors. One of them was Furuseth. He was offered the post of secretary but declined. However, when an 1887 strike failed and the union appeared shipwrecked, he agreed to take command. First he took control from Burnette Haskell's politburo and placed it in the hands of the sailors themselves. He worked fourteen to sixteen hours a day; he lived and breathed sailors' unionism. There was little money in the treasury, sometimes not enough for his pay of ten to fifteen dollars a week. It mattered little to Andy, his tastes were simple. He was an ascetic who lived in a bare room with but two changes of clothing. His sole luxury was a sea chest full of books. In 1934, at the age of eighty, his life savings were $2000. When his sister's farm was threatened by foreclosure, Andy sent her $1800 of his "fortune." When the writer of these lines interviewed one of Furuseth's last surviving cronies on San Francisco's Embarcadero and asked if it were true that the head of one hundred thousand dues-paying members of the International Seamens Union lived simply, the man snorted, swore, and said, "Christ! He didn't have a goddam thing!" The old German's exclamation was more effective than John L. Lewis's description of Furuseth's "life of self-deprivation and Spartan simplicity."

Furuseth began a speaking campaign, making hundreds of talks and thousands of friends. His accent was "Skandihoovian"; he spoke over his listeners' heads at times; he had a tendency to ramble. But his honesty came through in all its granitic toughness. He brought the power of the press to bear on the violence and brutality of a sailor's life with the *Coast Seamens Journal,* whose brilliant editor, Walter J. Macarthur, conceived the idea of a "Red Record" column, listing the hellships and the documented brutalities of their masters and mates. It was the most effective propaganda possible, and Furuseth reprinted the stories as a pamphlet, sent it to the nation's press, and put copies on the desks of all congress-men. He got the California Bureau of Labor Statistics to in-vestigate the seamen's lot, to find out "how the sailor has been kept purposely in his acknowledged degraded condition to render him a will-less commodity in the hands of unscrupu-lous speculators." In two years, Furuseth had the union back on its feet. He promptly resigned and went to sea. He was called back to save the C.S.U. from Haskell, who was plotting a harebrained revolution under the banners of the Socialist International.

Furuseth almost wrecked the union himself in 1887, when he fought the Steamship Sailors Union, thinking it was a fraud, a company union. He realized his mistake, did a *volte-face,* and merged the two to form the Sailors Union of the Pacific in 1891. He resigned again but had to come back. He was essential. He was also becoming a national figure, as he jour-neyed to the East Coast, the Great Lakes, and even to Great Britain, to try to put together an international union of sea-men. Samuel Gompers described him as being "on fire with zeal to free the seaman." Others began to call him (fondly, not sarcastically) "St. Andrew, the Sailor." Louis Adamic said that "Freedom was Andy's religion."

Internal dissensions and the great depression of 1893 threatened the union again, and employers threw charges of hoodlumism at his men. The Norwegian replied with a ser-mon of sorts: "The labor movement received its charter on Mount Sinai when God, through Moses, handed down the law in which we read, 'Thou shalt not steal,' to which Thomas Carlyle, the truth-speaker of the nineteenth century, adds, 'Thou shalt not be stolen from.' " That same year the union almost foundered when a crimp named Blind John Curtin had his establishment dynamited. The Sailors Union was blamed, although Furuseth said his men were innocent. At

106

this low point the Norwegian's battle cry became "Tomorrow is also a day!"

Furuseth studied maritime law and politics; he appealed to Congress for reform and finally went to Washington as a lobbyist for seamen. Samuel Gompers once described him to San Francisco's sailors, "Furuseth has stood at the doors of the Capitol, like a panther watching, like a lion attacking. No scheme has been hatched against you that he has not exposed and, by exposing it, defeated it." Although the press despaired—"the difference between a deepwater sailor and a slave is $15 a month"—Furuseth never gave up. His first real victory for human rights for sailors was the Maguire Act (1895), which prohibited allotments of a sailor's pay to crimps and which forbade the seizure of his clothes for debts. It also abolished imprisonment for desertion. Sailors were at last able to quit their jobs just like any other human beings. Called an anarchist and tailed by police, Andy educated Congress on the plight of the merchant sailor. He showed that American vessels lagged behind other nation's in working conditions and provisions. Although American bottoms handled only 20 per cent of San Francisco's trade, American seamen accounted for 235 of the 391 cases of scurvy in the San Francisco Marine Hospital. His scathing scorn finally got under the tough hides of congressmen when he compared the U.S.A. to "civilized nations," and asked, "Do *they* organize societies to protect dogs and cats and other animals and permit men who may not defend themselves, short of mutiny, to be beaten? *They* protect the animals and the seamen, too!"

The culmination of Andy's crusade for justice was La Follette's Seaman's Act of 1915, signed into law by Woodrow Wilson. There would be no more shanghaiings, no more beatings, no more arrests for quitting one's job. In the Senate gallery Furuseth, tears streaming down his face, cried "This finishes the work Lincoln began!" The rest of Andy's life was anticlimactic, and he fell out of favor during the Depression of the 1930's when he opposed the violent 1934 San Francisco Waterfront Strike. He was hissed and booed by his own men. He died on January 22, 1938, and was accorded an honor never before given a labor leader—his body lay in state in the Department of Labor. According to his wishes, his ashes were scattered at sea ("as far from land as possible"). When the *Schoharie* hove to in mid-Atlantic for the ceremony, the captain addressed his crew: "Fellow shipmates, we are assembled here to execute the wish of Andy Furuseth, an unselfish worker for the betterment of seamen who, through legal means, has done more to secure improved conditions under which you work than any other man." To this, the earlier words of Senator La Follette to San Francisco's sailors might well be added: "Except for his intelligent, courageous and unswerving devotion to your cause for twenty-one years, you would be bondsmen, instead of freemen, today."

The public in its paranoia insists on clutching villains to its bosom. Furuseth is thereby forgotten while Wild Bill Hickok and Clyde Barrow are fashioned into fraudulent folk heroes. The Norwegian sailor's name is little known today to masses of Californians, although he was as important to the building of civil rights and a humanitarian philosophy in government as was Leland Stanford in the construction of a transcontinental railroad and a university. The only monument to Andy Furuseth is a modest bust by Jo Davidson in front of the Sailors Union of the Pacific headquarters on Rincon Hill, overlooking San Francisco Bay. The gaunt, hawk-nosed face and wild mop of hair vouch for the words of William Green, of the American Federation of Labor, that Furuseth was, "physically, the replica of an old Viking."

On the base of the monument are the words of Furuseth

in answer to a friendly warning from Fremont Older of the San Francisco *Bulletin* that he might be pitched in jail for violating a court injunction in defense of his sailors. The few words tell Andy Furuseth's story better than all those which have gone into this sketch:

"You can put me in jail, but you cannot give me narrower quarters than as a seaman I've always had. You cannot give me coarser food than I have always eaten. You cannot make me lonelier than I have always been."

HENRY GEORGE

(1839–97)

Many best-selling books in America have been works of nonfiction, but few if any economic treatises have been genuine best-sellers in this country, at least until quite recent times. *Progress and Poverty,* by Henry George, was the great exception. Its contemporary rivals as best-sellers were books like *Quo Vadis?, In His Steps,* and the Utopian novel *Looking Backward,* not such economic classics as Thorstein Veblen's *Theory of the Leisure Class,* which was a disappointment in terms of sales though a very important book. Interestingly, *Progress and Poverty* was not the work of a Manhattan financier or an Ivy League professor but of a humble ex-sailor like Andy Furuseth. Henry George swallowed the anchor (gave up the sea) in order to devote his life to social and economic reforms. In this role he fought the same battle as Furuseth against bullying mates and land sharks who denied sailors their rights as human beings. But he went far beyond this immediate area of injustice and attempted to set right the whole economical scheme of things in the United States. He did not succeed, but the self-taught George became an economic innovator and reformer who influenced the thinking of many men in this field of study, and his writings made him world famous by 1880.

Henry George was born in Philadelphia on September 2, 1839, and acquired much of his idealism from very religious parents, although he rebelled against this upbringing later in life. Schooling was a great disappointment to him. It did little or nothing for him. George remembered the idleness of high school and the contrasting pleasure of being able to go to work as an errand boy at the age of thirteen years. He continued his education by reading widely all of his life. In 1855 he sailed as a foremast hand on the *Hindoo,* an old Indiaman bound for Melbourne and Calcutta. He first saw the tyranny of masters when the captain jailed the whole crew when it asked to be discharged in an Australian port.

Back home, George drifted into the other calling which he liked, printing. He learned typesetting but quarreled with his foreman and had to quit his job. He then got a steward's post on the new U. S. Lighthouse Service steamer *Shubrick,* which was sailing to San Francisco at the end of 1857 armed with six brass cannon and a device for squirting scalding water on boarders, just in case the North Coast Indians chose to be hostile. In San Francisco, young George joined the Fraser River gold rush but got only as far as Victoria, British Columbia. En route, he learned from his shipmates (California miners) why they were so anti-Chinese. They were convinced that the Orientals would drive wages down to the starvation point for them and their families. George began to muse on the problems of property and profits. He recalled, "It impressed me, the idea that as the country grew . . . the condition of those who had to work for their living must become not better, but worse."

George returned to San Francisco, dead broke, but got some part-time typesetting jobs so that he could live in R. B.

Woodward's predecessor of the "Y," the What Cheer House. This temperance hotel for men boasted one of the best libraries on the Coast, and Henry George made good use of it. When printing jobs were unavailable, George worked in a rice mill and tried to walk to the Sierra gold mines. The farm work which he took along the way, to keep body and soul together, was so rigorous, however (the hardest physical work he ever did in his life), that he gave up and returned to the city, determined to make a living either as sailor or printer. He shortly gave up the sea for printing, and when he came of age in 1860 he joined the typographical union.

With five other printers, all as poor as he, George founded a small daily, the *Evening Journal*. Its staff included the romantic John Rollin Ridge (Yellow Bird), poet laureate of the Cherokees and the instigator of the Joaquín Murieta legend, but the paper plunged George deeper in debt, although he slept in the office to save money. With his clothes in rags and his toes peering from holes in his shoes, he had to sell out.

At this inopportune time, Henry George fell in love with Annie Fox. Her uncle and guardian objected to him as a suitor because of his poverty and Annie had to separate the two men when they almost came to blows. The young people ran away on December 3, 1861, to get married. The elopement almost misfired when the driver of the carriage hired by George balked. He told the latter that he had a bullet in one leg already from an earlier role in just such a romantic adventure. George persuaded him to remain but at a discreet distance from Annie's Happy Valley home. So poor was George that he had to borrow a suit of clothes decent enough in which to be married.

The couple moved to Sacramento, where Henry was a part-time typesetter on the *Union* and performed such odd jobs as collecting tickets at a Mark Twain lecture. Again he quarreled with his foreman and was fired. It was back to San Francisco when salesman Henry failed to sell a single clothes wringer in a five-day canvass of Alameda County. He joined in a job-printing office when times were so bad that he had to barter printed labels and business cards for firewood, milk, corn meal, potatoes, and the cheapest fish on the Coast, sturgeon. His wife pawned her pathetic handful of jewels and trinkets, saving only her wedding band. A child arrived to make the family's destitution worse, its members now victims of the grinding poverty which Dickens depicted in his novels. When Annie's second baby was born, the doctor told Henry, "Don't stop to wash the child; he is starving. Feed him!" Long years later, Henry George remembered that desperate moment as proof of the brutalization of decent men by hunger. "I walked along the street and made up my mind to get money from the first man whose appearance might indicate that he had it to give. I stopped a man—a stranger—and told him I wanted $5. He asked what I wanted it for. I told him that my wife was confined and that I had nothing to give her to eat. He gave me the money. If he had not, I think I was desperate enough to have killed him."

This low ebb in George's life marked the turning point in his career, although it was not discernible at the time. That spring of 1865 he began to write in the little house he had found for his brood at nine dollars a month. In his diary, he noted, "I have commenced this little book as an experiment— to aid me in acquiring habits of regularity. . . . I am starting fresh." One essay was on laws relating to seamen; another on the supernatural; a third on Lincoln's assassination. In 1866 he was promoted from printer on the San Francisco *Times* to reporter, then editorial writer and, finally, managing editor. With a salary of fifty dollars a week, poverty seemed far astern. The first article which won him local fame was in the *Overland Monthly*. He wrote on the future of the West after the completion of the transcontinental railroad and, instead of echoing the chorus of boosters, predicted that while interest would decline, so too would wages. And he credited California's early prosperity to the fact that "the natural wealth of the country was not yet monopolized—that great opportunities were open to all."

In 1868 George visited New York as an agent of the San Francisco *Herald,* seeking its admission into the Associated Press, whose news wire service was essential, even then, to the success of the Far West paper. He was given a lesson in monopoly; the AP refused and when he set up his own little wire-service bureau in a corner of a coal company office in Philadelphia, nullified his efforts by pressuring Western Union, whose telegraph wires to California he would have to use. On the trip, too, he was struck by the monstrous wealth in the cities, on the one hand, and the contrasting poverty which had been his own lot only a few years back. He resolved to try to do something to change the situation.

Back in California as editor of the Oakland *Transcript,* George came up with a partial answer, at least, when he saw what railroad building was doing to speculation in land. "With the growth in population, land grows in value and the men who work it must pay more for the privilege." He would explore and build upon this idea until he came up with his single-tax thesis of economics. The Central Pacific Railroad, whose subsidies he opposed, of course, gave him his next lesson in monopoly, arranging for his defeat in the race for an Assembly seat. So he renewed his crusade via the printing press and in 1871 published a thousand copies of a work he titled *Our Land and Land Policy*. This tract contained many of the ideas which, honed and polished, would bring him world fame in his best-selling book, *Progress and Poverty*. He became a leading advocate of the Australian secret ballot at this time, too.

On December 4, 1871, George emerged as editor-partner in the Coast's first penny newspaper, the *Daily Post*. (He had to persuade the Bank of California to import one thousand dollars in one-cent pieces, so rare was the coin in affluent California.) He became a real crusader for reform, anticipating California's muckrakers. Nominally Democratic, the *Post* was the organ of no party or faction. He meant it to oppose centralization and monopolies of all kinds. The established press derided "George's fad," but it was an exciting paper because of its open attacks on entrenched interests. When he investigated the House of Corrections, George had to push past the bully who ran it, who was blocking the door with his hand on the butt of his pistol. When he criticized Chief Crowley of the San Francisco Police Department for not closing Chinatown's gambling dens, a partisan of the chief struck him in the face and threatened him with a pistol. When he supported an investigation of a swindle in school supplies, he angered City Hall. When he supported the efforts of ladies to campaign for local option at election time, every saloon in San Francisco (and there were hundreds!) turned on him. The journalist Arthur McEwen remembered the incident: "Subscribers withdrew by the thousands and advertisements were withdrawn by the column, but that made no difference to George." A money panic forced Henry George to give the *Post* to his creditors on November 27, 1875, but only after he had written a proud chapter in Western American journalism. The greatest story of his *Post* career was his exposé of maritime cruelty, particularly his scoop on the hellship *Sunrise*. When the police would do nothing to arrest the brutes who had beaten and killed several crewmen, George offered his own reward, hired his own detectives, and got the guilty buckos tried and sentenced.

Henry George had his faults. In his youth he was anti-Mormon; all of his life, because of his pro-labor stance, he was anti-Chinese. He editorialized in favor of lynching a man once when it appeared that the murderer would escape justice because of his wealth and influence. During a printer's strike, he had worked as a scab. Thus, when he lost the *Post,* he was not above begging for a political favor from the man he had helped into the gubernatorial chair, William S. Irwin. The latter gave him the sinecure of the post of State Inspector of Gas Meters. At the same time, he began to lecture as well as write on social and economic matters and was even mentioned for a chair in political economy at the University of California, Berkeley. But the post never materialized. He damned traditional economists for complicating the simple, for hairsplitting, and for defending the status quo and thereby aligning themselves with the rich against the poor. He likened Leland Stanford to the autocratic "King-maker," the Earl of Warwick, and asked rhetorically of Stanford, with his 2200 miles of railroad of millions of acres, "Would it add to the real power of our simple citizen to dub him an earl?"

September 18, 1877, saw Henry George, in the midst of a riotous depression, beginning his magnum opus. In March 1879, he sent the manuscript of *Progress and Poverty* to Harper & Bros. and Scribner's and other firms. There were no takers. Even Herbert Spencer's house, D. Appleton & Company, was not interested. The editor's letter of rejection is a classic: "We have read your *ms.* on political economy. It has the merit of being written with great clearness and force but is very aggressive. There is very little to encourage the publication of any such work at this time and we feel we must decline it." An old printer friend made plates for George, after the latter set the first two sticks of type himself for luck, and the budding economist issued his own Author's Edition. Appleton reluctantly agreed to publish a trade edition, but English houses would not touch it even if George sent them the plates free of cost. American newspapers derided "little Harry George's hobby," but the book began to sell. In fourteen months it went through five large editions. Soon it was the New Testament of single-tax groups erupting all over the nation. It was addressed to the people, not to economists, and it was written clearly and lucidly. Mary Austin remembered thinking of the book, when she was a child, as "something like the Bible, only more important."

In 1880, George ceased to be a Californian. He lived in the East, toured and lectured in various parts of the world, became an international personality. He wrote other books and articles and twice ran, unsuccessfully, for Mayor of New York. In the second race, he overtaxed himself and succumbed to an apoplectic stroke on October 29, 1897. About one hundred thousand people passed his bier when his body lay in state in New York.

Many of George's ideas were not new, but neither were they borrowed. He was largely ignorant of the classics of Malthus, Mill, Marx, and Ricardo. He was that rarest of birds, a perfectly original thinker. Today, Henry George's single tax is defended by only a hardy rear guard, but it may be due for a revival, as current practices seem unable to cure the inequities in an affluent society. Basically, George believed that every man has a natural right to work the land, and when he has to pay rent for the "privilege" he is being robbed. Taxes should be leveled on land alone, all others abolished. He did *not* preach land confiscation or forced redistribution, as some say, nor argue against the concept of private property. He was against monopolization of land and speculation in land, not ownership of it. He said, "It is not necessary to confiscate land;

it is only necessary to confiscate rent." With the end of the artificial fluctuations of our economic life due to the abolition of land speculation and monopoly, the cycles of inflation and depression would level out and America would see the end of poverty.

San Francisco did not know what to make of Henry George. John Russell Young remembered: "I never see *Progress and Poverty* without recalling the pathetic circumstances under which it was written and [without] honoring the courage of the author. . . . San Francisco did not appreciate him; had never given him recognition. He would speak of it as cold and barren, ruled by strenuous men too busy with mines and wheat and empire-building to listen to prophecy." Had he sought fame, wealth, or power, the city might have understood Henry George. But what can one do with a man who answers a fan letter from a reader by writing, "I do not think I shall be proud of it [*Progress and Poverty*] as men are proud of writing a successful history or novel. The feeling is one of deep gratitude that it has been permitted me to do something."

If Henry George's entire philosophy had to be condensed in a piñon nutshell, three sentences from his Fourth-of-July oration of 1877 will suffice: "Wealth, in itself, is a good, not an evil; but wealth concentrated in the hands of a few corrupts on one side and degrades on the other. . . . Here is the test: Whatever conduces to the equal and inalienable rights of men is good—let us preserve it. Whatever denies or interferes with those equal rights is bad—let us sweep it away!"

A. P. GIANNINI

(1870–1949)

Amadeo Peter Giannini, founder of the most behemoth of banks, the Bank of America, was once described as being one of only two men in all history (Henry Ford being the other) to take on Wall Street in a butting match and to win. He was born in San Jose, California, on May 6, 1870, of Genoese stock on both sides and enjoyed a pleasant childhood in the orchards and fields around San Jose's hay-scow port of Alviso except for the shattering tragedy of his father's murder by an embittered debtor. In his early years, he was interested not in finance but in the soil and its products. When his mother and stepfather, Lorenzo Scatena, moved the family to San Francisco to go into the produce commission business, A.P. was much more interested than a twelve-year old would have been expected to be. Soon, young Amadeo was spending as much time tagging after "Pop" Scatena as he was hitting the books. His mother did not approve of his getting up at 2 A.M. on a school day in order to accompany Pop to the Produce District, but Amadeo was strong as a bull and stood at the head of his class, more often than not, even though he "moonlighted." He helped Scatena first by writing personal letters to farmers and

119

attracting more business. When his stepfather jokingly promised him a gold watch when he should deliver his first carload of oranges, A.P. took him seriously. In just a week he had a consignment of two carloads from Tustin—and a brand-new watch.

When Amadeo was fifteen, he ended his formal schooling with a six months' business college course which (naturally) A.P. finished in five months. He then began to call on farmers along the Sacramento River. His distaste for wasting time and his efficiency in its use led him to overtake and pass his more leisurely business rivals. Farmers found that they could trust him absolutely; he never pulled a fast one on them, as did some commission men. He drove himself and he drove his horses, hard, "right to the glue factory," sniffed one disapproving liveryman, but he did relax, occasionally, with sandlot baseball or by attending the theater. At nineteen, Lorenzo made him a one-third partner in the Scatena & Company business. He was already its outstanding asset. He could not be bluffed. Not only was he honest, he had that knack of conveying his honesty and trustworthiness even to strangers. He brought in not only business but goodwill.

Young A.P. occasionally made small loans to farmers and orchardists, charging no interest, in order to tide them over bad economic times. This was his casual introduction to banking. He married in 1892 and continued to prosper. In 1899, he played a role in the temporary defeat of party boss Chris ("Christ Himself" or "Christ Almighty") Buckley by working over the latter's pocket borough of North Beach (the 44th Assembly District) and winning it for reform, instead of corruption, by a six-to-one vote. Then, a little over thirty, he retired down the San Francisco Peninsula, dabbling in real estate.

When A.P.'s brother-in-law died and left him executor of his estate, he was catapulted into banking by being elected a director of the former's Columbus Savings and Loan Association. When some board members opposed his plans, he dropped out and started his own bank when Scatena agreed to help him, upon the promise of always giving as much consideration to a poor man in his bank as to a magnate. In fact, said A.P., he intended his bank to be specifically for the people who had never used one before. He was vice president and manager of the Bank of Italy, which he opened on October 17, 1904. He shook his head at the bankers who, like doctors, waited for customers to come to them. A.P. advertised and went after business like a hog after mast. Most of his rivals were fooled by his one-room institution and wrote his institution off as a colony (i.e., Italian) bank which would always be small potatoes. But not only local *paesani* were banking with him, nor only commission house men. He allowed no wild speculation with bank funds; he accepted no salary himself; he limited all directors, including himself, to no more than one hundred shares of Bank of Italy stock. Within a year, the "baby bank" had resources of a million dollars.

The 1906 earthquake and fire were A.P.'s first great test. With two aides, he threw his entire cash reserve (eighty thousand dollars) into a pair of produce wagons and escaped from the burning city to San Mateo, where he hid the gold coins in the ashpit of his fireplace because he did not have a safe. When San Francisco's bankers urged a bank holiday, a six-month moratorium on debts, and the issuance of script in lieu of cash to withdrawing depositors, A.P. rebelled. He snorted that *that* was no way to rebuild a city. Instead, he set up shop behind a plank on two barrels on the Washington Street Wharf. Each day, he brought ten thousand dollars with him in order to conduct business as usual. Giannini's action had very healthy effects upon the stricken city's morale as well as upon its finances. The other banks got back in operation and, by the end of the year, were doing as much business as before the fire. But the Bank of Italy's business had doubled.

The next great test was not the Graft Trials, in which A.P. was on the side of reform, of course, but the 1907 financial panic and its aftershocks. Playing a hunch, A.P. had hung onto every ounce of gold which he could collect, using silver and paper for transactions as much as possible. Although it hurt his philosophy, he cut back on loans. He acquired new depositors. Thus, when hard-money sources dried up all over the banking map, A.P.'s firm was an exception. And he handed out the gold upon demand! Next, when most West Coast banks were refusing loans, even at blue-sky interest, he advertised for borrowers at the same old rates. When rumors started a run on the rival Crocker National Bank, A.P. honored its depositors' passbooks and set aside a portion of his gold reserve for that bank's management.

The panic brought into being the Federal Reserve Act, but it also led to one of A. P. Giannini's outstanding contributions to American life, branch banking. He had heard Woodrow Wilson, when president of Princeton University, boost it; he examined the system during a visit to Canada and saw that branch banks weathered financial storms much better than small unit (single) banks with insufficient reserves to draw upon in times of stress. Also, he saw that the branches were able to carry on a wide variety of banking services which were beyond the reach of any locally capitalized institution. That year of 1907, he opened his first branch, in San Francisco's Mission District. The second one was in San Jose. He was convinced that branch banking was essential to California's prosperity, especially in regard to agriculture. He saw his branches as buffers protecting farmers and horticulturalists from weather, crop, price, and profit fluctuations. He said, "We have the richest soil in the world in this state. Branch banking will be the steady foundation on which we can build the strongest, happiest, most prosperous state in the Union."

Giannini pioneered other concepts of modern banking and, in fact, remade the image of the business. He broadened operations and services, made banks comfortable rather than forbidding places of business by removing interior walls between offices (which he called "spite fences") and bars and cages, bringing customer and bank officers into close contact. Once-aloof bankers were soon on firstname terms with even modest depositors. He held to his promise to never slight—to favor, if anything—the worker, the dirt farmer, the small businessman as compared to the speculator or the landed gentry. And A.P. "knew" money. He worked with it as a sculptor worked with his clay. He admitted that there were two sides to every question, yes—his side and the wrong side. But, most of the time, A.P.'s side *was* synonymous with the correct one. Out of common sense, integrity, drive, and money sense, A. P. Giannini was building a banking empire.

Southern California, particularly, owes a debt to A.P.G. Snooty San Francisco hardly deigned to look down its nose at cow-town Los Angeles before World War I. Promoters in the south had a hard time getting money out of the financial capital of the Pacific Coast—until A.P. came along. Against initial hostility, he put branches in L.A. and opened up the area for investment growth. After World War I brought prosperity to both Northern and Southern California, A.P. finally consented to succeed Pop Scatena as president of the Bank of Italy with its seven branches and $22,000,000 in assets. Although A.P. had his blind spots—he did not invest in oil or that sure-fire commodity, California land, to any great extent (although he did back the motion picture industry, and early)—he was creating enemies as he grew more powerful, and he could not shrug off the very *bigness* of his bank, third-largest in the country by the 1930's. His use of a holding company to buy other banks caused some people to dub him a monopolist as he evaded the governmental taboo on interstate branch banking, too. He survived the Crash of 1929 but hand-picked the wrong man to run his Transamerica Corporation. During the Depression this executive seemed intent on a "fire sale" of the holding company's assets. (A.P. suspected that Wall Street was mixed in the fight, attempting to crush the upstart Italian banker from the West.) It was a desperate fight for control of the corporation and of the bank, but A.P. finally won. Then he set about getting a demoralized bank back on its feet. It took him forty-two days, but he reversed the trend of deposit loss and soon was helping restore prosperity not only to his depositors but to the entire state. He backed Franklin D. Roosevelt against his conservative fellow-financiers, telling them that "the day of concentrated wealth in a few hands is past"—and then, ironically, suffered at the hands of trust busters sniffing out monopolistic practices. Transamerica Corporation and the renamed Bank of America were forced to go their separate ways, but A.P. was proud to see his "baby bank" of 1904 pass up Chase National in 1945 and become the biggest bank in the world.

A little less than four years later, on June 3, 1949, A. P. Giannini died. President Franklin D. Roosevelt had said earlier, "In my opinion, A. P. Giannini has done more to build California through his great bank and his personal efforts than any other Californian." But A.P. was not thinking in terms of building California. Asked what he was proud of in his banking work, he referred to his small-loan program and said, "I often like to think that I've helped clothe and feed and educate some small boy in the Napa Valley who, fifty years later, may make a contribution in the world of medicine that will ease men's pain in centuries of better living to come. I like to think that I've helped to clothe and educate some little girl in the Sacramento Valley who, one day, may write a great book that will warm many a human heart, in years ahead."

AGOSTON HARASZTHY

(1812–69)

"He is a very efficient officer, but of late has been engaged a great deal in his private affairs. When he came here it was supposed that he was very poor. It is now generally believed that he is worth some thirty or forty thousand dollars, owns a large ranch, etc. . . . I consider him an unsafe man and would recommend his removal."

The words were those of U. S. Treasury agent J. Ross Browne, the Government's confidential investigator into California corruption in 1855. The "unsafe man" was Count, or Colonel, Agoston Haraszthy, the impressive, full-bearded Hungarian who was melter and refiner in the San Francisco Mint.

Haraszthy's spectacular career had begun in Futtak, Hungary, on August 30, 1812, when he was born to a noble family. He served in the royal Hungarian bodyguard to the Emperor Ferdinand of Austria until either Hungarian separatism or the democratic spirit led him to join in revolutionary activities which anticipated Louis Kossuth and the Revolution of 1848 by a decade. Banished, he landed neatly on his feet in Wisconsin, where he pioneered in farming and in a steamboat line. But, at heart, Haraszthy was a vineyardist and wine-lover so that when his grapes did not prosper in Wisconsin's harsh climate, he packed up, on Christmas Day, 1848, and headed for Southern California.

In San Diego, Haraszthy flourished. He was sheriff of the county and was elected to the State Legislature in 1851. Still, he had not found the ideal soil and climate for his wines so he migrated to Northern California and, after an insane attempt to plant wine grapevines in the wind- and fog-swept dunes of San Francisco, discovered Sonoma County's Valley of the Moon. He also won a key post in the U. S. Mint because of his brilliance.

When J. Ross Browne uncovered his "carnival of corruption" in San Francisco, the Mint lay at the heart of it. Haraszthy, whatever the degree of his guilt, was bumped from his position. This blot on his record was speedily forgotten by Californians, who are still in his debt as the effective Father of the California Wine Industry. Near General Vallejo's Lachryma Montis vineyard (Tears of the Mountain), Haraszthy established between 1856 and 1868 his Buena Vista Vineyard and Winery. He was elected a director of the California State Agricultural Society and a member of a new commission established by the Legislature to "report on the improvement and culture of the vine in California." He soon dominated the commission. When the Legislature failed to appropriate money for him to go to Europe to collect wine grape cuttings for California, he paid his own way and brought back not only three hundred varieties and one hundred thousand cuttings but a mysterious black pinot type of grape which is today the most widely planted red wine grape in the state, the unique zinfandel. (He presented a bill for his expenses to the Legislature but was never paid.) As a result of his study trip, he brought out (1862) the first book on

California wines, *Grape Culture, Wines and Wine-making* . . . , now a classic of Californiana.

Haraszthy quickly came to dominate the wine-making scene in California. He sent one of his sons, Arpad, to Europe to study champagne-making methods. His labels began to win awards in world-wide competitions, bringing fame to California's wines in general. At this juncture, the canny capitalist William C. Ralston moved in and formed the Buena Vista Vinicultural Society with Haraszthy, opening offices in New York, Chicago, Philadelphia, and London. Ralston did not understand the lore and art of wine making; all he knew was *profit*. He tried to get Haraszthy to speed up production and a falling-out occurred. The financier easily maneuvered the Magyar out of the society.

A disgusted Haraszthy had to make a fresh start in 1866. He decided to leave wine making to his sons while he took over a sugar plantation near Corinto, in Nicaragua. On July 6, 1869 Colonel Agoston Haraszthy's brilliant career was cut short. The count disappeared from his plantation. His body was never found. But his sons pieced together the pattern of events of his last day. He had set out to inspect a sawmill site on his property, alongside an alligator-infested stream cutting through his Finca San Antonio. He had apparently tried to cross the stream by the branch of an overhanging tree, but the limb broke under his weight and dropped him into the waiting jaws of the alligators below for a grisly and bizarre death.

BRET HARTE

(*1836–1902*)

The man who gave Mark Twain a helping lift-up in the early part of his career was born Francis Brett Harte in Albany, New York, August 25, 1836. A precocious youngster, he read Dickens at an early age, starting with *Dombey and Son,* and published his first poem when he was eleven years old. He must have been half-proud and half-ashamed, because the cheap little paper in which his verse appeared poked fun at its inadequacy.

Harte was a poor boy who had to work hard to support himself, but he survived and managed to come to California in 1854. Here, he was anything but the wild-and-woolly Westerner he is often taken for today because of his short stories of miners, prostitutes, and gamblers in the Low Sierra. In fact, his first writings in California—for the *Golden Era*—were described by his definitive biographer, Franklin Walker, as mere "sugar and water poems." He held a variety of jobs in addition to the most unremunerative one of poet. Harte was briefly an expressman, a tutor, and a newspaperman. It was in the last capacity that he finally made his initial mark in California. While reporter and printer's devil for the *Northern*

Californian in the little town of Union (now Arcata) on Humboldt Bay, he was left in temporary command by the editor-publisher, who went on a trip. A group of murderous hoodlums of the town chose this time, February 1860, for a raid on the peaceful *rancheria* situated on Gunther Island. There, they massacred sixty Indians, mostly women and children, without provocation and with impunity. The acting editor was outraged and wrote a story which he headlined "INDISCRIMINATE MASSACRE OF INDIANS—WOMEN AND CHILDREN BUTCHERED." In the account he stated, "We can conceive of no wrong that a babe's blood can atone for." Details of subsequent events are shadowy and unclear, but it appears that Harte was given a *very* short time in which to get out of town. In any case, he fled to San Francisco on the *Columbia.*

Once in the city, Harte found a patron in Jessie Benton Frémont, an author in her own right. She was sure that he had writing talent and, as usual, Jessie was correct. Most of his early works were contributions of patriotic poems to the press during the Civil War. He next became a member of the staff of the popular literary journal the *Golden Era*. His first real success was the story *M'liss,* a precursor of his finest local color yarns, and a considerable improvement over such sentimental poems as his verse *The Valentine*. Harte, who now shortened his name to the version familiar to us, was a truly gifted writer, but, almost from the first, he flawed his productions by inserting literariness—references to Homer, and so forth. These were dragged bodily into stories which were otherwise largely realistic (if romanticized) pictures of life in California. He also held himself back too much. The opposite of fiery, volcanic Mark Twain, Bret Harte was cautious, careful, and painstaking. He wrote and rewrote and *re*wrote.

In 1864 Bret Harte helped found the new literary periodical

The Californian, as a successor to the old *Golden Era.* He also contributed to it some good pieces, including the verse parody *To the Pliocene Skull.* By 1865, he was already the city's outstanding literary light, its resident poet. That year, he edited the first collection of California verse, modestly excluding his own work. The volume, *Outcroppings,* was mediocre at best, but it set off a long war of words among those whose poems were included and the many Pindars whose works Harte had not picked for inclusion. Harte was ready for his best work when he was chosen editor of the astonishing *Overland Monthly,* the best journal ever to appear on the Pacific Coast. Not only were his contributions among the best the magazine ever published but they were among the finest pieces of writing he ever did in his career: *Tennessee's Partner, The Luck of Roaring Camp,* and *Outcasts of Poker Flat.* In these and other stories of the Mother Lode, Harte skillfully mixed humor, pathos, and narrative, even if he did borrow a great deal from his fellow-Westerners Alonzo Delano and Dame Shirley, as well as from Dickens himself. Although he taught school in Lagrange and hiked into the gold diggings, he was there so briefly and in only one area, Melones, that he had to borrow background from Delano and Shirley because they were much more at home in the mining camps than he was. (This unfamiliarity with the gold regions made the geography of Harte's stories incredible, even with the help of writers Delano and Shirley.)

Harte was natty, dapper, and something of a dandy. He was in no real sense a bohemian in dress or life style. He was thoroughly—if not happily—married. (When he came home from his work in the surveyor general's office or the Mint, he expected to be able to put in two hours of writing. More than seldom, his wife dreamed up household chores for him to do in order to prevent him from writing.) Although he was meticulous about most of his writing, which was now in the *Atlantic Monthly* as well as the *Overland Monthly,* it was a work he had tossed off, *Plain Language from Truthful James,* which seized the public fancy (as *The Heathen Chinee*) and brought him national fame.

By 1870, Harte was soured on the Far West. He felt that people on the Coast did not appreciate his talents. When the *Atlantic Monthly* offered him the then fantastic sum of ten thousand dollars a year, he hurried East. Many people in San Francisco cried, "Good riddance!" for Harte's aloofness had turned into snobbishness. He was not above the petty business of "cutting" people (i.e., failing to recognize them on the street) when they no longer measured up to his exalted social standards. Harte even accused the *Overland Monthly* of abusing his reputation and he attacked Californians in general as being guilty of the most shameless ingratitude toward him, plus what he termed "blundering malice."

But the blunders were largely Harte's. No sooner had he broken with the West, which he depicted so well, than his work began to skid downhill. Even though he settled himself comfortably in London, and was well received there, his reputation continued its downward spiral. Eventually, he was forced to admit, sadly, to his wife, "I grind out the old tunes on the old organ and gather up the coppers." He lived out a long life by doing hack work until he died in 1902. Unfortunately, some of his later stories were so imitative of his earlier work, yet lifeless, that they were sometimes unconscious parodies.

Bret Harte's reputation remains firmly on his short stories of the Sierra foothill camps. Their humor is much quieter than the rollicking brand which was Twain's. But, now and again, Harte delivered a quip or two which were of Twainian caliber, such as when he named the fashionable church of San Francisco's nobs "St. Croesus's," or pointed out why San

Francisco had suffered in the earthquake of 1861 while Oakland had emerged scot-free—"There are some things the earth cannot swallow." Aficionados of California literature are delighted by Harte's teasingly few ventures into light parody and satire, such as his verse in the March 30, 1867, *San Francisco News Letter* titled *California Madrigal*. In these stanzas Harte demolished the superboosters of California's paradisiacal climate. Here, in three stanzas of the madrigal, is how a *real* Californian saluted the coming of spring:

O, mark how the Spring in its beauty is near
How the fences and tules once more reappear,
How soft lies the mud on the bank of yon slough
By the hole in the levee the waters broke through.

Once more glares the sunlight on awning and roof
Once more the red clay's pulverized by the hoof,
Once more the dust powders the "outsides" with red
Once more at the station the whiskey is spread.

Then fly with me, love, ere the summer's begun
And the mercury mounts to one hundred and one,
Ere the grass now so green shall be withered and sere
In the spring that obtains but one month in the year.

CHARLES MALLORY HATFIELD

(1876-1958)

"Hatfield the Rainmaker"—where else but in Deepest, Darkest Southern California would such a savior come paddling to the rescue of drouth-stricken cities? Water, or the absence of it, has always determined the destiny of Los Angeles and San Diego no less than of the desert Southwest. It is no accident that many folk heroes of Southern California, like Charles Hatfield and William Mulholland (curiously, half folk-hero and half folk-villain) were involved with water. If we throw in salt water, we find Phineas Banning and Stephen White.

It has often been said of Los Angeles, as of Cambridge University, that there are so many lunatics there that the moon must never set. But Hatfield should not be written off as either a flimflamming con man or as an eccentric or quack. He was no run-of-the-twig dowser, no water witch (or warlock) seeking subterranean water with willow switch or hazel wand. Hatfield pulled water down, not up. He bled the very skies to nourish the parched earth. Because San Francisco is tolerably well watered, Hatfield ventured no closer to the city than Crows Landing, in the San Joaquin Valley. For this reason, he is unknown today in the north while firmly imbedded in the folklore of the southland. The knowledgeable Carey McWilliams considered him to be the first folk hero of Southern California.

Hatfield had a go at rainmaking on his father's ranch in Gopher Canyon eleven miles east of Oceanside in 1902. It took him many attempts, but he finally got the precipitation he desired. The modest Hatfield denied that he could make rain, or make it rain; he confessed only to the ability to persuade moisture to drop from the clouds. He used no witch's wand, only "evaporating tanks" on towers. He filled them with a top-secret brew of noisome chemicals. The rising fumes then would "overturn" the atmosphere, as he put it, causing rainfall. During the long Southern California summer drouths, Hatfield's evaporaters came into increasing demand.

The Rainmaker received his first bona fide contract in Los Angeles in 1903. He was so successful that the grateful landowner gave him double the fifty-dollar fee he had asked. After he had set up his tanks, the clouds delivered an inch of rain in a five-day period. Naturally, his reputation spread quickly.

Charles Hatfield considered himself a meteorologist and a disciple of William Morse Davis, a geologist at Harvard whose book *Elementary Meteorology* impressed the Californian. Hatfield was led to discover chemicals which had an affinity or attraction for the moisture in the sky overhead. When these were in harmony, rain would fall. Actually, wittingly or not, Hatfield belonged to an old school of rainmakers—Espy, Dyrenforth, Gatham, and Powers—all of whom believed heat (fire) or concussion (explosions) would trigger rainfall. Gatham was on the right track—that of the cloud seeders of today. He prescribed not only concussion but also the cooling of air currents with carbonic acid gas. Hatfield was willing to sell his formulas to the Government but not to any individual.

Some persons estimate that Hatfield performed his experiments five hundred times. In 1916 he claimed to have carried out seventeen successful contracts and his onetime fifty-dollar fee was more likely to be five thousand dollars or ten thousand dollars. In Los Angeles he produced eighteen inches of rain in the first four months of 1905, and when asked to fill the Lake Hemet Land and Water Company Reservoir for four thousand dollars, he raised the water level behind the dam by twenty-two feet. But it was in 1916 that Hatfield the Rainmaker hit his peak—or, rather, went too far.

The Moisture Accelerator, as he called himself, met with the San Diego City Council on December 13, 1915. He was offered a contract to cure the local drouth and fill the Morena and Otay reservoirs. If he succeeded, he would be given ten thousand dollars; if he failed, he would not get a red cent. One councilman thought the whole idea was ridiculous, but the four others passed the motion of acceptance of the contract. Hatfield had until December 20, 1916, to fill the reservoirs, but he needed no such amount of time. Without even waiting for the contract to be drawn up, he took his brother, Paul, and started building a twenty-foot tower at Morena instead of the four twelve-footers he had used elsewhere. It was January 1, 1916. Atop it he placed an eight-foot platform, fenced, and on it he mixed his chemicals in galvanized tanks. Onlookers saw and smelled fire and noxious smoke and heard explosions from the tower's top. Colonel R. C. Wueste, of the city's waterworks, guessed that the chemicals were a compound of hydrogen and zinc.

Some San Diegueños say that Hatfield pulled down a few drops that New Year's Day. Certainly it rained on January 9; the lakes began to fill and the drouth was broken. Morena got 12.73 inches and Otay 4.66 inches. But it began to pour again on a January 14 and did not let up until the nineteenth. Morena Reservoir was filled with eighteen billion gallons of water. It had never before been even half full. It began to overflow the dam and San Diego was flooded. People were hauled about downtown in a horse-drawn fire wagon. Ranches and towns were inundated, highways, bridges, and railroad tracks were washed out, telephone and telegraph lines snapped. Ironically, the flood even cut off the city's water supply and resort had to be made to local wells. Attendance at the San Diego Exposition practically zeroed. A thirty-foot-high silo weighing thirty tons was deposited right side up, a mile downstream from its foundations by the raging San Diego River. The Colorado River flooded a thousand people out of their homes in Yuma, and Long Beach, Los Angeles, and San Pedro were awash too.

San Diego was cut off from the rest of the world except by sea and the S.S. *Yale*. The steamer brought food and mail to the city from Los Angeles. Worse hit were neighboring San Ysidro, California, and Tijuana, Mexico. Only fifty persons were homeless in San Diego, but on the border three were killed and a hundred left homeless. Even Hatfield had to admit that his San Diego experiment had been something special: "This was a phenomenon that I was never able to repeat . . . The most potent that I ever made."

With the skies clearing and the Morena Reservoir more than full, the Hatfields dismantled their tower and, traveling incognito as the Benson brothers (in case some flooded-out ranchers were a little peeved), made their way to San Diego. But before repairs could be made to the flood damage, another rainstorm broke on January 26. Winds reached fifty-four knots, breaking all records for the area, and 2.41 inches of rain fell in just twenty-four hours. The waters topped Sweetwater and Otay dams and ruptured them. With a great roar which the press labeled "the Crack of Doom," thirteen billion gallons of water formed a forty-foot-high surge which scoured the Otay Valley. Death estimates went as high as fifty but slipped to fifteen to twenty and were probably still too high. Perhaps a dozen people lost their lives. But damage was enormous. And San Ysidro and Tijuana were hit for a second time by flooding, and the new Tijuana race track was partially destroyed.

According to Southern California legend, self-appointed vigilantes were beating the muddied bushes for the Rainmaker, ready to string him up. But "Mr. Benson" was in San Diego, hoping to be paid for services rendered. An angry, sodden City Council welshed on the agreement. Its members said that they had hired him to fill the reservoirs, not to wash away the city. The city attorney reminded him that it had only been a verbal agreement and it was, therefore, not binding because it had not been written down and signed. He refused to pay the ten thousand dollars.

Rainmaker Hatfield filed suit and about a year later served a summons on the Mayor of San Diego. He argued his case before mayor, council, and city attorney, but they refused payment even when he offered to compromise at four thousand dollars, the actual cost, he said, of putting four billion gallons of water into Morena Reservoir. They cried, "Act of God!" and used the same argument to escape from three and a half million dollars of damage suits against the city. (Two honest councilmen, it must be said, urged that he be paid, in all fairness.) After all, said the city attorney, there was no *proof* that Hatfield had summoned the rain. He was correct, of course. (In fact, a heavy rain had fallen on December 30, before the Rainmaker even got his tower up.) When the council offered to pay him if he would accept all responsibility for the flood, absolving the city, Hatfield backed off.

Damages were already estimated at six million dollars. The suit was finally dismissed by the court on May 28, 1938.

Hatfield did not quit. He "precipitated" as far from home as Texas, Alberta, Dawson City, and Honduras—where he doused a forest fire. Perhaps his greatest trick, even superior to the San Diego affair, was his turning of Saharan Randsburg, in the Mojave Desert, into a fair replica of Venice. In just three hours, he loosed forty inches, it is said, of water on the desert mining community! Small wonder that, in time, Southern California became scared to death of Hatfield. It was obvious that the Great Precipitator did not know his own strength, that he could not control the volume of delivery of his product when under contract. Still, through the 1920's he was called upon to break drouths, and newspapers and public placed bets on whether he would win or lose in these gambles. It was a phenomenon akin to the football pools of London.

Stanford's scholarly Dr. David Starr Jordan debunked the off-beat alchemist in *Science* magazine in 1925. The professor attributed Hatfield's amazing success to his diligent study of weather charts and extraordinary skill at predicting changes in the weather. Jordan said that Hatfield would wait until the people despaired of a dry spell's ever ending, then would promise relief in thirty or sixty days, and usually won. But Hatfield was not put out of business by David Starr Jordan, but by Boulder Dam. The delivery of cheap water from Boulder/Hoover Dam was a lot more dependable than that of the Rainmaker. During the Dirty Thirties, when much of the High Plains blew away, Hatfield was quoted as saying that he had no doubt that his methods would save the tremendous losses of the Dust Bowl. But he was not called upon to perform his weather magic.

Eventually, Hatfield settled in Glendale as a sewing-machine salesman. He made just one visit to San Diego after the 1916 debacle, in 1946. The Rainmaker died in obscurity in Pearblossom, California, in January 1958. An editorial in the April 18 San Diego *Evening Tribune* lamented that he had never passed on his skill, his magic or gift, which had nearly washed San Diego into the sea.

JOSEPH HECO

(1837–96)

Chinese settlers came to California long before the Gold Rush—even if we refuse to believe the legend of Hui Shen's voyage to the Monterey area in A.D. 499. During the Gold Rush itself, tens of thousands of coolies came to the mines to make their fortunes. But the Coloma discovery made virtually no impression on Japan. No argonauts set sail for California from Japan, for a very good reason. Migration from Japan without governmental permission was a capital offense. In 1637, by imperial decree, Japan sealed herself off from all intercourse with the outside world, promising to reward with death any Japanese who either learned a foreign tongue or dared to travel abroad.

Not until 1860, seven years after Commodore Matthew C. Perry wrenched open Japan's closed doors, was immigration to the United States possible. That year, the first diplomatic mission of Japanese reached San Francisco on the U.S.S. *Powhatan* and the *Kanrin Maru*. These were the "swart-cheeked princes" of Walt Whitman's poem *A Broadway Pageant*. But Japanese did come to California long before the members of the diplomatic delegation. All were unwilling visitors, castaways and victims of shipwreck. Perhaps as many as a hundred junks and sampans were swept across the Pacific by the relentless Kuroshiro, or Black Current. As early as 1815, three survivors were rescued off Santa Barbara by an American brig. When American and other ships tried to re-store Japanese castaways to their country, they were fired upon by shore batteries. When rescuers persisted, Japanese officials firmly refused to readmit the pariahs.

The first Japanese-Californian was Nakahama Manjiro, rescued in 1841 after being shipwrecked on an uninhabited Pacific island where he subsisted for 108 days on sea birds and their eggs. He was taken to the U.S. by his rescuer, Captain W. H. Whitfield of the whaleship *John Howland* and educated as John Mung. He lived in Hawaii for a time and sailed as a whaler, came to California during the Gold Rush, but decided in 1851 to return to his homeland for good. With great courage, and fearing that he would be put to death, he landed with two companions in Japan. He was not heard of again until St. Patrick's Day, when the *Kanrin Maru* sailed into San Francisco Bay, the first Japanese ship to cross the Pacific deliberately. Newspaper reporters found her captain and sailing master to be the onetime castaway, now a samurai, wearing two swords.

However, the real pioneer of California's Japanese-American community is not Manjiro but Hikozo Hamada, who took the name Joseph Heco in California. Born in Komiya on the Inland Sea in 1837, he was only thirteen when he sailed with his father on a trading voyage in 1850. Just after leaving Uraga, the *Eiriki Maru* was caught in a storm and lost her rudder. She drifted, helpless, for fifty days. Unlike some castaways who starved to death on refuse and fish scales, the industrious crewmen of Heco's junk caught fish and even distilled drinking water from the sea while fuel lasted. At last, they sighted a ship, the first Western vessel Heco had ever seen. He recalled that it was "a strange vessel, so huge and black, and the strange creatures on board her; for all we knew, no human beings at all."

Captain Jennings of the American bark *Auckland* proved to be very human and kind and at 10 A.M. on February 8, 1851, he landed the seventeen Japanese in *Sanfuranshisuko,* the great port of the state of *Karuhoniya.* Once ashore in San Francisco, Heco was wide-eyed at its variety of wonders. He gave rapt attention, equally, to everything, whether chewing tobacco and pipes, roulette wheels, the chain gang, or the masquerade ball which he attended in his silken kimono.

Joseph Heco and his companions were given a home aboard the revenue cutter *Polk,* where the Irish master-at-arms, Thomas Troy, appointed himself their guardian. Only Heco was interested in learning English, but his fearful elders put a stop to it temporarily. As he later recalled, "If I learned a foreign tongue and went home, I, and they, also, would be put in confinement, besides suffering a very serious punishment, the exact details of which they were not certain of."

The Japanese were transferred to naval vessels for repatriation, but Heco and two others, Tora and Kame, decided to become Americans and Californians. They sailed back to California with Troy in 1852 to try the gold mines. This plan did not work out, but Heco sailed to Monterey, Catalina Island, and San Diego in the cutter *Frolic* and then back to San Francisco. There, Troy got them positions aboard the revenue cutters *Frolic* and *Argus* and the coast-surveying ship *Ewing.* But a steward's life soon palled on the young and adventurous Heco. He was intelligent, too, so when San Francisco's collector of customs, Beverly C. Sanders, offered him an education, he leaped at the opportunity. Sanders introduced him to Senator William Gwin, Sam Brannan, and other California notables, then took him to a Catholic school in Baltimore. In Washington, President Franklin Pierce offered Heco an appointment to West Point, but the Japanese politely refused, preferring to enter Catholic University.

Joseph Heco returned to San Francisco in 1854, where Sanders put him in school, but when the financial panic of 1855 bankrupted his protector, Heco went to work for Macondray & Company, merchants, in 1856. He was baptized a Catholic and, on June 30, 1858, became one of the first, if not *the* first, Oriental to be naturalized a citizen of the United States. In 1858, he also secured the appointment of captain's clerk (and interpreter) on Lieutenant J. M. Brooke's Pacific surveying expedition. He left the *Fenimore Cooper* in Hawaii because he had been seasick during the entire passage. However, he managed to go on to Japan, where he went into business as a commission merchant, employing his old protector, Thomas Troy.

But the proud Heco did not find his position a happy one. As a mere merchant, he was looked down upon by the samurai. So he returned to San Francisco in 1861 and went on to Washington. There, in what must be, surely, one of the most gigantic pre-CIA bungles in our history, he was arrested as a Confederate agent! Soon released, he won the appointment of interpreter at the American Consulate in Kanagawa, now Yokohama. The post allowed him to wear Yankee diplomatic uniform, ensuring him of sufficient respect and "face," so essential in his homeland.

Heco's last visit to San Francisco was in May of 1862, en route to his consular post. The naturalized American citizen, who had shaken the hands of three or four American Presidents, and who had hobnobbed with the great and not-so-great of San Francisco, Baltimore, and Washington, finally chose the attractions of Japan over those of his adopted home, *Karuhoniya*. He founded the first Japanese newspaper in 1864 and was a highly respected citizen until his death on December 12, 1896.

144

GRACE HUDSON

(1865–1937)

There is little doubt that, one day, Grace Hudson will be given the honor due her as the finest painter of California's Indians who ever lived. At present, she is little known even in her own state except to aficionados of American Indian history and lore and to art collectors and dealers who have recognized her genius. So zealously have they bought up her paintings that, when one occasionally reaches the market now, it is likely to be priced in the thousands of dollars. She has a following today, and, if a small one, it is a very devoted and loyal group of partisans.

Born Grace Carpenter (1865) in Potter Valley, in Mendocino County north of Ukiah, Grace had a twin brother, Grant. Since the birth of twins was rare in the Indian population, the Carpenter infants were the subject of much interest and almost veneration on the part of the Pomos. For her part, Grace Carpenter early showed a sympathy and love for the misjudged and much-maligned "Digger" Indians of California, whose skill at basketry, she saw, was unrivaled anywhere in America.

Grace Carpenter was lucky in that, although she was born in a rural (in fact backward) county, hers was a stimulating and intellectual family. Her father, A. O. Carpenter, was the founder of the Ukiah *Herald,* but he was also, at one time or another, the county's assistant assessor and deputy collector of revenue for the federal government. He was also a pioneer photographer of the Redwood Coast. Where her brother Grant's taste ran to law and to writing (*Chinatown Tales,* etc.), Grace's gifts lay in art. As a child, she excelled in drawing. After she finished grammar school in Ukiah, her parents sent her to Virgil Williams's California School of Design, which boasted Raymond Yelland and Amelio Tojetti among its art instructors. Under their tutelage, Grace Carpenter soon became a mature artist, winning the Alvord Prize for the best crayon study in competition when she was only in her early teens.

In 1890, Grace married Dr. John Hudson of Ukiah, who was, more and more, abandoning his medical practice in order to study the Pomo Indians of the locality, their art, customs, and language. His wife helped him to compile a Pomo dictionary, to collect baskets for the Field Museum of Chicago (now the Chicago Natural History Museum), and to serve as that museum's ethnologist on the Coast. Most of Grace Hudson's subjects came to be Pomos, often children, although she went to Hawaii in 1901 and painted some of the kanakas of Hilo and other areas. Her skill at painting the Pomos led the Field Museum to commission her to paint a series of portraits of Oklahoma's Pawnee chiefs, in 1904. She was very kindly received by them, especially by Eagle Chief and his wife. After a European trip in 1905, Grace Hudson made her home with her husband in Sun House, still standing in Ukiah, or in one or the other of their summer camps on Mill Creek, Batimma, and Matu.

Grace Hudson's work first attracted wide attention in January 1893, during the Mechanics Fair in San Francisco. She exhibited her oil painting of a Pomo papoose, furious at being left strapped in his willow cradle, titled *Little Mendocino.* A friend of Grace's, who saw the art show before her, and who was unaware of her contribution to it, told her about the painting of "an ugly little Indian" which was the hit of the display. There was such a crowd of admiring people around it that she had not been able to get near it. For this painting, Grace Hudson won a silver medal. She sent the painting on to the World's Columbian Exposition in Chicago; there it won honorable mention.

During her lifetime, Grace Hudson painted some six hundred works. Her Indian portraits, especially of the very old and very young, are most treasured today. The cultural details of her canvases are an unobtrusive delight to laymen and anthropologists alike—the infant, Betoon, plays on a furry pelt with dolls made of oak galls, twigs, and feathers; adult women wear necklaces of clamshell disc beads or of madrone berries; the medicine men sport their traditional turbans. Her strong sympathy for the neglected and abused Indians of California shines forth in every one of her Pomo portraits. If they are at times overly romantic and sentimental in a Victorian way, most of them capture marvelously the elusive, somewhat sad dignity of the red race, and many are superb historic documents.

The great majority of Grace Hudson's paintings are charming examples of representative art. At first she had to sketch her reluctant models hastily by baby-sitting the Indian children, but, once she won their full confidence, the adults were willing to pose properly for her. The result was a superb series of portraits of the survivors of a decimated tribe which once was as gifted artistically as its memorialist herself.

On March 23, 1937, Grace Carpenter Hudson died. She was buried in Ukiah Cemetery under a tombstone of her own designing, a shaft of basalt topped by a mourning phoenix. Grace Hudson's paintings explain her importance to California's artistic and cultural history in a way which no words can equal.

JAMES B. HUME

(1827–1904)

Jim Hume is not half as well known to Californians as he should be. He was Wells, Fargo's first—and greatest—chief of detectives and, in fact, one of the West's great lawmen of all time. But because he preferred the simple title of special officer and because he used his brain instead of a gun, he has never enjoyed the press of many lesser men who wore stars in the American West.

Born in Stamford, upstate New York (January 23, 1827), he moved to Lima, now Howe, Indiana, before heading for California with his older brother and friends. Although 1850 was a cholera year, they made it safely across the plains to the gold mines, and Hume began ten years of prospecting in the rugged cañons of the Sierra Nevada foothills. In this decade, he got enough gold to keep himself in beans and bacon, but little else. So it was that in 1860 he began a career in public service in Placerville, old Hangtown, as deputy tax collector, then city marshal and chief of police. He was a born lawman and cleaned the town up so neatly that the sheriff of El Dorado County appointed him undersheriff. This was just in time for his first big case, in 1864, a case which is surprisingly

149

little known even to history buffs although it involved the most bizarre stage holdup in California. Two coaches were stuck up, in tandem, on the night of June 30, 1864, at Bullion Bend, just east of Placerville. The dual holdup was rare enough, but Hume found that the bandits were Confederate guerrillas, raising money to help the Confederate Army in this unusual fashion! Jim Hume and other officers trailed the road agents all over California before the former finally arrested most of the guilty men in San Jose.

Because Hume was a Democrat, and his party was out of favor as a result of its identification with the South and slavery, he lost when he ran for sheriff in 1865. But he was reappointed undersheriff and in 1867 won great local fame for putting the Hugh DeTell gang out of action, although he was wounded in the arm in a gunfight with the outlaws near the south shore of Lake Tahoe. But Hume was primarily a detective, not a violent gunslinger. He was at his best tracking outlaws or figuring out the *modus operandi* of criminals at a time when fingerprinting was unknown and even the collecting and study of clues at the site of a crime were amateurish. Jim Hume had a whole bag of tricks which he used to secure arrests and convictions, too. He put away the Emmons Gang, for example, which had preyed exclusively on Mother Lode Chinese for years with impunity because the testimony of Oriental witnesses was inadmissible in California courts of that day. Hume's method was simplicity itself, but no one before him had tried it, perhaps not caring enough about the lot of the Chinese. He nabbed one of the gang, the weakest, put him in isolation, and pressured him enough to get him to peach (i.e., squeal) on his pards. Simple? Yes. But it worked and the Chinese of the Mother Lode were able to breathe easier, without fear of beatings and robberies.

Hume was rewarded for his fine record by being elected

sheriff of El Dorado County in 1868, and he plunged right into more cases of murder, arson, and robbery but went down to defeat, with his party, in the next election. The local paper, the *Mountain Democrat,* lamented, "Personal spite and sore-headed disaffection in our own ranks have defeated one of the best and most deserving officers this, or any other, county has ever had in its service." But Hume had no time to waste in grumbling and he was too good a man to be out of a job for long. Wells, Fargo, hurting badly from a rash of express holdups, hired him as the company's first chief of detectives. But the firm gave him a leave of absence when the State of Nevada appointed him deputy warden in order to clean up the Nevada State Penitentiary after the Big Break of September 1871, in which twenty-nine cons escaped in a murderous break. He restored order, morale, and discipline and then headed for California again.

Once at work for Wells, Fargo, Hume kept in close contact with local officers all over the state, built up a rogues' gallery of photos of criminals, and filled bulging scrapbooks with clippings on cases and trials. His first major case in his new job was a Grass Valley stage holdup which he cracked because he had an *exact* description of the loot. When a small piece of gold turned up, he recognized it as a hunk cut from a bar of bullion taken from the coach. He closed the case successfully but not before he got himself tangled in the first of a long series of quarrels with law officers who, out of jealousy (and, in some cases, dishonesty), refused to co-operate with him. He had no time for quarreling, however; in the year of 1875 alone, Wells, Fargo lost $87,000 to robbers. He was all over the map in frenetic pursuit of bandits. It was much too much of a job for one man, even a dozen men, but Hume gave the job all he had.

Seldom did he have to actually "ride shotgun" on an express shipment of treasure. But when Wells, Fargo sent $240,000 in gold pieces to Los Angeles in 1875 to save a bank which was going bust, Hume was tapped for the job of guard. He and his aides got the money safely to its destination although road agent Dick Fellows tried to get a crack at it. (He bungled the job.) Sometimes, Hume had the unpleasant duty of investigating inside jobs, too, as when Wells, Fargo treasurer Charles Banks swindled the firm and was so fearful of Hume's long reach that he fled all the way to Rarotonga in the Cook Islands of the South Pacific.

In his detective work, Hume ranged farther and farther from home. He spent a lot of time in the 1880's in lawless Arizona Territory, for example, and there had the most humiliating experience of his life. He was asleep in a coach which was held up between Contention and Tombstone and he was relieved of his two fine pistols. Early, he saw the transition taking place from stage robbery to train robbery, and he told newspaper interviewers in 1887, "Stage robbery is, comparatively speaking, a thing of the past. What with the extension of the railroads, closing down of many of the mines, and the adoption of the money order system, there are no longer inducements for the higher grade of criminal talent to engage in the business."

During the 1880's, Hume and his chief assistant, Jonathan Thacker, got out a report on fourteen years of criminal activity versus Wells, Fargo. It was jammed with interesting statistics. In that time, bandits carried out 313 successful stage holdups and bungled thirty-four more. Half of the eight train robberies attempted were successful, plus twenty-three burglaries. The good news in Hume's so-called *Robbers Report* was the figure for convictions of the criminals involved —206 road agents, twenty train robbers, and fourteen burglars. Only two Wells, Fargo messengers had been killed and six wounded, along with four stage drivers killed. Four more drivers had been wounded, and four passengers killed and two wounded. Hume's shotgun guards had killed five bandits, while five more had been killed resisting arrest and seven had been lynched by angry citizens. Real proof of the profits of road agentry was Hume's total of treasure stolen during the period—$415,312.55, no mean sum in the hard dollars of that era.

As Hume grew older and train holdups popped up all over the West, he had to delegate much of the field-work to younger men while he supervised investigations from his San Francisco office. Thus, he was in and out of his last big case, that of the "war" between the Southern Pacific Railroad and suspected train robbers John Sontag and Chris Evans. The elusive pair even won Hume's grudging admiration, which was added to large public sentiment in their favor because of the widespread hatred for the "Octopus," the bullying S.P., which, literally, ran California from Capitol to whistle stop in those days. Hume's other great case involved Black Bart, the greatest stage robber of all time. Again, Hume did not personally snap the cuffs on Bart, but the arrest was made by an assistant hired by Hume to do one thing—get Black Bart.

Among Hume's outstanding assets was courage, and not only in the common physical sense. He had the courage of his convictions. Hume was as stubborn as a mule; there was only one man who could make him change his mind—himself. But when he found that he was on the wrong track he always switched to the right one. Hume was absolutely devoted to the ideal of justice. He won many enemies on the "right" side of the law as a result. If he was convinced that a dyed-in-the-wool scoundrel was innocent of a particular charge, he would —and did, several times—take the side of the felon against the decent people who acted out of a simple belief in "Good riddance." Hume was very distressed when a murderer of a stage passenger in 1879 got life and his accomplice was hanged only because he did not have a friend in court. When the wrong gang was accused of the Gage Station train heist in New Mexico in 1883, Hume had to persuade the press, the public, and the peace officers that they were after fall guys, not the guilty. He steered them toward Kit Joy and his gang, the real culprits. Sometimes, he had to protect prisoners, like Bill Sykes, from brutal deputies and jailers. In the case of William Evans, accused of killing Hume's friend, Wells, Fargo guard Mike Tovey in 1893, the detective tried to appear in court in behalf of the accused, a disreputable oaf, who he *knew* was not the murderer from the evidence. Hume was virtually thrown out of court and had to take his case to the newspapers.

Jim Hume lost and was vilified for taking the part of a ne'er-do-well like Evans, "who deserved everything he got." The detective had to endure the personal enmity of many law officers who felt that he was some kind of a traitor. In the end, Jim Hume won. In 1907, the San Francisco *Call* carried a headline which read: "INNOCENT MAN WILL GO FREE AFTER 13 YEARS." On December 29, 1909, the railroaded Evans was released from San Quentin. But it was too late for Hume to celebrate his vindication. He had died three years and five months earlier, still in harness, on May 18, 1904.

COLLIS P. HUNTINGTON

(*1821–1900*)

Probably the most cordially hated man in the entire history of California was the state's greatest capitalist and railroad magnate-lobbyist, Collis Potter Huntington. He was the driving force in the Big Four and became a national figure who spent much time in the East, selling company stocks and bonds, borrowing cold cash, and fighting off the threats of competition in the West from rival rail lines. But he was more Californian than New Yorker, or anything else, although he claimed that the Golden State's mild climate bred weaklings.

Huntington attracted epithets and invective the way garbage draws flies, and the general opinion of C.P. in California was that he was a ruthless pirate. Newspaperman Arthur McEwen said that he had the soul of a shark. Adolph Sutro put in a good word for him by observing that he had never been known to steal a red-hot stove. The San Francisco *Examiner* described him as being "ruthless as a crocodile," and an anonymous critic remarked upon his "scrupulous dishonesty." No pioneer was more greedy, more selfish—or more able. The public be double-damned was Collis's view. His attitude was documented when his confidential letters to his associate,

David Colton, were made public after the latter's death. His profane and cynical disregard for the public good and his willingness to bribe Congress in order to have his way did much to contribute to the image of the Southern Pacific as a grasping "Octopus."

Withal, he was a cheerful pirate—jolly at times, presumably when the plunder was good. Although miserly, he was not dour. His New York office was almost as barren as a Trappist's cell. The blame for the mustard-colored sheds which passed for S.P. stations can be laid largely to Huntington's penury too. As ill-mannered and arrogant as he was grasping, he won the grudging respect of his enemies because of his business acumen. Huntington cared neither about the number of his enemies, as numerous as autumnal leaves, nor their respect, for he despised not only politics, speeches, interviews, and the press but even personal popularity itself. (In his seventies, he mellowed somewhat and aped other multimillionaires with travel and fancy homes, but in his salad days he wanted only to be left to hell alone. People could do as they damn pleased as long as they did not mess with him. His only weakness, in fact, was a sensitivity about his bald spot, which led him to wear, virtually around the clock, a black skullcap like that of an Orthodox Jew.)

As might be imagined, Central Pacific Huntington was a New Englander, born in Harwinton, Connecticut, on October 22, 1821. He learned to hoard early, even for a New Englander, and had a hundred dollars squirreled away by the time he was a fourteen-year old hired hand. He enjoyed (in every sense) his reputation for parsimony throughout his life. He believed firmly in working hard, saving hard, and spending little. He had no scruples in business, treating it like love and war. His commercial cunning was unrivaled. Even though saddled with free-spending Leland Stanford, Huntington managed an effective "poverty lobby" in Washington to get Congress to cancel, scale down, or fund the Central Pacific's debts. When the Government had agreed to pay forty-eight thousand dollars per mile for construction of the C.P.R.R. in the California mountains, as opposed to only eighteen thousand dollars in the flatlands, the Big Four, in order to fatten the kitty by a half million dollars, moved the Sierra Nevada range twenty-four miles westward by proclaiming Arcade Creek to be the foot of the mountains, only seven miles east of the state capitol! Charlie Crocker is often given credit for this geographical sleight-of-hand, but it smacks more of Huntington's genius than Crocker's.

As the brains of the Big Four, Huntington had the alchemical touch of Midas himself, and was soon the Croesus of American railroading. But he never claimed to be a "railroad man," and he was not. He treated the railways which he collected, like the S.P. and the Chesakpeake & Ohio, not as utilities but as merchandise to be bought and sold. Profit was everything. The transcontinental railroad was a dream and a challenge to Judah; to Huntington it was a speculation.

Although he was strong and healthy and had endurance enough to work long hours at his desk until he was up in his seventies, Collis disliked manual labor. He worked as a miner in California for exactly half a day. Shoveling gravel from creek bottom to shore was not his idea of how to make money. As a shrewd Sacramento merchant with Mark Hopkins, he prospered mightily by learning one effective way of making profits, and that was to corner the market on something— anything. Deprive the public of something it wanted—shovels, blasting powder, iron—and it would come crying for it, willing to pay through the nose. This simple technique worked splendidly for Huntington. He spent time in San Francisco, too, buying a dory and field glasses and rowing out between the Heads to intercept profitable cargoes and paying deposits in gold dust from a pouch on his belt. By the time the vessels were warped up to the Embarcadero, C.P. had the cream of the cargo.

The antisocial Huntington was anti-intellectual, too, and contemptuous of art and letters. Formal education was a waste of valuable time. He had only one brush with literature. This occurred when the *Examiner* published Edwin Markham's poem *The Man with the Hoe*. It was a sensation which transformed a Lagoon Valley schoolteacher into the Poet of the People. The Socialists used the grinding poverty of the hoeman in Millet's painting and Markham's poem as effective anticapitalistic propaganda. Huntington was incensed and, although it must have hurt to throw away money on poesy, posted a $750 prize, via the New York *Sun,* for the best poetic answer to Markham's work. Of five thousand submissions, John Vance Cheney's *Responsibility* was adjudged the best.

Huntington liked his surviving partner, Stanford, less and less as the years passed, but he kept quiet for the sake of business even when the ex-governor rudely shouldered aside his friend, A. A. Sargent, in order to run for senator. The vindictive New Englander bore his grudge for five years before he took his revenge. In exchange for the promise that he would destroy the embarrassing papers he held documenting Stanford's political maneuvering in "the Sargent matter," Huntington got the ex-governor to step aside as S.P. president. The new president then calmly went back on his word and broadcast that Stanford had not only bought his election but had purchased it with funds from the railroad's treasury, "to defeat the people's choice." Small wonder that Stanford never wanted to speak to him again, telling the press that he would trust Huntington, in future, only so far as he could "throw

Trinity Church up the side of Mount Shasta." Eventually, and probably for the sake of business, Huntington apologized.

C.P.'s benefactions were virtually nonexistent. He gave a little money to Negro colleges as well as to poet Cheney. Probably his largest philanthropic gesture was his founding of the modest Westchester, New York, Library and Reading Room, in the Bronx. (Little did he guess what it suggested to his nephew, Henry.) He died on August 14, 1900, and it is said that the six policemen at the funeral, hired to keep the expected crowd in order, were outnumbered only three to one by mourners. Since he had no sons, Collis was succeeded to the commercial throne by his favorite nephew, Henry Edwards (Ed) Huntington. The latter was ostensibly a hard-driving carbon copy of the old man. But after marrying Collis's widow, Arabella, Henry found himself with more money than he knew what to do with, even when he laced the Los Angeles Plain with interurban railways to carry the fondly remembered Big Red Cars of yesteryear. So it was that the tight-fisted old scrooge of the Central Pacific plowed back some of his ill-gotten profits—unwillingly, to be sure, and via a proxy. Henry E. Huntington founded in 1919 the Huntington Library, Art Gallery, and Botanical Garden, one of the cultural jewels of California, in San Marino near Pasadena.

How "Highwayman Huntington" must have cursed, from the tomb, his spendthrift nephew's squandering of his wealth! And how the shades of Judah and Stanford, et al, must still enjoy the spectacle and the trick unconsciously played on Uncle Collis by the skinflint's philanthropic pet nephew!

ISHI

(1862?–1916)

Early in the morning of August 23, 1911, before the heat of the Sacramento Valley had set in, employees of a slaughterhouse near Oroville found an Indian brought to bay in a corral by the pack of dogs which lived on the abattoir's offal. But he was no ordinary Indian—he was a *wild* Indian, such as had not been seen by Californians for decades. The hastily summoned sheriff of Butte County, J. B. Webber, found the redman to be peaceable enough and he surrendered to the handcuffs without resistance. He was fatalistic—and he was starving. But the stranger was no more like the local Indians than he was like Webber's deputies. He was naked except for a ragged scrap of wagon canvas worn as a cape. He spoke no English or Spanish and even the local Indians and half-breeds could get nowhere with their Maidu, Wintun, and other tongues. Small wonder; they were addressing a refugee from the Stone Age.

When the story of the Wild Man of Oroville reached San Francisco, University of California anthropologists T. T. Waterman and Alfred Kroeber became most interested because, in 1908, wild Indians had been surprised and scattered by a

160

survey party in the Sierra foothills. Kroeber had sought the handful of aborigines then but with no success. He did not want to miss a second chance, so he hurried a telegram to the sheriff: "Hold Indian till arrival Professor State University who will take charge and be responsible for him. Matter important account aboriginal history." The two scientists guessed correctly that the stranger was the last survivor of the Yahi subtribe of the Yana. These were a people who had lived in the lower Sierra along Mill and Deer creeks east of Tehama. They had been virtually exterminated in a series of bloody punitive expeditions (for theft and murder) by settlers in the 1860's and 1870's. The most primitive of the Yana were the Yahi, believed to be completely extinct by most Californians. But not by Kroeber and Waterman.

Professor Waterman escorted the missing link between the Neolithic Age and the twentieth century to San Francisco, where he gave him a comfortable home in the Museum of Anthropology. The Indian found it a quiet and timeless place, although it was surrounded with the clangor and mad pace of the city. It suited him perfectly. Nowhere else would he ever feel so much at home, not even when he returned to his Mill Creek and Deer Creek hunting grounds for a visit. It was his good luck to be placed in the considerate hands of Kroeber, Waterman, and their friend, Dr. Saxton Pope. They all became close friends of the Yahi. Had he been given over to the Indian Bureau's tender mercies, he would probably have ended up in the Round Valley Reservation at Covelo, among unsympathetic (and possibly hostile) Indians of tribes which had, long before, made their varying adjustments to the twentieth century. He did not even get along well with a part-Yana interpreter the professors hired, in order to communicate with him, at first. The "wild man" was of great dignity and bearing, once he recovered from starvation, and had nothing in common with the interpreter.

The anthropologists never knew the true name of their new friend. It was Yahi custom never to reveal one's name. So they dubbed him Ishi (Man) and thus he was known ever after. As they learned his tongue and as he picked up pidgin English, they were able to piece together his story. He had been hunted like an animal from birth; he had seen his tribelet reduced by disease and white man's guns from three or four hundred people to just *five* when the surveyors stumbled on their Deer Creek hideout. For twenty-four years, from 1884 until 1908, the tribal remnant had lived there in the chaparral-choked gorge of Deer Creek, undisturbed and even unde-tected. When the four others scattered, Ishi never saw them again, nor did anyone else. He became the sole survivor of the Yahi. His own personal last stand was of three years' duration, until hunger drove him onto the valley floor, to write finis to what Ishi's biographer, Theodora Kroeber, has called the Long Concealment.

Protected by the scientists from the barkers and mounte-banks who would have made a sideshow attraction of him in California, the gentle and shy Ishi came to enjoy the curious but well-behaved multitude of visitors which came to the museum to see him. He was such a diligent worker (like a Japanese, he had almost an aesthetic obsession over neat-ness) in odd jobs about the museum that he was put on the university payroll as an assistant janitor. Although he was stolid and patient and of great dignity, he demonstrated other characteristics not attributed to the Indians so commonly and derogatorily lumped together as Diggers. He was friendly, warmhearted, kind. He was jolly much of the time and charm-ing all of the time. He was, in fact, a gentleman in every sense of the word. Any Yahi survivor, of course, could have served the university professors in their research on language and customs. But Ishi, the individual, completely won their hearts. He had few friends but they were close, mainly the three professors, the janitorial staff of the museum, and a Papago Indian, Juan Dolores, who used to visit the museum.

Ishi was gawked at by crowds, photographed by both still and moving-picture cameramen, and recorded on the primitive Edison cylinders which preceded phonograph disc records. In turn, he stared at the tall buildings, the automobiles, the steam trains, the Pacific Ocean, and the great crowds of people. He enjoyed meeting different kinds of visitors—like Chinese—and always welcomed, particularly, Caucasians who wore any kind of uniform. At the theater, he was much more interested in the audience than the performers on stage. He became accustomed to wearing Western style dress—even shoes, painful to him—and learned to shop for his food and other necessities and even to save a portion of his small monthly salary.

The Indian told his friends much about the mysterious Yahi people, now extinct save for himself. His fear of sleeping in moonlight with his head uncovered was pure superstition, but not so Ishi's use of frogs or toads on rattlesnake bites. This technique was paralleled by experiments at the Pasteur Institute in which extracts of salamander skin were found to produce immunization to snakebite poisoning. Ishi learned to accept surgery as a necessary and useful practice in the new world in which he found himself, but he was never comfortable at the idea of men cutting and tampering with another's body and spirit. He was even more concerned and disturbed by anaesthesia which, in his eyes, caused the soul to leave an individual's body.

But better than telling whites about Indian customs and traditions, Ishi showed them. He demonstrated his amazing skill with the ancient fire drill, at shooting with the bows and arrows which he made, in chipping out beautiful arrowheads from flint, obsidian, and even beer bottle glass. In the field, he showed his new friends how to hunt with bow and arrow, how to fish with hook and line, harpoon, and snare. He taught Pope archery; so well, in fact, that the doctor later hunted lions in Africa with bow and arrow! On the expedition to his old hunting grounds, Ishi was able to virtually re-enact his whole life for the edification of his professor friends. Other trips were scheduled to coincide with the acorn harvest and the salmon run, but the outbreak of World War I put an end to all such plans for the time being.

Worse, Ishi's good health began to decline in civilization. He had hardly arrived in San Francisco when he took his first cold. This turned into pneumonia. Next came the dread tuberculosis. Although he was given the very best of care, Ishi died of TB on March 25, 1916. By then, all who knew him were very fond of him. Without a trace of self-pity, always cheerful and content, full of patience, he was a boon companion to Kroeber, Waterman, and Pope. Waterman wrote to a colleague at the time of Ishi's death, "He was the best friend I had in the world." Pope, whom Ishi considered to be practically a fellow-Indian, because of his skill with the bow and arrow, was left desolate. Kroeber, in New York, wrote his friends to insist that they guarantee their lost friend the death rites of his Yahi religion. He (unsuccessfully) urged them to forbid any autopsy. "As to disposal of the body, yield nothing at all under any circumstances. If there is any talk about the interests of science, say for me that science can go to hell! We propose to stand by our friends."

Kroeber's friends could not protect Ishi from a post mortem. But they did the best they could. They gave him a quick cremation, placing with his remains a bow and arrows, acorn meal, shell beads, and some flakes of obsidian. The ashes of the last Stone Age man in the United States were not placed in an urn at Mount Olivet Cemetery but in a black pottery jar of Pueblo design, a last gesture which Ishi would have liked.

CAPTAIN JACK

(*1837?–73*)

California has had drama aplenty in its history, yet few stories of its past can truthfully be said to measure up to Greek tragedy. James Frazier Reed's banishment in the Nevada desert and subsequent rescue of his Donner Party persecutors is one valid example. Another is the story of Captain Jack, who was confronted with a dilemma, like Hamlet, and sensed a foreshadowing of tragedy and death in it but was unable to halt the turn of fate.

Jack was a subchief under Chief Schonchin of the Modoc Indians, a tribe which was small but proud and hardy, dwelling in northeasternmost California on the very Oregon border. American settlers, as ever, coveted the Modoc lands and pressured the Government into removing the Indians to the Klamath Indian Reservation at Yainax, in southern Oregon. The tribe was brought suddenly and forcibly to the American public's attention in 1872 and 1873 by newspaper headlines of a Modoc War and by Joaquin Miller's timely pastiche of fact and fiction, *Life Amongst the Modocs*.

Born Kientpoos circa 1837, Jack got his new name because of his fondness for military uniforms, buttons, and insignia.

He did have a claim to the chieftainship, however, and may have been the son of the chief of the Modocs killed in the Ben Wright massacre in 1852, following a massacre of emigrants at Bloody Point, on Tule Lake. In any case, he quickly demonstrated his genius for leadership and, as a native military tactician, gave nothing away to either Crazy Horse or Osceola. The conflict in which he participated rivaled the Seminole War both in hardships and cost per capita of hostiles involved. Estimates of money cost ranged from a half million dollars to a highly improbable (even if *every* rancher in Northern California filed a phony claim for war-damage indemnification) five million. Infantry and cavalry, reinforced by Oregon and California volunteer militiamen and Warm Springs Indian scouts, were used against Captain Jack and his warriors, the latter numbering perhaps eighty at most. The soldiers were armed with rifles, cannon, howitzers, and coehorn mortars. They requested grenades from Benicia Arsenal, but none were in supply. They patrolled Tule Lake in Whitehall boats, the small craft which normally ferried people from ship to shore in San Francisco Bay. Even poison gas was suggested as a weapon. Still, in five major engagements or skirmishes the Army won not a single clear-cut victory. Three Modocs were killed by soldiers; two more blew themselves to the happy hunting grounds by hammering at a dud howitzer shell out of curiosity. Four were hanged after a trial and one committed suicide. A few squaws and children died, too, in the bombardment of the Lava Beds. For this, the Army paid with 165 dead and wounded. Nobody won this war; everybody lost. (Except for the ubiquitous profiteering damage claimants.) Everyone lost morally in a war which was even more bloody, demeaning, and unnecessary than most Indian conflicts.

How did it all come about? Largely via governmental stupidity. Disregarding tribal boundaries, federal policy forced the Modocs onto the Klamath Reservation. There they were strangers, interlopers, and virtually enemies. The more numerous Klamath harassed them, so their chief, Captain Jack, led them back to their own land. He resisted the attempt of a military force to herd them back, and a battle was fought at Lost River in which the Army unit was forced to withdraw. This November 29, 1872, engagement was the first of the Modoc War. Captain Jack then moved into California's roughest *malpais,* or badlands. This was the Lava Beds area south of Tule Lake, a volcanic wilderness which the Modocs termed "The Land of Burnt-out Fires." Jack recognized it as a natural fortress. The Army, stung by its setback at Lost River and by the massacre of eighteen settlers by a warrior chief, Hooker Jim, and his band, sent a well-equipped force of four hundred men after Captain Jack in January. After an all-day battle, the soldiers—who had marched out boasting that they would have "Modoc steak" for breakfast—came reeling back, bloodied and exhausted, from Captain Jack's Stronghold. (This natural fortification is now the heart of Lava Beds National Monument.) Their loss was nine dead and thirty wounded. None of the Modocs was even scratched. No wonder General John Schofield described the war as "a conflict more remarkable, in some respects, than any other before known in American history."

Badly whipped by a handful of so-called renegades, the Army was allowed to lick its wounds while President Grant's "Quaker Policy" was tried. General E. R. S. Canby and other peace commissioners agreed to meet with Captain Jack under a flag of truce. Jack was in favor of returning to the reservation and continuing passive resistance. The shaman, Curly Headed Doctor, advocated bloody warfare. Schonchin suggested the murder of the commissioners. Jack spoke against this, but the war party clapped a woman's shawl and bonnet on him and taunted him with cries of "Woman! Coward! White-faced squaw!" Jack was shamed into participating and, of course, as war chief, claimed Canby as his victim. The Modocs treacherously fell upon the commissioners and killed two, including General Canby, and wounded another. Thus ended Act I of the tragedy of the reluctant murderer, Captain Jack.

The Government responded by throwing a thousand soldiers against the Modocs and, although the soldiers had to pay dearly for each foot of tufa and cinders, the warriors eventually lost their horses and even their water supply. Jack's little army, outnumbered twenty-five to one, began to disintegrate. Sixty-five Modocs surrendered while the rest scattered in hiding. The next act of the tragedy saw murderers Hooker Jim and Shacknasty Jim and two other warriors hiring out as "bloodhounds" for the Army, to run down their erstwhile general. On June 1, 1873, Jack's legs gave out and he was captured. The war was over.

The Government tried six Indians by court-martial for violation of the rules of war, i.e., killing the peace commissioners. President Grant commuted the sentences of two of them to life imprisonment, but Jack and three others were sentenced to be hanged on October 3, 1873, at Fort Klamath. Now, Jack saw Act III unfold. The bloodiest of his war party faction, men like Hooker Jim, who had hunted him down like an animal, were allowed to testify against him at the trial and were granted immunity for their crimes. Jack's last words testified to his recent, bitter education in American justice. He glared at the "bloodhounds," who were among the gallows crowd, and told Colonel Frank Wheaton, "I feel that while these men—Bogus, Shacknasty Jim, Hooker and Steamboat— are free, they have triumphed over me *and* the Government."

Civilized folk were not through with the "savage" even when Captain Jack was cut down from the gallows. That night, some enterprising citizen dug up Jack's body and rushed it to Yreka for embalming. Tradition has it that the corpse was exhibited in a sideshow in Washington D.C., at ten cents a look. Eventually, the warrior chief's head was taken to the Surgeon General's Museum in Washington and, reduced to a skull, was displayed as a specimen of Indian anatomy.

HELEN HUNT JACKSON

(*1830–85*)

So fantastically popular has been the novel *Ramona* that the modern public often thinks of Helen Hunt Jackson as a one-book author. Perish the thought! "H.H.," born Helen Maria Fiske in Amherst, Massachusetts, on October 15, 1830 and twice married, was a prolific writer with almost three dozen novels to her credit plus scores of magazine and newspaper articles. *Ramona* was her last work, barring posthumously published writings, and the culmination of twenty-eight years of authorship.

Some critics would say that she is remembered for the wrong book, and Mrs. Jackson herself hoped to be remembered more by her nonfiction exposé of the mistreatment of America's Indians, *A Century of Dishonor,* than by her propaganda novel. But *A Century of Dishonor* was only a modest success, where *Ramona* has gone through three hundred printings, has been widely translated, made into movies, has fathered plays and pageants which are California's answer to Oberammergau and has created a whole Ramona school of souvenirs, relics, pseudo-sites and hokum-history until "Ramona's Marriage Place" in San Diego is more of a tourist attraction than

Mission San Luis Rey. In short, *Ramona* has been effective, whether for good or for ill.

Mrs. Jackson hoped that the novel would be the *Uncle Tom's Cabin* for the Indians. This was not quite the case. Harriet Beecher Stowe's book was a kind of detonator for the emancipation movement, but *Ramona* won more generalized sympathy for the Indian than outright help. Although the author had also sent every senator and congressman a copy of *A Century of Dishonor,* at her own expense, results were negligible. Like many another memorialist, Mrs. Jackson found no deafer ears in the world than those on Capitol Hill.

What *Ramona* did to Southern California is saddening, for the author's intentions were so honorable. It did not wipe out the bigotry and injustice from which the Indians suffered in southern California more than the Mexicans and Negroes. All it did was to create a synthetic California of the past peopled by Spanish dons, gentle Franciscan padres, and noble redmen. The predominantly white Protestant population of Los Angeles and its surroundings, growing at a fantastic rate, now swooned schizophrenically over the good old days existing largely in Helen Hunt Jackson's mind. They mastered a (still) mind-boggling ambivalence and managed to keep their actual Indian and Mexican neighbors "in their place" while adoring the cardboard "Spaniards" and mission neophytes of Mrs. Jackson's romance. Stewart Edward White and Gertrude Atherton soon arrived as reinforcements in the great Ersatz History campaign until, today, the pitiful but proud handful of genuine historic sites in California's Southland is overwhelmed by the pseudohistorical charades performed in Disneyland, Knott's Berry Farm, and the pageants and plays from Hemet to Padua Hills. Were it not set in mythical Southern California, the whole astonishing phenomenon of actual

16. *Agoston Haraszthy*, honored pioneer of the California wine industry, served his apprenticeship in various vocations. For a time, he was an officer of the San Francisco Mint—until federal investigator J. Ross Browne discovered that altogether too much gold was escaping "up the flue" in Haraszthy's department instead of finding its way into the gold bricks being poured in the room above. *California State Library*

17. Most exotic of all California badmen was *Little Pete*, or Fong Ching, who managed a monopoly of Chinatown rackets after a brief setback (five years in the state pen for suborning a jury, etc.), only to be murdered in a barber chair just off Waverly Place. *Author's collection*

18. A rougher-hewn sort of John Muir was *Galen Clark,* Yosemite's other watchdog. Clark tried his hand at writing but could not come closer than a Spanish league to "John o' the Mountains" as an author. However, he was his equal as a mountaineer and should be remembered as one of California's bona fide mountain men, like Grizzly Adams. *California Historical Society*

19. Once overenthusiastically described as a mining wonder of the world after first having been put down as "Sutro's Coyote Hole," the Sutro Tunnel near Dayton, Nevada, was bored into the base of Mount Davidson in order to drain the depths of the Virginia City mines of the water which was strangling them. It was successful but it was too late; the boom was ending, the major leads pinching out. Still, *Adolph Sutro* made a fortune out of it and, praise him, reinvested it in books for the Sutro Library of today's San Francisco. *Nevada State Highway Department*

20. California's badmen have run less often to greasy buckskins and tobacco-tinted whiskers than the wrongdoers of other frontier territories, largely because of the early civilizing influence of metropolitan San Francisco. Thus Charles Boles —better known as *Black Bart*, Wells Fargo's nemesis—is not out of uniform, at all, with his derby, double-breasted salt-and-pepper suit, cane, and fancy lapeled topcoat. *Wells Fargo History Room*

21. *E. J. (Lucky) Baldwin's* luck soured in 1898, when his magnificent hostelry, the Baldwin Hotel, the early rival of San Francisco's Palace, burned to a heap of rubble at Market and Powell streets. It was Baldwin's great monument in the north. Luckily, his Southern California monument has been spared by time. It is, today, his old estate in Arcadia, transformed into the Los Angeles County Aboretum, complete with lake, Queen Anne cottage, and peacocks. *Historical Collections, Security First National Bank, Los Angeles*

22. *Luther Burbank,* of Santa Rosa, bearer of California's greenest thumb of all time, was as much a wizard in his day as Thomas A. Edison, and if gardeners were only half as aggressive as TV salesmen he would be remembered with equal ease by the public for his "inventions," like absurd spineless cactus and superb Shasta daisies. *Redwood Empire Association*

23. Neither rain, sleet, snow, nor dark o' night stops a bronzed *James Marshall* from pointing out (perhaps in disgust?) the gravel bank where he should have made a fortune but did not when he found gold in the South Fork of the American River at Coloma and, thereby, stood California—and the world—on end in '49. *California State Division of Beaches and Parks*

24. One of the few true pioneers of California who managed to hang onto his wealth despite the hordes of squatters and Philadelphia shysters which flocked to the Promised Land was *John Bidwell.* The gracious style of living of this gentleman farmer of the Sacramento Valley can be deduced from the Bidwell Mansion, still standing in Chico. *Joseph Baird*

25. *William Mulholland* was en route to great fame as California's water wizard when the San Francisquito Dam disaster was blamed on him. Whatever responsibility—if any—he had for the tragedy, he deserves to be honored by Los Angeleños by more than Mulholland Drive. It was Mulholland who, quite literally, made L.A. possible by finding enough water for the thirsty metropolis. *Los Angeles Department of Water and Power*

26. The still largely unsung hero of the Central Pacific end of the transcontinental railroad was *Theodore Dehone Judah,* its Sierra engineer and lobbyist, who had to sell the idea to the Big Four as well as to Congress and the general public. Before he could enjoy the fruits of his success, he died. *Southern Pacific Photo*

27. Even the severest critics of Governor *Leland Stanford,* the bluff extrovert of the Central Pacific, Southern Pacific, and Big Four, should forgive him for any sins against the public weal because of his astonishing penance—the creation of a "Harvard of the West" in California, in the shape of Stanford University. *Southern Pacific Photo*

28. Perhaps the most beloved of all of California's many adopted sons is famed writer *Robert Louis Stevenson.* The sickly Scot, who died at the age of forty-four in Samoa, lived the most pleasant months of his life in the summer of 1880 atop California's Mount St. Helena, in an abandoned shanty at the ghost town of Silverado. This charming picture of R.L.S. is also one of the rarest photographs of the author in existence. *Robert Weinstein*

history being set aside for a synthetic brand would be absolutely incredible.

Of course, as Lawrence Clark Powell has pointed out, *Ramona* was (and is) misread, like Swift's *Gulliver's Travels*. Intended to shock America into righting the wrongs done the Indian, it has been taken over by the masses as a costume love story, a historical romance, and a children's classic. *Ramona* documents a "vanished" way of life which never really existed in the form which Helen Hunt Jackson gave it, although there are many grains of truth and insight scattered over her romanticized landscape. She was too much a product and a victim of her times. *Ramona* bears too much resemblance to the sentimental and trite romances of Fanny Fern and other female disfigurers of American literature. What saved *Ramona* from the fate (oblivion) of the potboilers of its day was Helen Hunt Jackson's motivation. She felt deeply about the plight of the Indians and she did yearn for a return to a simpler, better past which she thought she perceived in the mission period of California history. This concern brought a kind of vitality to her morality play between book covers. Perhaps, because of her compassion and zeal to reform Indian policy, Spiller's definition of literature in his *Literary History of the United States* applies to *Ramona:* "any writing in which emotional or intellectual values are made articulate by excellent expression."

Literature or not, *Ramona* is now a document of California history. Where its depiction of mission-days California is faulty, it is a candid mirror of the curious, ambivalent, intertwining of romance, prejudice, and nostalgia in Southern California's ex-New Englanders and Iowans. They wanted to set down roots in California but preferably not in the clayey adobe of reality but in the shifting silver sands of more comfortable legend. (To their minds, there were still too many

173

"dirty" Indians and Mexicans loafing about the fringes of Arcady's real estate tracts and speculative colonies.)

Curiously, Mrs. Jackson herself duplicated the process. She was originally as anti-Catholic as she was anti-Mormon, and her first opinion of California's Indians was "hideous." She ended up by eulogizing both monks and natives. Her love for the Southern California back country was almost unique, too. She disliked San Francisco; put Santa Barbara down as a smug, stodgy, and New England sort of a place; detested Paris; hated Denver; and found little of interest in Edinburgh. She made enemies on the very ranchos she idealized (in an earlier state) by her meddling and was such a busybody that she angered her San Diego hotelkeeper by interfering when he disciplined his child.

Although Helen Hunt Jackson's poetry was briefly held in high repute, like Bayard Taylor's, it is certain that she would be forgotten today had she not visited California in 1872 and had she not heard a lecture in Boston in 1879 by Chief Standing Bear of the Ponca. The former gave her the backdrop she would need; the latter turned a petulant and intolerant snob into a zealous crusader for Indian rights.

Helen Hunt Jackson visited California on three occasions between 1881 and 1885 but not to write *Ramona*. She was gathering material for four articles on the state and its missions which *Century* magazine had asked her to write. She visited every mission and studied in Hubert H. Bancroft's library and the archives at Santa Barbara Mission just as she had crammed in New York's Astor Library while writing *A Century of Dishonor*. Don Antonio Coronel was her best informant, but she visited the Cámulos, Guajome, and other old ranchos to sop up local color. She dug deeper into the Indian rancherias when President Chester Arthur appointed her a special Indian commissioner to investigate the condition

174

of the so-called Mission Indians. She ranged all over the back country with her Spanish interpreter, Abbot Kinney, finding the Indians existing in squalor and misery, intimidated by squatters and being kicked off their land by "legal" buyers.

The germ of the idea for *Ramona* came to Helen Hunt Jackson in a sudden flash in Colorado Springs in October 1883. By December 1 she was holed up in the Berkeley Hotel in New York, writing away. Legend to the contrary, she did not write the book in bits and pieces in missions and ranch houses. The theme haunted her and drove her to a frenetic writing pace of two thousand to three thousand words of finished copy every day, although tension and overwork made her ill.

When the book appeared, its author thought it a failure rather than the huge success which it was. This was because her best-seller was accepted as merely an idyll of California's mythical days of the dons. "Not one word for my Indians!" she cried when she read the reviews, "[and] I put my heart and soul in the book for them."

Ill with cancer, Mrs. Jackson died in San Francisco on August 8, 1885. Her last act was to laboriously write a letter to President Grover Cleveland. It was both pathetic and hopeful. "From my deathbed I send you [a] message of heartfelt thanks for what you have already done for the Indians. I ask you to read my *Century of Dishonor*. I am dying happier for the belief I have that it is your hand that is destined to strike the first steady blow toward lifting the burden of infamy from our country and righting the wrongs of the Indian race."

There are several schools of thought about *Ramona's* worth, besides that of the simple-minded who would oust Proust from the library's shelves to make room for it. One group, of course, applauds Mrs. Jackson for a good try at ameliorating the Indian's sorry condition. Another faction condemns her for aborting the sickly legend of Olden California with its fraudulent figures now commercialized into a heavy industry in Southern California. Many of these critics throw up their hands over Helen Hunt Jackson's congenital inability to spell Spanish names. Gaspar in her hands becomes Gaspara and poor Salvatierra ends up Salvierderra. Proof, perhaps, of the unconscious influence of her 1869 stay in Italy is her rendering of her hero's name not as Alejandro but the Italianate Alessandro. Still a third group of partisans, led by Dr. Lawrence Clark Powell, honor the book as Southern California's first novel and as a respectable example of the creative process of the writer. Mary Austin—who should know —praised *Ramona* as an authentic and faithful historical novel, if a romantic one. Certainly, Mrs. Jackson took the simple materials of observation, local history (largely the story of runaway lovers Ramona Lubo and Juan Diego), local color, and oral tradition and wove them into a story which has intrigued thousands of readers for more than eighty-five years. Already, *Ramona* has lived far longer than most American novels ever will.

HIRAM JOHNSON

(*1866–1945*)

The grass-roots phenomenon which was the Progressive movement grew out of the social and political philosophy of both major parties as they were constituted circa 1908, when Theodore Roosevelt ran the Republicans and William Jennings Bryan dominated the Democratic Party. America was changing rapidly from a rural and agricultural economy to an urban-industrial civilization, and reforms in economic, political, and social areas of life were long overdue. It was necessary to eradicate such fringe deficits of the Industrial Revolution as child labor, city slums and poverty, sweat shops, trusts and monopoly.

William Howard Taft's failure to carry out T.R.'s reform policies led to a movement for a Progressive Party, per se, and much of its leadership came from the West in such men as Congressman George Norris of Nebraska, Senator Robert La Follette of Wisconsin, and Hiram Johnson of California. Roosevelt's Progressive, or Bull Moose, campaign of 1912, with its planks of tariff revision, women's suffrage, and minimum wage standards, succeeded in splitting the Republican Party and electing Democrat Woodrow Wilson. However, by now, the latter's party was progressive in spirit, itself, although World War I stifled the movement. The Progressive Party and Progressivism itself were effectively wiped out by the turn to conservatism during the 1920's, although elements of the philosophy were later apparent in Franklin D. Roosevelt's more radical and thoroughgoing New Deal of the 1930's.

One of the major figures of the Progressive movement was Hiram Warren Johnson, a founder of the 1912 Progressive Party. Born in Sacramento, California, on September 2, 1866, young Hiram studied law and entered the University of California, Berkeley, but, like Frank Norris and Jack London and others, became a dropout. He failed to finish his junior year. He married in 1886, became a shorthand reporter and again studied law until he was admitted to the bar in 1888. He and his brother helped his father, Grove Johnson, with the reform ticket which finally ousted Sacramento's long-entrenched city bosses. Muckraker Lincoln Steffens, born in San Francisco in 1866 also, described the boys when, armed with pistols, they had to act as virtual bodyguards for their father as he took on the crooked politicos of the capital city. In 1891, the aggressive Hiram got into a name-calling quarrel with the D.A. which ended in a fistfight. There was no doubting the crusading zeal of the two Johnson boys.

Unfortunately, such was not the case with their father. When he was elected to Congress, he underwent a transformation and became conservative, siding with the Southern Pacific Railroad interests, which ran California like a hobby. Hiram left his father's firm and joined with Independent reform interests even though he had to fight his father. His group won; the reform candidate secured the mayoralty.

In 1902, Hiram and his brother set off to conquer new worlds. They went to San Francisco (ten times the size of Sacramento and still three times the size of L.A.) and opened a law firm. There, Hiram won nation-wide fame in the San Francisco Graft Trials. He became one of Fremont Older's crusading allies against boss Abe Ruef and his henchmen. Others who joined the fight included District Attorney William H. Langdon; Attorney Francis J. Heney; Rudolph Spreckels, the sugar heir and surely the most social and well-off reformer of California history; and Detective William Burns. Langdon retained Johnson as an assistant district attorney and the latter's reputation for pugnacity suffered not at all when once again he traded blows with the opposing attorney during one of the Graft Trials. But the crusade was cooling fast as business interests suddenly lost heart when bribe-*takers* were investigated as well as bribe-givers.

Suddenly, the crusade got going again when a witness's home was dynamited and when an ex-con, Morris Haas, shot Heney down in court. Langdon had Johnson take Heney's place as chief prosecutor in Abe Ruef's trial and, although Abe had "fixed" four of the jury, he was found guilty and sentenced to San Quentin. Fremont Older, in his San Francisco *Call,* described most vividly the courtroom drama: "Never in the history of criminal jurisprudence in San Francisco has there been voiced in any court a more terrific denunciation of any man than the lashing of Abe Ruef by Hiram Johnson. . . . For two hours and a half the flood of invective poured from Johnson's lips in overwhelming torrent. . . . His summing up of the evidence was a masterful gathering together of the loose threads of testimony scattered through the thousands of pages of the record. . . . 'We know this man is guilty,' he declared sternly. '*You* know he is guilty. Dare you, then, acquit this man who came into court with streaming eyes and admitted his guilt? Dare you acquit him?' "

At this point in his political career, Hiram Johnson became interested in the direct primary and, through it, in the whole philosophy of Progressivism. Under political bossism, California's primary elections had long been farces. Johnson was quoted as saying that the direct primary would put the government back where it belonged—in the hands of the people. Again he had to fight his conservative father, now in the Assembly, and again he won and the direct primary was voted into law. Johnson next became a leader in the Lincoln-Roosevelt Republican League of Edward A. Dickson, of Los Angeles, and Chester Rowell, of Fresno, which was fighting to "emancipate" California from the strangle hold of the so-called Octopus, the Southern Pacific Railroad monopoly. Johnson was elected vice president of the league.

Although as late as 1907 he had insisted, "I am not a politician in any sense of the word. I have never held and never will hold any public office," he allowed himself to be persuaded to run for Governor of California as the Lincoln-Roosevelt Republican League's candidate on a platform built of one huge plank—the overthrow of the political power of the S.P. He saw his reluctant candidacy as a sacrifice, but he was determined to win: "I am going ahead, making the fight as a Progressive Republican on the Roosevelt lines. I am going to make this fight an endeavor to return the government of California to the people and to take it away from the political bureau of the Southern Pacific Railroad Company."

Johnson won the 1910 election, barnstorming the state in his newfangled automobile. As governor, with the help of the Legislature he removed California from the clutches of the S.P. machine, gave the Railroad Commission new muscles, and saw measures through to regulate railroads. He also helped carry out other needed political and social reforms. The initiative, referendum, and recall became realities. Machine politicians battled the last-named with particular tenacity but lost when Governor Johnson stated, "Under an elective system, the recall should be applied to *all* officers. It will make no weak judge weaker nor a strong judge less strong. It will be a warning and a menace to the corrupt, only."

Hiram Johnson was Teddy Roosevelt's running mate in the losing Presidential campaign of 1912, but he was re-elected as governor in 1914 by a landslide—460,495 votes to his nearest opponent's 271,990. In 1917, still a Progressive, he secured a Senate seat. By 1920, Johnson's reforming zeal had congealed and it appeared to be a case of "like father, like son." He moved around to a conservative political stance, which he retained in the Senate until his death in 1945. He was an isolationist who opposed both the League of Nations and the United Nations, and he was a stubborn opponent of Franklin D. Roosevelt's foreign policy. Liberals and conservatives join in agreement that he was one of California's outstanding governors, but the former were greatly disappointed by their onetime crusading hero, who changed so markedly in outlook after 1920.

THEODORE D. JUDAH

(*1826–63*)

The real heroes of the transcontinental railroad were not the panatela-smoking captains of industry who persuaded the Government to underwrite their speculations so lavishly with money and land grants, but the men who actually built the line. These were the bogtrotters from Ireland and the coolies from Canton who worked as graders, tunnelers, and track layers. Equally deserving of praise is the conceptualizer, the planner, the engineer—really the *builder*—of the Central Pacific Railroad over the Sierra, which brought into being the Union Pacific and the link-up with the East. This was "Crazy" Judah.

The Big Four financiers of the Central Pacific have long enjoyed the center of the proscenium. But off in the wings of history stands the real star, who would probably have up-staged Leland Stanford, Mark Hopkins, Collis P. Huntington, and Charles Crocker—had he lived beyond his thirty-seventh year. Without him, the Big Four would have either remained in, or reverted to, the status of small businessmen, lost to history.

Judah was born in Bridgeport, Connecticut, on March 4,

1826, attended Rensselaer Polytechnic Institute in Troy, New York, and obtained practical experience in engineering in the construction of railroads and bridges. In 1854, he was called to California to plan the Sacramento Valley Railroad, the first in the state, which he ran to its Folsom terminus in 1856. Judah surveyed other railway and wagon road routes but, already in 1856, was developing his grand concept of a Pacific Railroad over the Sierra to link California with "the States." He went East and attended three sessions of Congress, lobbying in behalf of his proposal. According to his wife, the transcontinental line became an obsession with him: "Everything he did from the time he went to California to the day of his death was for the continental Pacific railway. Time, money, brains, strength, body and soul were absorbed. It was the burden of his thought, night and day, [and] largely of his conversation till it used to be said, 'Judah is Pacific Railroad crazy.'" So monomaniacal was Judah that even Newton Booth, later Governor of California, was heard to say on a Sacramento street circa 1862, "There comes Crazy Judah!" Everyone, especially overland and Panama immigrants to California, prayed for a railroad across the plains and mountains to the Golden State, but, of all Californians, only Theodore Dehone Judah seemed to be doing something about it, even if it earned him the reputation of being both a bore and a candidate for the asylum because of his crusade for an "impossible" trans-Sierra railway.

But Judah was a pragmatic visionary; a planner as well as a dreamer. He saw that the beautiful thirteen volumes of the pioneering *Railroad Surveys* would never be enough to get solid support for a transcontinental railroad; something more concrete was necessary. At first, all that he could do was to imitate the reports with his own pamphlet, *A Practical Plan for Building the Pacific Railroad.* He deplored the speculative nature of the projects and the rivalry over routes. He stated, flatly, that he could build the line in just ten years, raising the capital from private sources. (He later realized that Government subsidy would be necessary.) Judah knew that a real *survey*—with mileage, number of tunnels and bridges, total cost estimate—was necessary, not another reconnaissance. He estimated that he could carry out this survey for $200,000 and build the railroad for $150,000,000.

Because of Congressional inaction, the California Legislature (probably pushed by Judah) called a Pacific Railroad Convention in 1859 in San Francisco. As its prime mover, Judah was the natural choice as envoy to carry a memorial to Congress. He wrote bills for congressmen, lobbied for them, publicized the Pacific Railroad on tours of New York, Ohio, and Illinois, and found the Vice President's Room in the Capitol turned over to him as a display area for his maps and reports.

But still Congress failed to act, and Judah returned to California to actually lay out the route over the Sierra. This was the concrete action which he was now sure was necessary in order to get Congressional support for his plan. He examined Beckwourth Pass; a route through Georgetown which paralleled the Placerville stage road; the Nevada City-Henness Pass; and the Dutch Flat-Donner Pass (or Summit) route, which he found best. Judah issued a pamphlet and began drumming up stock-subscription agreements. He did well in the mountain towns but not in San Francisco, where financiers, remembering the losses of the Sacramento Valley Railroad in the recent recession, wrote him off as lunatic—an enthusiastic one, to be sure, but still a loony.

In Sacramento, Judah had better luck. He got the support of a group of businessmen including the Big Four—Stanford, Crocker, Huntington, and Hopkins—and formed the Central

Pacific Railroad of California, with Stanford as president. It was Huntington, however, who supplied Judah with funds and men to start his survey. It was not long before the dynamic Judah had a formal *Report* for the directors on the line's survey, completed to the Truckee River at the east base of the mountains by September 1861. He told them that river routes were impracticable because of the deep gorges of the side cañons and tributaries which would have to be crossed. With his motto, "Avoid the cañons," Judah found his way on high ground to the Truckee and managed to avoid the obstacle of the second summit of the Sierra entirely. "That the elevation overcome in crossing the summit of [the] Sierra Nevada is greater than that upon any other line of road in the United States is true. But," he emphasized, "it is no less true that the grades employed in reaching the summit are less than the maximum grade employed on important roads in the United States."

Judah's engineering brilliance resulted in a right-of-way which rose almost to seven thousand feet but which followed the Sierra's divides, or ridges, from gap to gap until the easy descent of the Truckee River was reached to Nevada. So skillfully did he lay out the line that maximum grades were only 105 feet per mile, and no major rivers or cañons had to be crossed. The highest bridge was only fifty feet above Little Bear River. Here and there, he was overly sanguine. He dismissed snow at the summit as being a real problem and had no plans for snowsheds. He overestimated the revenue to the railroad from the Washoe mines of Nevada. But, by and large, it was a splendid plan and survey, and when Crazy Judah returned to California from Washington, it was with a Pacific Railroad Act signed into law by President Lincoln on July 1, 1862.

Work began which would not end until the joining of the

C.P.'s rails with those of the Union Pacific in 1869 at Promontory Point, Utah. Judah ignored the cries of "Swindle!" leveled against his Big Four associates by their enemies, but he grew impatient with the progress of the railroad and resented the fact that the foursome did not take him into its confidence. Nor did he like Huntington's ascendancy of influence over his friend, Stanford. Apparently, Judah disapproved of certain sharp business (monopoly) maneuvers in the matter of contracts, too, and absolutely refused to sign an affidavit establishing the point where the base of the mountains lay. The company being given a greater subsidy for higher, difficult terrain, it was to their advantage to move the foothills all the way to tidewater if possible. Judah said, flatly, of the curious geography of his associates, "The foothills do not begin here, according to our surveys."

Finally Judah had had enough. He got the Big Four to buy him out for one hundred thousand dollars with the option of his buying them out, at the same sum, each. He headed East, almost certainly with the idea of finding replacements for the Big Four. His chances of success were good. He was now widely known in the Eastern United States, and respected. Had he succeeded, the subsequent history not only of the Central Pacific and Southern Pacific railroads, but of the state and the whole West, would have been different.

But, while crossing the Isthmus, Judah contracted one of Panama's innumerable fevers, possibly typhoid. He died (November 2, 1863) shortly after arriving in New York. The Big Four had its way. After his death, Judah was attacked by partisans of other railway routes across the Sierra Nevada, men who did not allow common decency to get in the way of vested interest. But Leland Stanford was correct when he wrote, "Mr. Judah's character as an engineer, respecting which he was particularly sensitive, and [as] a man of integrity, stands too high to be reached by such infamous assaults."

The best proof of Judah's excellence as an engineer is the fact that his original route is, virtually, still the main overland rail connection between California and the rest of the nation. Moreover, the major motor vehicle and truck route to California, Interstate Highway 80, follows his trans-Sierra route to the Golden State. Historian Thomas H. Hittell called Judah a genius; poet Edward Robeson Taylor dubbed him the Prince of Engineers. He was an idealist, a dreamer, too, but the very best kind of one—a *practical* dreamer, who changed the face of the country and the shape of American history.

DENIS KEARNEY

(*1847–1907*)

Denis Kearney started out in life much like Henry George, as a common sailor. In the prime of his political life he borrowed reform ideas from the latter and was, in turn, the subject of an essay by George. But Kearney was much more violent than George—and not within a country mile of the latter as an original thinker. Born on February 1, 1847, in Oakmount, in County Cork, Ireland, Kearney was first officer of a coasting steamer when he married and settled down in San Francisco in 1872. He bought a drayage firm, became a staunch union man, took out his naturalization papers, and taught himself to read and write at a Lyceum for Self-Culture and in the new Public Library. The stocky Irishman began speaking in public and became charmed with the sound of his own voice. But, for a sailor, he took a wrong tack and began lambasting the "shiftless and extravagant" working class and its love of tobacco and booze, both of which he despised. His oratory was sometimes boring, and his delivery offered more brogue than logic, but his emotionalism and colorful language appealed to the horny-handed unsophisticates who made up his audiences.

When an anticoolie riot of unemployed workers occurred during a July 1877 depression, Kearney joined the old "Lion of the Vigilantes," William T. Coleman, whose Committee of Safety was speedily nicknamed the Pick-handle Brigade, for its chief weapon. The brigade helped the police turn back the mob, and both Chinatown and the Pacific Mail Steamship Company docks (where Chinese laborers were landed) were spared the torch. But, suddenly, between July 23 and August 22, 1877, when the Workingmen's Trade and Labor Union was formed with Kearney as its secretary, the Irishman did a complete about-face. From a defender of the Celestials he became their chief persecutor. His battle cry—"The Chinese Must Go!"—became a household slogan across the nation. Even Kearney apologists are hard-pressed to explain such a switch, although such 180-degree changes of course are not unknown among extremists. It has been blamed on resentment following a rebuff from Senator A. A. Sargent when Kearney presented some grievances of the Draymen and Teamsters Union. It has been laid at his anger after luckless dabbling in stocks. Did someone in Labor simply "get to him"? Or did he belatedly see that his hunger for power would be assuaged by backing workingmen, with the power of the ballot, rather than voteless aliens? Naturally, Kearney would not say, so no one knew for sure.

Kearney's new political force soon absorbed the (Marxist) Workingmen's Party and took its name. He proposed to wrest the Government from the rich and to turn it over to "the people." En route to his goal, he promised to rid the state of land monopolists as well as coolie laborers. By a soak-the-rich tax program, Kearney planned to render great wealth impossible. The Party was careful never to call for violence; it promised to exhaust all peaceful avenues to its goals. Its chief soapbox orator, however, now escalated his party's epithets and demands. He had an intuitive sense of mob psychology, and he developed, overnight, into a first-rate demagogue, a genuine rabble-rouser worthy of Sather Gate or Provo Park in a later era. Kearney preferred to speak alfresco, so he packed the sandy vacant lots of the city. His following came to be known as the Sandlot Party. He spoke, and occasionally ranted, on Sundays, when news was slim and when the papers gave him a lot of type. He swore that he would never cease fighting the Chinese until there was blood enough in the streets of Chinatown to float their bodies into the bay. "Bread or blood!" he thundered at the capitalist, another pet enemy like John Chinaman. His threats of arson and hanging were not taken seriously, at first, and the press (irresponsible as ever) began to puff him up, using his vituperation, hate, and abusive insults as means to sell more papers. Much of his threatening was, in fact, mere bombast and bravado. But where the *Argonaut* called him a boor and "a pustule," the *Chronicle* all but adopted him. He reciprocated by urging upon his followers a boycott of the *Chronicle's* rival, the *Call.* Lord Bryce insisted, later, that the press "made" Kearney, just as TV today manufactures a candidate or a street-corner demagogue by sheer exposure to fearful or hate-filled audiences. Certainly, the *Chronicle* treated the Workingmen's Party as if it were a force when it was, really, more of a farce and thus, long before McLuhan, created something from next-to-nothing. Later, the paper recoiled from its rashness and attacked the Transylvanian monster it had helped to create.

By 1878, Kearney was the most feared single individual on the Pacific Coast. (Eventually, Henry George would run an autopsy on his movement in a national magazine, and Kearney would be the subject of work by artists Howard Pyle and Thomas Nast.) The philippic-flinging Irishman bragged that he was the people's dictator; that Judge Lynch was the only jurist he respected; that bullets would replace ballots in California; and that San Francisco would burn like Napoleonic Moscow. His defenders, who included (to some degree, at least) even Henry George, said that he was much misquoted, and it *was* noted that he qualified many of his threats with "ifs" and "buts." But no press, not even Frisco's, could misquote a public figure *every* time, and his urging the workingmen to form armed, paramilitary forces, and his likening the flagstaffs of Nob Hill to gallows, began to frighten a large number of people.

Many of Kearney's tirades were based on fact. His violence was a product of underlying abuses. The Chinese were pawns, caught and ground between opposing forces. (Kearney's deadliest enemy, Frank Pixley, hated the Chinese as well as Catholics, Irish, Germans, etc.) Much of his program grew out of popular unrest and was liberal and progressive rather than communistic and destructive. He urged a shorter workday; assessment of property at full value (the city was as full of tax dodgers in 1878 as it is today), and the creation of a State Bureau of Labor and Labor Statistics. As a result, Kearney's following was much larger than the total of floaters who attended his open-air speeches. His language grew more and more violent as his personal power increased and as "Kearneyism" became a national term. He threatened the Legislature with "hemp" (i.e., hanging); he predicted a San Francisco leveled to ashes and its ruins filled with roasted bodies. He boasted, "If I give an order to hang [Charles] Crocker, it will be done!"

The courts (just as in the 1960's) were distraught, weighing freedom of speech against public safety. Kearney was arrested several times and the city passed a "gag law" while the state enacted a strict riot act. But the Irishman was always out of jail in a few days, a hero, and both ordinances quickly became dead letters.

In 1879, the Workingmen's Party won Assembly seats, "captured" a railroad commissioner, and elected the bizarre Reverend Isaac Kalloch mayor of San Francisco after the publisher of the *Chronicle* shot him for insulting his mother. But now, at the crest of its power, the Party began to crack up. It had been kept alive largely by the mistakes of its opponents. A reaction set in; the Party lost the support of the nonviolent public. Kearney's colleagues, tired of the dictator who cast them aside if they did not become bootlicking yesmen, became rivals. Kearney was accused of not only selling out to the capitalists but of tapping the till, to boot. He was ousted from the presidency to which he had risen, and found himself leading only a splinter group. In June of 1880, he broke with the Workingmen's Party completely and joined the Greenback Party. This did not suit him and he floundered on to the Anti-Monopoly Party and, finally, the Democratic Party. Meanwhile, the Workingmen's Party had foundered after losing the San Francisco election of 1880.

Kearney's descent was even faster—if less spectacular—than his rise to fame and power. In 1884, he retired from politics entirely. In the 1890's, he inherited wealth and long before his largely unnoticed death on April 24, 1907, he had made a last *volte-face,* turning into a San Joaquin Valley wheat capitalist.

Unstable, inconsistent, and possibly insincere, Denis Kearney was a political shooting star, destined to burn out quickly. He was an agitator, not a thinker. Lord Bryce thought him a demagogue of a common type, full of noise, confidence, and discontent but without foresight or constructive talent. Henry George saw him differently: as the burning reflection of a hot resentment felt by the people trapped by the machine politics of a monopolist state. They were ready for a change —*any* change. Both observers, curiously, were largely correct. But Kearney was of a type not yet common to California; hence his swift rise and large following.

The Irishman knew the value of martyrdom and once said, "I hope I will be assassinated, for the success of the movement depends upon that." If he really meant what he said, he was doomed to disappointment. Not only did he have the ill luck to live out a long life, but the people of the state, tired of his ranting and clumsily veiled threats, dealt him the cruelest blow possible—they deliberately ignored him and forgot him. Still, for five years of his heyday, Denis Kearney had spooked the whole country and, in truth, had scared the bejesus out of the California Establishment.

WILLIAM KEITH

(*1838–1911*)

In vivid contrast to the violent careers of such raffish fellows as Tiburcio Vásquez and Harry Love was the placid life of painter William Keith. Yet there is not the most frayed shred of doubt that Keith did far more for California than such brutish fellows as Vásquez or Love, no matter how colorful (or, occasionally, charming) they might be. Born of stern Presbyterian stock in Oldmeldrum, Scotland (November 21, 1838), Keith migrated to New York as a youngster and was apprenticed there to a wood engraver. He easily mastered this craft and, in California after 1859, turned out posters, wine bottle labels, and engravings for book and magazine illustration. Yet he yearned for a career in fine art. His friendship with the first of California's major artists, Charles Nahl, and his marriage to artist and art teacher Elizabeth (Lizzie) Emerson in 1864 reinforced this ambition. Although he was so poor that the couple's wedding breakfast was out of a brown paper bag, as they sat on an Embarcadero wharf, legs dangling over the side, Keith set out to teach himself to paint. His wife was of help, of course, and the prominent California painter Samuel Marsden Brooks taught him to mix colors.

Almost from his very first watercolors, it was obvious that William Keith was gifted as a painter of the outdoors, which he loved so much. One of his first watercolors was of Yosemite, a scene of which he never grew tired in his entire life. By 1866, the San Francisco press was paying attention to him, *The Californian* printing an appreciative note on one of his pictures. About the same time, he made his first sale, and this double success further elated him. From watercolors he soon (1868) turned to his true medium, oil, and was, shortly, being collected by West Coast men of wealth and taste. One of these patrons of the arts, Benjamin P. Avery, made an estimate of Keith for the *Overland Monthly* that has held up well over the years. He praised the Scots-Californian for his "remarkable power, fidelity, and sentiment. His atmospheres are luminous. His woods have depth and richness. His coloring is full of the finest feeling. He imbues his pictures with poetry."

Because he loved to paint landscapes and to sketch from life, Keith often made field trips from his Oakland (and, later, Berkeley) home to Mount Tamalpais, the Sierra Nevada, Mount Shasta, and Castle Crags. When he opened the first of a series of San Francisco studios, in which he taught art and exhibited his own works, he painted as a sweatshop worker labored—from sunrise till dark. (Later, he cut his day, stopping his work at 4 P.M. to walk or visit friends.) While his canvases still betrayed an artistic naïveté and showed signs of some carry-over from wood-engraving techniques, galleries and libraries were beginning to exhibit "Keiths." But as an artist he was not satisfied; he worked hard on his drawing, color, perspective, and composition in a kind of second apprenticeship. Frequent sales now elated him since they made possible study in Europe to perfect his technique. He studied with Albert Flamm of the Achenbach school in Düsseldorf, but when the Franco-Prussian War broke out in 1870, he found it a convenient excuse to return to America. He was homesick for California, for one thing, and, for another, he feared with some grounds that he was falling into the static and mechanical style of painting typical of the German school, which he found so disappointing in the works of his California rival, Thomas Hill. Keith vowed to paint, and to study, entirely from nature, rather than in schools and galleries. He told friends that "a man who has the artistic instinct strong, needs only nature."

Once back in the United States, he painted in New England for a time but soon returned to California, where, in 1872, he met John Muir in Yosemite. He found that Muir inspired him almost as much as the wild Sierra scenery itself, which Muir knew so well and which he showed to Keith. These sketching trips into the High Sierra involved real hardship, but the burly, bull-necked artist was up to it and Muir's influence infused his work with new power and realism. The two men became fast friends, "Johnny" and "Willie" to each other, and Keith returned, year after year, to Yosemite. With Mount Tamalpais, just north of the Golden Gate, it was his most enduring source of inspiration. In 1875 he wrote, "Yosemite has yet to be painted; painters' visits of a month or so have not done it. Time is required to take it in and digest it or else the inevitable result will be artistic dyspepsia (in the shape of the conventional yellow and red rocks) which, perhaps, is the reason for the average Californian's disgust for Yosemite pictures. The cliffs are neither red nor yellow but an indescribable, shifting, gray, changing and shifting even as you work." It is true that no one, even yet, has really captured the soul of Yosemite in oils, photographs, or words, but William Keith came as close as anyone. He did with a brush what John Muir did with his pen, what Ansel Adams does with a camera.

It was Muir's influence which kept Keith's personal, natural style alive after his formal study in Europe. Although he disdained the sensational, melodramatic alpine style of Albert Bierstadt and others, which he termed Mock Heroic, some critics found still too much of the European (German) influence in Keith's work, making for somber, formal, and passive paintings which were technically correct but which muted the initial feeling and poetry and excitement of his vision and inspiration. Although he resisted showy lighting, excessive detail, and literalism, and gave up glazing his canvases, Düsseldorf style, and sought to put more art and emotion—and less precision—into his canvases, he was never completely successful in acquiring a "free" technique, much less anything resembling an impressionistic style. Perhaps, in the long run, it was a mistake for Keith to have studied in Germany. But it was this very formality of his paintings which won him the title of California's Old Master.

By now, wealthy patrons were collecting his pictures, some of which, like *California Alps,* fetched five thousand dollars, a fantastic price in the 1870's and '80's. Yet Keith himself realized that the picture, for all of the craftsmanship, skill, and technique which he had lavished on it, suffered from the same lack as that of many of Tom Hill's paintings—it had no spontaneity, no life. His answer was to work harder, turning away from huge, epic canvases akin to those of the Rocky Mountain School, saying "a panorama is not fine art," and adopting a more lyrical style, with the soft and true colors of reality.

By the 1880's, William Keith was California's premier artist and, to many Americans, the peer of George Inness, the acknowledged master of landscapes. More of Keith's pictures were exhibited in the East now, but his fame was still largely regional. (New York and Boston would accept California's

197

oranges but not its artists.) Gold and silver medals came to him, but mainly from California State Fair exhibitions of his work. Men like Theodore Hittell and Charles Lummis became great boosters of Keith but let friendship get in the way of good sense when they proclaimed him "another Corot" and superior to Claude and J. M. W. Turner.

No bohemian, Keith was a hard-working artist who happily remarried (Mary McHenry) in 1882, after his first wife died. He visited Europe again and tried portraiture but always returned to his first love, California landscapes. During his lifetime he was honored by having a Sierra mountain named for him; a sonnet by Poet Laureate Ina Coolbrith devoted to him. (Later, a plaque would be placed on the University of California track stadium, Edwards Field, to memorialize the site of his home, where he used to entertain faculty like "Professor Joe" Le Conte and students like Francisco I. Madero, later the martyred President of Mexico. In World War II, a liberty ship was named the *Keith;* streets in Oakland and Berkeley bear his name and two fine Keith Galleries are now in existence, at St. Mary's College and in the Oakland Art Museum.)

William Keith was at the height of his career in 1906 when earthquake and fire wracked San Francisco. He lost his studio and almost a lifetime's production of paintings. Asked why he did not rescue them while there was still time, Keith answered, "A policeman pointed a pistol at my head and told me to go back. He looked as if he meant business and I decided not to argue with him. So, I turned my back on the two thousand pictures I had in the Pine Street place and went back to Berkeley, to work."

After 1906, Keith worked even harder than before, turning out first-rate pictures at an astounding clip, to replace those of forty years' work, lost in the fire. A tribute to his artistic standing was the number of fake "Keiths" which now appeared on the market. In 1910, Keith was seventy-two years old and in ill health. He virtually retired from painting, and died on April 13, 1911. After his death, some critics called him a mere imitator of Inness (which he was not, any more than he was another Turner); still others, with more reason, put him down by asserting that he was "a true poet but a poor painter," meaning that he would be remembered, but more for the personal feelings he expressed toward the subject of his painting than for any artistic execution.

The final returns are far from being in on Keith or any other California artist. Artistic reputations ripen slowly and California is still a very young state. He is, today, something of a patron saint to the West Coast school of representational painters (as opposed to abstract artists) who make up the membership of the Society of Western Artists. But, although he had imitators during his life and later, he had only a handful of disciples, like Gutzon Borglum, who won fame more for his enormous Mount Rushmore National Memorial sculptures than for his oils. It is virtually certain that history will not rank Keith with Corot or Turner. However, his high place in the story of California art is assured, and he probably will be remembered as the state's outstanding landscapist. Someone called him "California's Constable," which is praise enough.

Although a representational painter, Keith wished to leave exactitude to photography, saying, "Accuracy of drawing in landscape leads to hardness and stiffness. . . . There is a quality of drawing in landscapes which only a landscape painter of long experience knows the difficulty of, and that quality is truth to the nature of the thing represented. . . . It is not *all* that lies before the eye that is the valuable thing. . . . It is the difference between science and art. . . . There is the element of accident which comes in and which makes a picture interesting and suggestive. . . . When I began to paint, I could not get mountains high enough or sunsets gorgeous enough for my brush and colors. . . . [Now], I am contented with very slight material—a clump of trees, a hillside and sky. I find these hard enough and varied enough to express any feeling I may have about them."

Keith believed that an artist's career consisted of three stages, like life's childhood, youth, and manhood. In the first, the young painter is swept with ideas and feelings and impressions which he is hard-put to express on canvas. In the median stage, he has the facts or techniques, but they tend to crowd out impulses and feelings. And here, said Keith, too many artists stop. In the last stage, there is a return to the wealth of feeling which, combined with the artist's increase in knowledge and skill, gives him great power of expression. Wrote Keith, "I have been laboring hard to get into the third state where I can express myself, subordinating the lesser to the greater. Some good friends may think that I am going too far, but I know that I am on the right road."

William Keith was, indeed, on the right road. His failure was in terms of actually reaching the point which he sought. But his greatness was in seeking it when lesser men would have been content with what he had—artistic competence, fame, and something of fortune.

JAMES KING OF WILLIAM

(1822–56)

The curiously named James King of William was originally humble James King. Born on January 28, 1822, in Georgetown, District of Columbia, he tacked on the suffix "of William" (his father's Christian name) in order to distinguish himself from the surfeit of Jim Kings in Washington. After a mundane existence in several careers, he migrated to Yerba Buena in 1848 to try prospecting in the Mother Lode. He soon found that he preferred gold lending to gold mining and by the end of '49 had his own banking house in San Francisco. Alas, one of his agents misused company funds and James King of William found his business wrecked. However, Adams & Company, Wells, Fargo's principal early rival in the express and banking fields, hired him to run its banking department. The great financial panic of 1855 carried Adams & Company to ruin.

Twice-bankrupted, King of William can be forgiven a certain amount of bitterness toward society and, particularly, toward the financial warfare raging in the city. But he did not stop with smoldering resentment; he stoked it until he became a self-righteous crusader, a reckless reformer who won (if he did not exactly earn) the title of "The Patriot Martyr of California." His fiery crusading made him a martyr, the only kind of human more dangerous dead than alive. As Dostoyevsky reminded us, "Men reject their prophets and slay them, but they love their martyrs and honor those whom they have slain." Martyrs are not always angels and sometimes are out-and-out scoundrels or frauds. Hitler's bully-boy Horst Wessel, for example, was both. James King of William should not be classed with the National Socialist street brawler, but he did personify the worst extravagances of public men—and particularly journalists—in the California of the "good old days." Innuendo, accusation, libel, threats, and even blackmail were all in the editor's bag of tricks, as of 1856.

King of William was only a little more vindictive and flagrant than his peers in the fourth estate. But by his excess he managed not only to get himself killed but also to bring into being the second Vigilance Committee which, by brute force, took over the city of San Francisco from its elected officials. This much-romanticized seizure demonstrated a disdain for the rule of law, for democratic procedure, and for civil rights. It was a dangerous adventure unworthy of whitewashing. Luckily, the leaders of the Vigilance Committee eventually returned control of the city to its proper custodians. But how did the committee come into being? It was virtually egged into existence by one man, James King of William, who was willing to barter his life in order to cleanse what he saw as an Augean metropolis.

The philosopher Josiah Royce labeled King of William a revolutionary who caused a regeneration of California society. This may be an overstatement; at least, the regeneration was not permanent. However, a revolutionary he was from the day he issued the first number of his newspaper the San Francisco *Evening Bulletin,* on October 8, 1855. His militancy was unequaled as he sought to lead public opinion, not follow it, report it, or reflect upon it. He was, in short, a propagandist before his time. He made his letters-to-the-editor column a public forum and lashed the citizenry with his editorials. He preached reform and righteousness with the fanaticism of a zealot. He used large helpings of invective, vituperation, and scurrility. He attacked gamblers, criminals, prostitutes, politicos, corrupt officials, spineless judges, and impotent editors. He has been rightly called the most aggressive and fearless editor ever to send a paper onto the streets.

But even King of William's enemy, Judge Ned McGowan (no saint!) was right, in considerable measure, when he summed up the patriot martyr of San Francisco: "Aimed at the correction of abuses, which undoubtedly existed in the San Francisco community, it was thought by hundreds of our best citizens that the example of unbridled license set by this paper to the press was far more dangerous in its tendency than even the evils it sought to eradicate." After referring to the "boldness, arrogance and, not unfrequently, reckless mendacity" which characterized the sheet, Judge McGowan drew a bead on King of William himself: "Day after day, this self-appointed censor fulminated his abuse indiscriminately on the innocent and the guilty, making shuttlecocks of the reputations of some of the best and most enterprising men in the state, till, emboldened by impunity, his apparent zeal in the cause of reformation ran into the wildest fanaticism."

The reckless reformer finally went too far, but before he did so he acted with such desperation that many observers felt that he was convinced that he had nothing to lose. It was as if King of William was seized by a death wish. Before he died atop a counter in the Pacific Express Building, on May 20, 1856 (as much from the clumsiness of a doctor—who left a sponge in his wound!—as from the gunshot), the crusader called David Broderick, a powerful politician, "an ungodly swindler" and nicknamed him Catiline, after Cicero's conspiring opponent. He warned the court that Charles Cora, the "Italian assassin and gambler," *must* be hanged (if guilty, of course) and predicted the fearful consequences of any attempt to rescue him by either a packed jury or bribes. He denounced the jailer in the same breath that he threatened the city with vigilantism, raging, "If Mr. Sheriff Scannell does not remove Billy Mulligan from his present post as Keeper of the County Jail, and Mulligan lets Cora escape, *hang Billy Mulligan,* and if necessary to get rid of the Sheriff, *hang him— hang the Sheriff!"*

In other editorials, King of William moaned, "Rejoice ye gamblers and harlots! Rejoice with exceeding gladness!" when the Cora jury was stalemated by disagreement. But, curiously, it was one of his milder editorials which proved to be his last. On May 14, 1856, he mentioned a fight between James Casey, a rough-and-tumble politician, and a man named Bagley. In a sense, King of William took the former's part, stating that Bagley was the attacker. But he could not resist blackening Casey's character by dragging his past reputation up out of the muck, and with the following words, James King of William not only wrote and signed his own death warrant but created the second Vigilance Committee and threw San Francisco into chaos: "The fact that Casey has been an inmate of Sing Sing prison in New York is no offense against the laws of this state, nor is the fact of his having stuffed himself through the ballot box as elected to the Board of Supervisors from a district where it was said he was not a candidate, any justification for Mr. Bagley to shoot Casey, however richly the latter may deserve to have his neck stretched for such fraud on the people."

The inevitable occurred on Montgomery Street on May 14,

1856, when King of William finally goaded someone, James Casey, into being the instrument of his fate. The pistol ball which Casey sent into his chest won for the crusader the martyrdom which he had so desperately sought.

PETER LASSEN

(1800-59)

If John Bidwell was Captain Sutter's most dependable and loyal aide in the settling of California, surely Sutter's most colorful lieutenant was Peter Lassen. The latter, a Danish blacksmith whose name should be Larson, for he was the son of Lars Nielsen, is today the best-known of all Sutter's associates except, perhaps, Bidwell. His name is attached to a national park and a national forest, a great peak and a California county as well as to trails and meadows. The variety and geographical separateness of these landmarks bearing his surname suggest Lassen's roving nature. Although a somewhat inept mountain man, by temperament he liked to wander and to explore new trails. His general independence and this roving nature led him to leave Sutter's employ after a few years. The Swiss was not particularly sorry to see him go. The two were often at odds, for Sutter preferred less individualistic subordinates. But he used his good offices with the governor to secure a land grant for Lassen.

Like Sutter, Lassen was a born optimist and a man accused of being harsh and stubborn at the very time that his Sutterian naïveté and gullibility allowed him to be fleeced by his two-faced critics. Arriving in Boston from Denmark in 1829, he made his way to California in 1840 on the *Lausanne*. When he and his companions tried to land at Bodega Bay, a Mexican officer and his soldiers refused them permission. The Mexicans were, however, "overruled" when Governor Rotchev, of nearby Fort Ross, Sutter's friend, threatened to intervene in the newcomers' behalf. While working for Sutter, Lassen made a trip up the Sacramento River from New Helvetia with Bidwell in search of some of Sutter's horses. Both men returned with a determination to own parcels of the rich riverine land. With Sutter's help, Lassen received his Bosquejo grant in 1843.

Lassen's fortunes suffered a reversal when he marched with Sutter to aid Governor Micheltorena in the 1845 civil war which ended with Sutter's defeat in the debacle-battle of Cahuenga. Again like Sutter, Lassen made a neat recovery from misfortune, and the Lassen Ranch, on Deer Creek near present-day Vina and between Chico and Red Bluff, became a small-scale New Helvetia. He imitated Sutter in employing a large number of Indians to plant wheat; he experimented with cotton, like his mentor; he raised grapes for wine and brandy; he set up a smithy which he operated personally. Soon, Lassen was winning a reputation for hospitality toward travelers which vied with that of Sutter himself.

When John C. Frémont marched his ragged force down out of the snowy mountains in 1844, Sutter outfitted the un-horsed men with mules from Lassen's herds. When Frémont returned to California in 1846, he visited Lassen Ranch and impressed the Dane so much that he named his planned settle-ment (now a ghost town) Benton City in honor of Jessie Frémont's father, Senator Thomas Hart Benton, the Pathfind-er's protector. Lassen was a guide for Archibald Gillespie when that cloak-and-dagger Marine lieutenant in mufti hurried to Oregon after Frémont with a still-secret message which led the latter to return to California in order to enter the Bear Flag Revolt and, ultimately, the Mexican War. The very night that Lassen overtook Frémont near Klamath Lake, he had to help fight off an Indian attack. Lassen remained with Frémont during some punitive forays against the Indians but took no real role in the Mexican War.

Peter Lassen returned to the United States with Commodore Robert F. Stockton in 1847 but was back in California by the fall of 1848 in time to supply hungry miners with flour and to plunge into the Gold Rush himself. He prospected on the Feather River around Rich Bar but, in the long run, was no more successful than Sutter. If '49er Alfred Baldwin is to be believed, Lassen briefly made good money out of the rush. The former claimed that the Dane paid him one hundred dollars a week for five weeks to mind his ranch while he led argonauts to California. The Lassen Trail, or Lassen Cut-off, was not popular; it was not a good route. In fact, it was so long and roundabout that disgusted travelers dubbed it the "Cape Horn Route." Neither mining nor guiding paid off very handsomely for Lassen, and he was soon surrendering parcels of his rancho in order to pay his debts.

"Old Pete" went broke in 1850. Some say he busted himself in speculation on a steamboat, *Lady Washington,* which ripped its bottom out on a Sacramento River snag. In any case, Lassen lost his twenty-two-thousand-acre Bosquejo Ranch and was forced to return to prospecting in earnest. Like Sutter, he preferred to hunt for the big strike (like mythical Gold Lake) rather than settling down to the dull work of panning out a living of a few dollars a day in the fashion of the mass of miners.

In Indian Valley, Lassen tried a new start with a trading post and truck garden but soon moved on to Honey Lake Valley, in the extreme northeast corner of California. Here, with

Isaac Roop, he pioneered not only the settlement of Susanville but also an evanescent Nataqua Territory, because the California State Government paid no attention to their area. It was here, of all places, in short-lived Nataqua (squeezed out of existence by the formation of Nevada Territory) that Lassen finally set down some kind of roots.

But he was still of a restless spirit and when he heard of a ledge of silver in Nevada's Black Rock Desert in 1859 he had to go and look for it with two companions, Wyatt and Clapper. Camped on what is now Clapper Creek, Wyatt was awakened at dawn on April 26 by the report of a rifle. He climbed out of his blankets and shook Clapper. The latter rolled over and Wyatt saw that his friend had a bullet hole through the temple. Lassen was on his feet, now, shielding his eyes against the low morning sun with one hand, attempting to find the ambushers, while his other held his rifle. Suddenly, another shot came and Wyatt saw Peter Lassen clap his hand to his chest. He cried out, "I'm a dead man!" and fell. Wyatt panicked and ran. He managed to get one of the horses and rode, bareback, to Susanville with the news of the ambuscade.

The party of men which rode out to bury Lassen and Clapper found no clue to their murderers. Most Californians blamed the redskins, for the Dane had dragged a skulking Digger into camp the night before his death. But a minority of Californians has always believed that Peter Lassen was shot by renegade white men. The murder of the pioneering Danish smith and mountain man remains, today as in 1859, one of the state's greatest unsolved mysteries.

JAMES LICK

(*1796–1876*)

There are several claimants to the title of "California's First Millionaire"—Sam Brannan and James Lick, for example, and, possibly, Captain Joseph Folsom. But even the partisans of the recusant saint, Brannan, would not dare to contest James Lick's pretension to the crown of California's Richest Eccentric. (Both Grizzly Adams and Emperor Norton disqualified themselves by being poor.)

Lick was a Pennsylvania Dutchman, born August 25, 1796, whose ancestral name was Lük. The turning point of his life came when he was twenty-two years old. The miller's daughter with whom he had fallen in love woke up pregnant one day. Young Lick tried to do the right thing, asking her father to be allowed to marry her. But the arrogant millowner, according to Lebanon County lore, dismissed the poor boy with a rhetorical question—"Have you a penny in your purse?"—followed by his own answer, "When you own a mill as large and as costly as mine, you can have my daughter's hand, but not before." Lick was hurt, and since he had more the temper of an Irishman than that of a phlegmatic Pennsy Dutchman, he shot back an angry promise—"Someday, I'll own a mill that will make this one look like a pigsty."

Shortly after making this hotheaded and seemingly idle boast, James left home with a single dollar in his pocket, to seek his fortune. In time, he became a piano maker, carrying his skill to Buenos Aires, Valparaíso, and Lima. He prospered in South America, in spite of endemic revolutions, so that when he decided to settle in California in January 1848 he brought thirty thousand dollars in cash with him. (This seemed like a million to the Customs House officials of the sleepy little port of less than five hundred souls.)

Immediately upon his arrival, Lick showed his sagacity by embarking on a great property-buying spree. Lots were cheap because news of the January 24 gold discovery did not gain wide currency until May. Lick spent $6762, in all, in 1848. By the fall of 1849, he was the richest man in San Francisco because of his land purchases.

Lick succumbed to the rampant gold fever, but ever so briefly. One taste of the rough life of the miners at Mormon Island was enough for him. He returned to the San Francisco Bay Area, this time to develop the Santa Clara Valley. On the Guadalupe River, near the town of Santa Clara, he bought a farm and millsite of many hundreds of acres. While he developed his estate, word of his eccentricity began to make him notorious throughout California. Rich as he was, he wore shabby old clothes and lived in a frame shack, sleeping on a mattress atop the frame of an old grand piano. He traveled in a rickety and patched-up wagon and never passed a bone or cow horn without stopping to toss them into the wagon bed. At home, he had a great heap of bones, hoofs, skulls, and horns, over which his neighbors shook their heads in bewilderment. (Eventually he buried them to enrich the soil of his gardens with calcium.) Once, when he hired a new gang of

211

workers, he had them plant a number of trees upside-down, with their roots in the air. Now his neighbors were convinced that he was daft. But the canny Lick was merely testing his laborers' readiness to follow his directions without question. Eventually, Lick built the first great luxury hotel in San Francisco, the Lick House. It was a proud forerunner of Ralston's and Sharon's magnificent Palace Hotel. Before his death in 1876, he established the Lick Trust so that his wealth would be spent in public benefactions such as financial assistance to the California Academy of Sciences and the Mechanics Institute Library. His greatest memorial was the posthumous Lick Observatory, the University of California's astronomical center on top of Mount Hamilton, near San Jose. There, in the base of a giant telescope, Lick was buried.

But the most congruous monument to the generous miser was not the Lick Hotel or the observatory, but "Lick's Folly." This was his Guadalupe River mill, a magnificent three-story building of redwood and brick, complete with dovecot and observatory. If the exterior was prepossessing, the interior was almost unbelievable. Lick used fine mahogany and some Spanish cedar for all beams and planking, and the floors were of exquisitely laid hardwood parquetry. It was a palace which Lick had built for his flour sacks.

Family tradition has it that Lick lost interest in his palatial mill once it was finished—and once he had sent a photograph of it to his home town, to show the small-town autocrat (if he lived, still) that James Lick was a man of his word. By the end of the 1860's, Lick had practically abandoned the flour mill. Because he revered the patriot Thomas Paine, he decided to give the building to a Boston corporation organized to build a Paine Memorial Hall. He fully expected the corporation to sell the mill and to use the money to help construct and maintain the hall, as well as to provide for visiting lecturers.

To Lick's disgust, the Bostonians sold the mill for twenty thousand dollars, a fraction of its cost, and then wrangled over the money. But the mill had been worth it. Lick's Folly had served its purpose. With it, the penniless lad of Stumpstown, Pennsylvania, had a kind of sweet revenge on Fate, which had treated him so humiliatingly in 1818.

JACK LONDON

(*1876–1916*)

Jack London's life was so adventurous—like Ernest Hemingway's, only more so—that even his best fiction pales beside it. It was also a life of misadventure for London, a gifted writer whose work was very hasty and uneven in quality, as critics have been quick to point out (critics who, presumably, have never had to hammer out hack prose in order to keep one paragraph ahead of the bill collector). Even when his prodigious output is weeded ruthlessly, there remains enough good material to demonstrate that London was touched with genius. It is no less sure, of course, that he failed to appreciate adequately or use this great gift in his hurried race through life.

London had none of the breaks so useful to a young writer in seeking to become established. He had to make it the hard way. He was illegitimate, impoverished, and poorly educated. If anyone had three strikes against him in youth, it was Oakland's Jack London. He was somehow aware, too, that Fate was not going to grant him the traditional threescore and ten years on earth, so he wrote furiously, as if to exorcise demons bent on dragging him to the lip of a grave. He explained to friends, "I shall not waste my days in trying to prolong them. I shall *use* my time." His credo was simple—"The proper function of man is to live, not to exist."

Jack was born in San Francisco on January 12, 1876, the son of a wandering Irish astrologer who wandered right out of the child's life about the time his mother married John London. Before he was ten years old, Jack was working in order to keep the family afloat in a sea of destitution. For fourteen straight years his true talents were frustrated and sublimated by the desperate need for grinding toil in laundry, power station, cannery, and jute mill—just to stay alive. Smallish wonder, then, that the lad was tempted by drink and crime, on the one hand, and the panacea of socialism on the other, as he shoveled coal (at ten cents an hour) for thirteen or fourteen hours a day. Of course, as rugged (and strenuous and muscular) an all-American individualist as Jack London was miscast as Comrade London. He lacked the docility to accept, on faith, dogma from on high, and all of his adult life he was torn by the conflict of the two disparate philosophies, socialism and the most ruggedly individualistic *laissez faire* capitalism.

London's career was so colorful, although his whole life lasted but forty years, that it would be impossible to summarize it adequately in a few pages. Suffice to say that he drew upon his rich treasury of personal experience—as slavey, hobo, sailor, oyster pirate, and gold miner—in order to create tales of romantic adventure which captivated the imagination of the entire literate world. His first great success was the classic dog story, *The Call of the Wild,* born of his Gold Rush experiences in Alaska and the Klondike. This book was followed by a string of best-sellers—*The Sea Wolf* (forty thousand copies sold *before* publication day!), *White Fang, Martin Eden,* and *The Valley of the Moon.* He filled the narrow interstices of time between his many full-scale books with short stories, essays, and journalistic articles. In the capacity of journalist, he reported on a variety of subjects from military actions of the Russo-Japanese War to the degradation of the London slums.

A born sailor, Jack progressed from a skiff on the Oakland Estuary to a little sloop, the *Razzle Dazzle,* then to a San Francisco Bay yacht, the *Spray,* before building his thirty-thousand-dollar dreamboat, the *Snark.* He sailed her to Hawaii, Tahiti, Samoa, and the Solomons before a severe case of sun poisoning put an unhappy end to the cruise. London apparently regained his health on his Sonoma Valley ranch north of San Francisco while making it as modern and efficient as any holding in California. He decided to abandon the sea and restless travel in order to set down roots on his ranch at Glen Ellen. His "anchor" was the huge stone and redwood "Wolf House," which he was building as a home. In Europe, it would have been the hunting lodge of royalty. With eighty thousand dollars sunk into this fieldstone castle, and only the finishing touches necessary before moving in, a mysterious night fire in 1913 gutted the magnificent structure. Three years of work was destroyed—along with one of Jack's cherished dreams.

Rootless again, Jack returned to his wandering, but dysentery, contracted in Veracruz during the U.S. invasion began to erode his health. He became depressed mentally, as a result, although a trip to Hawaii temporarily improved both body and spirit.

Jack London died suddenly on November 22, 1916, either a suicide or a victim of acute uremia, which had long been plaguing him. There are partisans of both possibilities today.

One way for a reader to get some appreciation of a writer's talent is to look at it in the "bud" stage. In London's case, his first published work was his first-prize-winning submission in a San Francisco *Call* competition of November 1893 for the "Best Descriptive Article." During his writing career, Jack London dramatized scientific, socioeconomic, and philosophical ideas in his works, but he was best as a writer of outdoor action stories, true or fictional. This talent was already evident when the seventeen-year old Oakland boy wrote his "Typhoon off the Coast of Japan," although he was not many years removed from his first taste of literature in Ina Coolbrith's Oakland Public Library, where he had devoured books of history and of voyages and travels. The short sketch is an important one in London's canon for, as his nephew, Irving Shepard, pointed out, "Typhoon" was the essential spark which ignited his creative genius, made him a world-famous author, and started a whole school of adventure fiction, with Stewart Edward White, Rex Beach, and James Oliver Curwood among Jack's most successful imitators.

Only in his teens, Jack London was, already, a master of descriptive prose. In one single paragraph the reader can sense the sullen, deadly malice of the typhoon testing the *Sophie Sutherland* in the Japan Sea:

"As day broke, we took in the jib, leaving not a sail unfurled. Since we had begun scudding, she had ceased to take the seas over the bow, but amidships they broke fast and furious. It was a dry storm in the matter of rain, but the force of the wind filled the air with fine spray, which flew as high as the crosstrees and cut the face like a knife, making it impossible to see over a hundred yards ahead. The sea was a dark lead color, as with long, slow majestic roll it was heaped by the wind into liquid mountains of foam. The wild antics of the schooner were sickening as she forged along. She would almost stop as though climbing a mountain, then rapidly rolling to right and left, as she gained the summit of a huge sea, she steadied herself and paused for a moment as though affrighted at the yawning precipice before her. Like an avalanche, she shot forward and down as the sea astern struck her with the force of a thousand battering rams, burying her bow to the catheads in the milky foam at the bottom that came on deck in all directions—forward, astern, to right and left, through the hawse pipes and over the rail."

HARRY LOVE

(18?–68)

Set a thief to catch a thief. Or, better, "Knavery is the best defense against a knave," as Zeno held. Harry Love, first, last, and only chief of the California Rangers, may not have been a thief by dictionary definition, but the ex-Texan was a cruel and vindictive hardcase, a tough hombre who proved a natural choice for the job of catching California's legendary bandit, Joaquín Murrieta.

We are assuming, of course, that there really *was* a man named Joaquín Murrieta as well as a legendary figure. Several Mexican bandits raided Mother Lode settlements in the 1850's, and some of them bore the popular Christian names of Hispanic countries. It was the San Francisco *Daily Alta California* which suggested on December 15, 1852, that the probable murderer of General Joshua Bean at San Gabriel was a *Mexicano* named Murrieta. Most reports of marauders in 1853 cited a Joaquín but gave no last name. If the guilty party was Murrieta, he was a cowardly scoundrel, for he preyed largely on unarmed and helpless Chinese miners. On the other hand, he was as slippery as an eel in eluding the pursuit of sheriffs' posses even when they were guided by Indian trackers.

When an exasperated Governor John Bigler posted a reward of one thousand dollars for the mysterious Joaquín or Murrieta, he mistakenly called him Carrillo. But he also attracted a first-rate man hunter in Harry Love. The latter, a mean-looking, mustachioed bucko with narrow-slitted eyes, followed developments in the Capitol carefully. There, the legislators were urged by Assemblyman P. T. Herbert, of Mariposa, to pay an additional five thousand dollars reward for Joaquín. Herbert's bill was tabled after objections in committee, but he came back with another bill, which created a force modeled on the famous Texas Rangers. This bill was passed into law and signed by Governor Bigler on May 17, 1853. The chief executive chose Harry Love to raise and head a twenty-man force because the Texan was an ex-peace officer, scout, Indian fighter, Mexican War veteran, and El Paso express rider —or so "Captain" Love claimed. He was charged with the extermination of Joaquín, whether his name was Murieta, Carrillo, Valenzuela, or whatever. The only rub as far as Harry Love was concerned was the brevity of the enlistment—only three months. The pay was good, $150 a month, each, and a chance at the governor's thousand-dollar reward.

Love put together as tough a band of roughnecks as ever graced a Mother Lode saloon. Among them were Judge W. H. Harvey, who killed Jim Savage, the White King of the Tulare Indians; Patrick Edward Connor, a general in the Civil War; Charles (Bloodthirsty Charlie) Bludworth, sometime sheriff of Merced County; James Norton, alias the Terrible Sailor; William J. Henderson, who once hanged a man, singlehanded; and Billy Henderson, who, eventually, cut off Joaquín's head at Love's behest. Some five of the twenty would ultimately die with their boots on. Many others claimed to have been members of the Rangers and some—William J. Howard and Horace Bell—actually put forth their claims to this dubious honor in published books. Most curious of all, perhaps, Assemblyman P. T. Herbert was not only a Ranger as well as an assemblyman, but, according to historian Joseph Henry Jackson, was familiar with a Colt, being the killer of a Washington, D.C., waiter.

Love first led his men in a scout, or reconnaissance, of the San Juan Bautista area and arrested a cattle thief named Jesús (again, no last name), who claimed to be Joaquín's brother-in-law. According to the war correspondent of the *San Joaquin Republican* at William J. Howard's ranch on Burns's Creek in Mariposa County, where Love was resting up, the Rangers were confident of catching their prey. The reason was revealed by Captain Love in a letter to Governor Bigler of July 12. Writing of his captive, Jesús, Love said, "He says he will take and show us to Joaquín if we will release him. I will try him a while, to see what it will end in." Love eventually sent Jesús to jail in Mariposa. Two other Mexicans, suspected horse thieves, were not so lucky. According to Love, they were shot when they tried to escape. The reporter said nothing of the *ley de fuga* but observed, "They were found dead on the wayside, perforated with half a dozen balls, each." Apparently, Love was not interested in taking prisoners.

On July 25, 1853, on the dry side of the Coast Range where Cantua Creek reached for the San Joaquin plain, Love overran the camp of a band of Mexicans. In the ensuing gun battle, four of the Mexicans were killed. Love described the affair in a report to the governor from Quartzburg on August 4: "Joaquín was immediately recognized and on his being aware of the fact, immediately sprang to his horse and endeavored to escape. He was closely pursued by some of the Company and, his being wounded, some of the men shot him dead before going far." In order to be sure to collect the governor's reward, Love had Joaquín and his lieutenant,

Manuel (Three Fingered Jack) Garciá, decapitated, taking the heads as evidence to Fort Miller to be preserved in liquor. Since Jack was shot in the skull, his head did not pickle well and had to be buried at the fort. Perhaps at this time his crippled hand was cut off as an alternative.

Many newspapers, like the important *Alta California,* dubbed the capture and decapitation a humbug, asserting that the head on exhibit did not resemble Joaquín Murrieta in the least. But Love stuck to his guns. He wrote the governor, "There is not the least doubt that the head now in my possession is that of the noted Joaquín Muriatta [sic], the Chief and leader of the murderers and robbers of the Calaveras, Mariposa and other parts of the State." Witnesses other than Rangers were few. Two prisoners were taken, but one conveniently drowned in Tulare Slough and the other was rumored to have been lynched in Mariposa. The grisly relics were placed on exhibition in Stockton and San Francisco, at one-dollar admission, and came to be accepted as bona fide evidence that Joaquín Murrieta and Three Fingered Jack were no more. Certainly, bandit raids attributable to them stopped, so the chances are good that Love happened upon the right band of Mexicans at Cantua Creek. (The 1906 San Francisco earthquake and fire destroyed the trophies when it wiped out Natchez's Arms Store and Pistol Gallery on Clay Street.)

Captain Love collected Bigler's thousand dollars but was hungry for more. He urged the extension of the Rangers' enlistment period, hinting strongly when he advised the governor, "I have good and reliable information of the existence and whereabouts of other bands of robbers but it will be impossible for me to visit all their strongholds on account of the short period of time before our three months expire. . . ." He planted similar seeds in the ear of the *San Joaquin Republican* correspondent, scaring him enough with his tales of bands of guerrillas swarming over California. The reporter wrote: "Harry Love says that Joaquín, at a pinch, could have raised two thousand [!] desperadoes to sack the country and announce himself [dictator?] at Sonora." Small wonder that the affrighted reporter added, "We think it would be desirable for the Rangers to be kept in the field. Harry Love knows the men who are leaders of the brigands, and is probably one of the only men acquainted with their haunts; his companions know not what fear is, having proved their worth, and merit the praise of all. . . ."

Love did not get his extension. He did much better. His cronies in the Legislature tapped the public till again and by an 1854 bill, for the relief of Captain Love for capturing "the notorious robber, Joaquin," pressed five thousand dollars on him. The politicians acted despite the skepticism of editors and others. The *Alta,* while not saying that Love was guilty of unjust acts, pointed out that he had shot down men *said to be* robbers and had taken others prisoner and seized their stock and property contrary to the laws and constitution. "To pay Mr. Love for such acts would be a dangerous precedent," warned the paper. "What did Love do with all the cattle taken from suspicious-looking strangers? How many men were killed by his Rangers? These are questions which should be answered. . . . A proposition for the relief of Captain Love is before the Legislature. Of what Captain Love wishes to be relieved is not stated in the Legislative Report but probably it is of an empty pocket."

Now, Yellow Bird, or John Rollin Ridge, the poet laureate of the expatriate Cherokees, picked up the story of Joaquín Murrieta and turned him into a trans-Sierra Robin Hood. More books followed his and, soon, Murrieta was a full-fledged legend. Love took advantage of the myth; in fact, he made a career out of his capture of Joaquín. He coasted for years on fame and notoriety, enjoying the nickname of "The Black Knight of the Zayante." When he sailed for the East on the clipper *Yankee Blade* in June of 1854, the *Golden Era,* of course, described the ship's outstanding passenger as "the renowned capturer of Joaquín." He was soon back in the news. A report from Aspinwall, Panama, held that Love and six other passengers from the clipper had formed up a Judge Lynch firing squad to punish C. E. Bingham for his treatment of Mrs. Woodward (née Susan Denin). One of seven pistols charged with powder was also loaded with a ball. All seven men then fired, blindfolded! at Bingham. The *Alta* could not verify the tale but it ran the story, as is, on July 3, 1854.

When he returned to California, Love settled down. He married the Widow Bennett of Santa Clara. By 1868, the aging Mary Bennett Love was so fearful of his rages and all-around bullying and beatings that she hired her foreman, Christian Fred Iverson, as her bodyguard. On June 28 of that year, the brutish temper of Captain Love finally exploded in his own face. He drove up Santa Clara's Grant Street in his buggy that day and loudly told two carpenters working on his wife's house that the damned Dutchman would enter the building again only over his dead body. That afternoon, Iverson returned from a business trip to San Jose with Mrs. Love. Her daughter, Samantha, tried to signal them away but, failing, then shouted a warning. Just then, Love, kneeling behind the fence, fired at the pair. Iverson reached for his pistol but had to handle the rearing horse, frightened first by Mrs. Love's screams and shortly by the whoosh of a charge of buckshot in a near-miss. Part of the charge cut Iverson's hand, but he got his gun out and, still out of effective pistol range, scuttled toward the house, sideways, to offer Love as little of himself as a target as possible. Shortly he fired; so did Love. To witnesses, the two shots sounded as one. Iverson missed but

Love's buckshot wounded him in the right arm. Iverson shifted his revolver to his left hand and fired but again missed. Love had no pistol and with his shotgun empty swung the weapon as a club, but missed. At close range now, Iverson shot him in the right arm. The old Ranger—Joaquín's nemesis—now fled ignominiously, crying, "Murder!" and begging the carpenters to intervene. The German caught up with him and clubbed him to the ground with the pistol. Finally, the carpenters grabbed him and held him back before he could finish off his ambusher.

When a doctor arrived, he found Iverson's wound to be minor but Love's arm badly shattered. He operated immediately in Mary Love's yard, but the captain died just as the amputation was completed. The coroner's jury ascribed his death to a pistol shot fired in self-defense. According to old Santa Clara tradition, a final ignominy was reserved for Love. The handwriting of the coroner's clerk was so bad that his "Harry Love" appeared to cemetery officials to be "Mary Love." Farfetched as it seems, the story is that the captain was buried as Mrs. Love. In any case, no stone now remains to mark the last resting place of the bloody California Ranger.

CHARLES F. LUMMIS

(1859–1928)

The individual who broke the image of the typical California librarian as a be-bunned, shushing old maid was a wiry and uninhibited Massachusetts man by the name of Charles Fletcher Lummis. His professional iconoclasm alone has endeared him to California's modern librarians, but it is his work as a pioneer publicist in behalf of "Sunny California," around the turn of the century, which makes him important enough to be remembered by Californians in general.

The rugged nonconformist was born on March 1, 1859, in Lynn, and celebrated his birthday, ever after, with March Hare parties. Guests at these affairs came to include such prominent folk as Modjeska, the Duke of Alba, Melba, and President Teddy Roosevelt. By then, Lummis was calling himself Don Carlos and was more Hispanic than the *duque de Alba* himself. He dressed in the wide-wale corduroy of the Peninsula, wore a broad-brimmed Mexican sombrero, moccasins, and Navajo jewelry of turquoise and silver.

As a young Harvard student, Lummis had rebelled against the rigid discipline of his Methodist-minister father and majored, seemingly, in athletics, poetry, and poker. The poems which he wrote he published in a little book of birch bark instead of paper, and sold fourteen thousand copies! Undisciplined at this stage of his career, Lummis became infatuated with a girl, fathered a daughter, and was more or less rescued from his predicament by marriage, but to another girl. However, he came down with what was diagnosed as brain fever and had to leave Harvard only three days before commencement.

Upon his recovery, Lummis edited the *Scioto Gazette* in Chillicothe, Ohio, when he was not absent on long hikes, hunting, fishing, or searching for Indian relics. He was soon enjoying ill health again—this time malaria—and he decided to quit Jedediah Smith's home town for healthful California. The adventurous and impecunious twenty-five-year-old editor offered to send the Los Angeles *Times* a series of reports during a 3507-mile walk across the continent to California. The *Times* took him up on the idea. The crossing of seven states and two territories took Lummis 143 days in all, including 112 days of actual walking. It won him the post of city editor of the *Times,* brought him to the eye of the public, and furnished him with material for another book, *A Tramp Across the Continent.* Unfortunately, the young Lummis had not as yet checkreined his tendency toward melodramatization, and his travel account, in parts, is about as trustworthy as one of Psalmanazar's or Münchausen's. But he did have adventures and he did suffer. When he marched triumphantly into the offices of the *Times,* he brandished an arm in a sling. He had broken it on the march and had set it while alone in the desert.

Charles Lummis became a strident reformer but nearly worked himself into an early grave. Proud of his strong constitution, he smoked too much, drank too hard, and worked twenty hours a day and slept but four. The result? A prodigious literary output—newspaper columns, magazine articles, and books—but also a paralyzing stroke which sent him to New Mexico for a recovery demanding more than three years. It was, apparently, his iron will which pulled him out of it, more than anything. When Lummis returned to Los Angeles in 1896, it was just in time to be appointed editor of the promotional magazine *Land of Sunshine*. Within a few years, with this instrument, Lummis became the state's greatest public relations man. Somehow, he was able to mix successfully the oil and water of literature and publicity. The little booster magazine, during the ten years of Lummis's editorship, became a rival of the famed *Overland Monthly* of San Francisco, with which it merged in 1923. He lured to his pages such writers as Mary Austin, Joaquin Miller, Charles Warren Stoddard, Ina Coolbrith, and Edwin Markham, and such artists as William Keith and Maynard Dixon. But whether it was the personal journalism of his editorial pages, the blatant boosterism of his advertisers, or the bona fide literature of his talented writers, Lummis dedicated himself completely to "selling" California and its satellite, the Southwest of Arizona and New Mexico, to America.

But Lummis's nature was such that he always wanted to turn to something new. He was not content to play the part of a chamber-of-commerce crusader. He formed the Landmarks Club to save California's missions, today among the state's architectural and historic treasures but in the 1890's tumbledown ruins. He formed the Sequoyah League to secure justice for America's Indians. He wrote a dozen popular books on the Southwest. He facetiously defined the area as "Anything far enough from the East to be Out From Under." In 1905 he was appointed city librarian of Los Angeles and rocked the bibliothecal boat with a series of reforms. Most of his radical innovations—an advisory staff "senate," an outdoor reading patio, critical evaluation of textbooks, etc., were merely ahead of their day, but his marking of books with a hot branding iron was actually a throwback to the custom of eighteenth-century Mexican monastic libraries. Even when the strait-laced ladies of the reading room could accept his new ideas, they were alienated by his bizarre dress, flamboyant personality, and liking for girls and apricot brandy. And many of them were *not amused* when he formed an association called the Bibliosmiles, "a Rally of Librarians who are, Nevertheless, Human," which he dedicated to antiossification and antifossilization of the profession.

Lummis resigned his position in 1915 after transforming a lending library into a genuine reference and research institution. He turned to a new love—the creation of the Southwest Museum. This institution, overlooking the Arroyo Seco, is now nationally known for its Indian collections and its library. At the same time, he began to build a home of rugged stream boulders with his own hands. He called it El Alisal, the Sycamore Grove. It is now the headquarters of the Charles F. Lummis Memorial Association and of the Southern California Historical Society, and is a registered historical landmark. The rustic building was quite likely the inspiration for Tor House in Carmel, with its Hawk Tower. This was the home of poet Robinson Jeffers, once a contributor to Lummis's *Out West* magazine.

Lummis was an amateur historian and ethnologist of considerable talent, but he should be remembered more as a promoter of Southern California and the Southwest. Lummis, in fact, popularized the term the "Southwest" (in its limited meaning—Arizona and New Mexico—where once it had been a shifting geographical term including even Arkansas and Oklahoma). With his many books, his editorials, his articles and talks, the magazines he edited, Lummis fixed the imagination of the populous East on the "new" Old Southwest and Southern California. He was worth all the chambers of commerce south of the Tehachapi Mountains rolled into one.

To his friends, the flamboyant Lummis was a Renaissance man in a corduroy suit. To others, he was a shallow, cocky egoist who was addicted to superlatives and sentimentality in his writing. Charles Lummis did spread himself a little thinly; no one could hope to become expert in the many fields he explored. Yet, in spite of his vanity and the thinness of his scholarly veneer, he was an important figure in Southern California history. He was dynamic, a changer as well as a doer, a catalyst bringing literature to a cultural desert. He was devoted to laudable causes—anti-imperialism, antibigotry, etc.— but paramount was his desire to supplant the frenetic pace of modern times with the leisurely attitudes of old Spanish California.

Modesty was not one of Lummis's virtues, but he did not do badly in choosing an epitaph. He might have taken the motto from his *Out West* masthead: "To love what is true, to hate shame, to fear nothing without, and to think a little." Instead, he chose the following epitaph for his ashes at El Alisal:

> He founded the Southwest Museum
> He built this house
> He saved four missions
> He studied and recorded Spanish America
> He tried to do his share.

Many more famous Californians have done less.

Charles Lummis, today, is one part hero, one part humbug, and one part villain. Ironically, all of the things which he hated—crowds, hostility, the mad pace of the East—have all come to California and largely because of the booster movement which he pioneered. He would be appalled today by the tasteless architecture, din, bad manners, strangulating traffic, and scarified landscapes under Southern California's yellowish canopy of smog. But he would be proud of the progress of the two institutions which still bear his brand—the Los Angeles Public Library and the Southwest Museum, two tropic isles in a dead sea, two oases in a cultural Kalahari. Unknowingly, jokingly, he had predicted Los Angeles's fate in 1899, when, in forming his Bibliosmiles, he warned, "The whole tendency of civilization is to run together in an undistinguishable mass."

TOM MAGUIRE

(1820?–96)

Horatio Alger would have balked at ghosting Thomas
Maguire's atuobigraphy. Can one imagine an *illiterate* New
York cabby leaving his hack stand in order to bring culture
to San Francisco and to absolutely dominate West Coast
theater for decades? And at a time when it was still common
for bigots to tack up signs on places of business reading "No
Irish Need Apply"?

Tom Maguire's exact birth date and birthplace are unknown.
Tom was secretive about the event but not because of any
doubts of legitimacy; rather, he was as sensitive about his age
as any of his prima donnas. Barely able to write his name (if
that), the dapper and handsome gentleman who came to be
called "The Napoleon of the Stage" had to dictate every one
of his pronouncements to more learned menials. But he was
as shrewd as he was uneducated, as ambitious as he was im-
perious and proud. He was, in short, more hero than humbug.
He fooled the critics when his first wife died. Emma (Little
Em) had supposedly been the brains of the family, but Tom
went right on in his flamboyant career with no fewer and no
more ups and downs.

Maguire's introduction to the theater was in his managing the bars of the balcony and gallery of New York's Park Theater in 1846. Greasepaint got into his blood there, and when he came to San Francisco to run a saloon on Portsmouth Square he turned the vacant second story into the first of his several Jenny Lind Theaters. Tom was not quite the first impresario in San Francisco, but when his chief rival, Doc ("Yankee") Robinson left town, Maguire began a virtual monopoly of the stage business for years and launched a career as "The Napoleon of Impresarios." When fires repeatedly wiped out his theatrical houses, he built a splendid place of Australian sandstone. This yellow palace, with its pink and gilt interior, bankrupted him, and he was glad to unload it on San Francisco as its new City Hall for two hundred thousand dollars.

Now he built his grandest theater, his monument—Maguire's Opera House. He hired Junius Brutus Booth, Jr., as his manager and brought Junius, Sr., and Edwin Booth west to perform. He introduced San Franciscans to Edwin Forrest, John McCollough, Dion Boucicault, David Belasco, and James O'Neill (playwright Eugene O'Neill's father). He brought Modjeska, and the daring Adah Isaacs Menken in *Mazeppa,* and scouted the prosceniums of the United States for new stars. Although he had never spent a day in school, his education as a theatrical entrepreneur was almost perfect. Maguire had an ear for good singing and an eye for dramatic or comic talent. He introduced the Coast to minstrelsy, burlesque, and Japanese acrobats and jugglers as well as legitimate drama. Totally uncultured personally, he was thrilled by *Carmen* and *Faust* and patiently absorbed one hundred twenty thousand dollars in losses over ten years in order to establish a tradition of grand opera on the Coast along with Shakespearean drama, when his audiences would have been content with the black-

233

face minstrels, the then daring plays like *Camille* and *East Lynne*, and such premature leg shows as *Mazeppa* and *The Black Crook*, which he also offered. The *Call* applauded his public-spiritedness: "We need not say how pluckily he has met this financial strain. It is the admiration of our public." But no one helped him financially with his culture crusade.

Newspaperman Charles McClatchy was undoubtedly correct when he observed that Tom Maguire owed more money to more people than any other theatrical man in America. He made and unmade millions. Maguire was the Columbus of credit on the Coast. Once he discovered that marvelous natural resource of California, he simply could not be stopped. He never blinked at the most outrageous salary demands of his leading men and ladies. He liked to hold court before lunch on the sidewalk in front of his Opera House steps, and the handsome devil could have been an actor himself, with his diamond rings and stickpin, fine clothes, and handsome head of prematurely white hair. His vanity and hot temper proved to be positive assets in the rough-and-tumble world of provincial theater. He knew all of the tricks of survival, including the unscrupulous ones, and was almost (but not quite) accused of setting fire to the rival Metropolitan theater and drugging one of its leading men! He was always good newspaper copy whether scoring a theatrical scoop, throwing a hostile critic out of the house, or being arrested, sued, threatened, or attacked physically, as when he called an actress a hussy. Mostly, Tom's frays were matters of copyright theft or of libel, but once or twice he was hauled off for assault and battery.

Like most untutored men, Maguire had certain completely blind spots. His howlers entertained the readers of local papers who learned, for example, that Edwin Forrest was not only the star of *Coriolanus* but its author, too. He was completely taken in when a reporter tried to sell him on an idea for a play about a crazy Dane, some ghosts, and a girl who drowns herself. The obtuse and humorless Tom called the idea pure trash, adding, "Why, it's the most infernal, confounded rot I've ever heard of." And the producer of several versions of *Hamlet* went on to say, "They wouldn't play it in a melodeon!" Occasionally, Tom Maguire was generous and he gave a spiritualist the free use of one of his theaters on Sundays, and held a benefit to support the "agitators" of the Plasterers Protective Union who were fighting for an eight-hour workday. He had more friends than enemies, and received testimonials including a thousand-dollar silver service from the former. His downfall came, largely, from his daring, his gambling with new productions—which, of course, was his greatness—and from his extravagances. He liked gilt, frescoes, scrollwork, crystal chandeliers, velvet drapes, and satin curtains in his theaters. He spent six thousand 1867 dollars to remodel his Opera House for Edwin Forrest's debut. The papers called it a "temple of the muse," but Forrest was a flop and Tom lost ten thousand dollars more. In the 1870's, he had the Alhambra plus a new Opera House, and a third theater in blueprints, but his luck turned when he tied in with Lucky Baldwin and the Baldwin Theater. The two could not get along and Tom's secretary, David Belasco, had to play go-between.

The stage was now set for a real disaster. This came in 1879, when Tom Maguire completely misjudged the sophistication of San Franciscans. He tried to turn Frisco into Oberammergau by putting on Salmi Morse's Passion Play and invoked the hostility of clergy, press, and would-be ticket purchasers, all still rigidly Victorian in matters religious. God-fearing Christians of both the Catholic and Protestant persuasions turned on the bewildered Maguire to denounce him for blasphemy. Jews accused him of proselytizing although the author,

Morse, was Jewish. The debacle was complete. The Board of Supervisors passed an ordinance forbidding the impersonation on stage of scriptural characters; Christ (i.e., James O'Neill) was arrested; others of the cast were fined; Morse fled to New York and committed suicide. A crushed Maguire gave up the holy war into which he had blundered.

Tom Maguire returned to his old haunts in Manhattan, hoping to make a comeback during the 1880's. He failed completely, became destitute, and was being kept alive, by the time of his death, January 20, 1896, by the Actors Fund. San Francisco's footlight czar had failed, but not before instilling a taste for theater in the roughest and farthest flung of America's cities. He was forgotten, to be sure, in 1896 (and, largely, in 1969), but the comments of the San Francisco *News-Letter* and the *Figaro* of 1873 are still valid: "The public are indebted to Mr. Maguire for the last 20 years for all of the first-class entertainments given in this city . . . He has, upon several occasions, lost heavily and, nothing daunted, he—like Phoenix—rises from the ashes."

WILLIAM L. MANLY

(1820–1903)

Physical bravery is far easier to identify than moral courage. Jedediah Smith is more recognizable as an example of the American hero than is, for example, Andy Furuseth. Yet the muscular variety of genuine courage is sometimes confused with mere recklessness, bravado, and foolhardiness.

Possibly the "purest" case of human courage in the history of California is that of the well-named William Lewis Manly (who often spelled his name "Manley"). In 1849, he demonstrated the most authentic and laudable kind of manliness by rescuing the Bennett-Arcane Party, trapped on the floor of Death Valley with food and water dwindling away to nothing. Thirteen men died in Death Valley that season and, but for Manly's courage, the bulk of the emigrant party might well have shared the fate of the unlucky thirteen.

The discovery of Death Valley by the Bennett-Arcane and Jayhawker parties has many of the elements of the Donner Lake story, including drama, tragedy, and heroism, although not the final horror of cannibalism. James F. Reed would rival Manly in heroism were it not that a "vested interest" drove him to rescue efforts—his wife and children were trapped in the Sierra snows. In Manly's case, he was a bachelor who, out of sheer courage, compassion, and selflessness (like the tragic would-be Donner rescuer, Charles T. Stanton) gambled—with his life—when he had everything to lose and nothing to win but the thanks of the succored.

Before his moment of truth in the desert, Manly had a rather unusual career. Born on April 6, 1820, at St. Albans, Vermont, he helped carve a farmstead out of a forest at a time when the clearing of a single acre might be a full year's work for a man. The family was too poor to afford draft horses but could yoke a few oxen to relieve the straining backs of the boys. Like so many New England families, however, the Manlys eventually gave up fighting the flinty soil and settled upon a Government claim in one of Michigan's oak openings. But here, as in the case of many other California Argonauts, the "agur" (ague) played a decisive role in Manly's life. He declared that he would rather catch chipmunks for a living on a peak in the Rockies than own the biggest farm in malarial Michigan. He fled westward and when he found Wisconsin healthier settled down to a life of hunting and trapping, content even without his Rocky Mountain peak.

Manly was no more immune to the news of California gold than the rest of his generation. He gave up his traps and headed for the Far West in '49. Near Fort Laramie, U.S. troopers warned him that it was too late in the season to cross the Sierra, so, rashly, he led a half-dozen men down the Green River in an old ferryboat which he had found buried in the sand. When the boat was wrecked, he and his men took to canoes axed out of logs, but finally the cañon became absolutely impassable. The voyagers struck overland toward Salt Lake and the overland trails.

Lewis Manly, as he called himself, joined a friend, Asahel Bennett, and a party called the Sand Walking Company, which decided to take the Old Spanish Trail to San Bernardino. Unfortunately, like the doomed Donners of 1846, Manly, the Bennetts, the J. B. Arcanes, and a party of single men called the Jayhawkers (although they were mainly from Illinois, not Kansas) were tempted by talk of a five-hundred-mile shortcut westward from Mountain Meadows. On the edge of the desert already, they found that the terrain grew worse and worse, more barren and dry with each mile. Even a crack shot like Manly was lucky to bag a jack rabbit in several days of hunting. He confessed that he wished he were not duty-bound to stand by the women and children, who slowed down the company's progress. But had he left them, he would have considered himself morally guilty of murder and he determined to stick by them, come what might.

At Furnace Creek, the travelers had to begin killing and eating their oxen. Incredibly, the terrain grew even worse, culminating in a flat valley between eight and fifteen miles wide and far below sea level in altitude. It was obvious that there was no game to shoot there and almost no water to drink. Bennett proposed that the two youngest and strongest men available go ahead to get supplies from a settlement for the remainder of the party. He would wait for them for ten days. (The period stretched to almost four weeks, in the end.) At first, not even Manly would volunteer, but, finally, he agreed to go and a young Tennessean, John Rogers, joined him. Their supplies were a few spoonfuls of rice and tea and the jerky of an ox so far gone that about seven-eighths of all the dried meat taken from the creature's bones was packed into the two men's knapsacks. They had half a light blanket, a seven-shot rifle, a double-barreled shotgun, and two sheath knives. About sixteen people counted upon them for rescue.

Tormented by thirst, Manly and Rogers found only salt water at first on their march toward the sunset over mountains as barren as the moon and cut by arroyos in which the memory of flowing water must have extended back to Paleolithic times. Providentially, they found a little bit of ice near Telescope Peak, which they called simply "the snow mountain." This probably saved their lives. They passed the dead body of one of their erstwhile trailmates, then overtook the Jayhawkers, now almost as badly off as the Bennett-Arcane group. Climbing up out of Death Valley and over the Panamint Range, they found no settled ranchos but, instead, the Panamint Valley, the Basin Ranges and the Owens Valley, and the rugged Sierra itself. On they trudged between Tejon Pass and Mount Wilson (somewhere in the Palmdale area) into the land of "cabbage tree" yuccas—Joshua trees. The land began to improve slightly and Manly was able to kill a crow, a hawk, and—manna from heaven—a quail, which gave them the squarest meal they had had in a long spell. Pushing on, they found an equally heaven-sent creek of live water, then horses and cattle. Ultimately, about New Year's Day of 1850, Manly and Rogers saw a sight which the former insisted he would never be able to describe adequately—a green meadow near the modern town of Newhall. Tears of joy rolled down his face; he and Rogers had made it through!

The Mexican Californians of Rancho San Francisquito and Mission San Fernando treated them most kindly, and when Manly hurried back with supplies on packhorses and a mule, one *señora* gave him four oranges to carry to the little children suffering in the Godforsaken valley. His course lay via Elizabeth Lake and then his outward trail through "75 miles of perdition." It was thirty miles between water holes, and they usually held not more than a pail or two of the precious liquid. The horses failed and had to be abandoned, but the two men struggled on with only the little mule. They passed the grave of a Jayhawker, then the still unburied body they had seen earlier. Next, they reached the sulphur spring which they had left twenty-five days earlier.

After passing another corpse, they reached the wagons, next day. On the alert for Indians, for there was no sign of life about the vehicles, they approached the camp. Finally, someone crawled out from under a wagon bed and called to them. Then the croaking cry went up. "The boys have come! The boys have come!" All were still alive at the desert well. Mrs. Bennett cried, "Good boys! Oh, you have saved us all! God bless you, forever! Such boys should never die!" Manly learned that, earlier, some of the despairing party had said, "If those boys ever get out of this cussed hole, they are damned fools if they ever come back to help anybody."

The women tried to ride the strongest oxen but were thrown, so everyone had to walk out but the very youngest children, who were carried in hickory shirts lashed to oxen like packsaddles. When the party reached the summit of the Panamints, the men turned, raised their hats, and gave a name to the valley which they had cheated of sacrifice. "Good-by, Death Valley!" they shouted.

From Providence Springs and the Walker Pass area of the Sierra's eastern wall, Manly and Rogers led the exhausted, hungry men, women, and children on a now familiar route. From Red Rock Cañon they made their way to the blessed Newhall meadows via Soledad Cañon before reaching the safety of the ranch country.

When their strength returned, the emigrants scattered. Manly went to the gold placers and prospected but eventually settled in the San Jose area. He died there on February 5, 1903, still honored by his neighbors for his feat of heroism and endurance performed fifty-three years ealier.

JAMES W. MARSHALL

(*1810–85*)

The man who turned the world upside-down in 1848, by the simple act of picking up a yellowish, metallic speck from the tailrace of John Sutter's sawmill was forced to live out a long, embittered life of anticlimax. Still, his name will never be forgotten in the history of the American West—although it is often mistakenly given as "John" Marshall. He was born James Wilson Marshall on October 8, 1810, on a farm in Hunterdon County, New Jersey. Marshall is still sometimes confused with his employer, John Sutter, because both were involved in the discovery of gold. Both men suffered the ignominy of being thrust aside and into public discard after having made history, but the two were more dissimilar than alike. Where Sutter was a planner, a schemer, and a dreamer of considerable imagination and skill, Jim Marshall was but a simple—if eccentric—man who was never quite able to live up to the role expected of him in Gold Rush California.

Marshall's chief talent was in his hands. After an early career as a farmer in Missouri, he came to California to work for Sutter and to soldier in the Mexican War. He made himself into a pretty fair carpenter and wagonwright. So scarce were these skills that when Sutter picked Marshall as his mill-wright to build a grist mill near his fort and a sawmill far up in the Sierra Nevada mountains, he not only put Marshall in complete charge of the work while he remained at the fort but paid him with a half interest in the future proceeds from the mill's lumber production.

On the South Fork of the American River in the Sierra, Marshall found a site recommended for a mill earlier by some of Sutter's scouts. With his stamp of approval on Coloma—Beautiful Valley to the Indians—Sutter gave him the go-ahead. Marshall's crew of workmen, both whites and Indians, were diligent (especially the Mormon ex-soldiers), and by New Year's Day, 1848, the foundation was in and the brush and stone dam almost completed. When the structure was finished and the mill irons and flutter-type wheel in place, the mill was seemingly ready for business. However, when Marshall tested it, he found that the raceway was too shallow and without sufficient fall. The wheel would not operate freely because water tended to back up in the ditch under it. So Marshall put a gang of Indians to deepening the tailrace by day and at night he flushed away the loose gravel and sand in it by opening the floodgate.

On the twenty-third of January of 1848, Marshall was making one of his regular inspections. Idly, he picked up a piece of quartz from the race. Somewhere he had read that quartz was often associated with gold. That night he gave orders to shut the headgate early in the morning and to pack dirt, leaves, and sawdust around it to make the ditch as dry as possible. While his men were at breakfast that morning, he sauntered along the tailrace. Stopping, he reached into six inches of icy water and brought up some dull yellow *chispas* not even half the size of a pea. He laid one on a boulder and hammered it with another rock. It was malleable! That ruled out the brittle iron pyrites, or fool's gold. But could it *really* be gold, undiscovered by Sutter and his Mexican predecessors in California? Marshall was nervous and excited but unsure. He picked up a few more specimens and, knocking a dent in the crown of his old slouch hat to hold them, carried them over to his workmen. Discarding all his doubts, he announced to them, "Boys, by God, I believe I have found a gold mine."

The initial skepticism of the hired hands was replaced by gold fever, and all were gleaning nuggets before long, after their regular workday was over. In a driving rainstorm, Marshall took word to Sutter. Insisting upon the greatest secrecy, he asked his employer to make a series of tests on the mineral. When he was done, the Swiss echoed Marshall's feeling, saying, "I believe this is the finest kind of gold!"

The partners agreed to keep the discovery a secret until the mill should be in full operation, knowing how disruptive of normal work would be the news of a gold strike. Marshall hurried back to Coloma and Sutter followed shortly. The latter found gold himself, swore his workers to secrecy for six weeks, and then, with Marshall, signed a treaty with the Coloma Indians which gave the partnership sole lumbering and mining rights in a tract of some ten to twelve square miles surrounding the mill.

Unluckily for Marshall and Sutter, Colonel Richard B. Mason, Military Governor of California, held the lease to be invalid because individuals could not make such treaties with Indian "nations." Almost at the same time, a leak developed in the veil of secrecy which Marshall and Sutter threw over the discovery. A young son of one of Marshall's workers told a teamster who had brought supplies to the mill. He, in turn, told a barkeep at Sutter's Fort who spilled the beans to Sam Brannan. The latter kept a store at the fort and, eager for

29. The success of *Theodore Judah's* dream, the transcontinental railroad, all but put wagon trains out of business during the 1870s, replacing them with the "emigrant cars" made famous by California-bound Robert Louis Stevenson. In the photograph above, a belated caravan arrives at a gentle pass somewhere in the sage east of the Sierra and finds it pre-empted by an iron horse and its roadbed. *Southern Pacific Photo*

30. A crowd lined the Cascades, man-made rapids (still to be seen from Highway 99) at the southern terminus of the Los Angeles-Owens River Aqueduct where it flows into the San Fernando Valley en route to Los Angeles proper. The date was November 5, 1913, when the first water sluiced down the slope, to complete the work of *William Mulholland*. *Los Angeles Department of Water and Power*

31. One of the best-loved—and most tragic—individuals in all American history was *Ishi,* sole survivor of the Yana tribe and California's last Stone Age man. When he died, with great dignity, it was as a victim of disease brought to his world by civilized man, a greater killer of his people than even the Winchester and the Colt. *University of California Press*

32. Like Ernest Hemingway, author *Jack London*—"the Sailor on Horseback" —lived as adventurous a life as the hero of any of his stories. London was always at home on boats, whether at the tiller of his little sloop *Razzle Dazzle* during his oyster-pirating youth or at the wheel of his *Snark* in the South Seas. *Redwood Empire Association*

33. Something of a Southern California version of Captain John Sutter was *Benjamin D. Wilson,* better known during his California period as Don Benito Wilson. The ex-Tennessean was an Indian trader and fur trapper who migrated early (1841) to California and settled on a ranch near Riverside. He was one of the earliest and most prominent advocates the California Indians ever had, as well as a good friend of the Mexicans, his wife's people. *Los Angeles Department of Recreation and Parks*

34. Not the first Japanese to live in California, *Joseph Heco* (born Hikozo Hamada) was really the founder of the state's Issei, Nisei, and Sansei colony because he did enjoy living in California and became a naturalized American citizen. His predecessor, Nakahama Manjiro, had visited California from Hawaii during the Gold Rush, but only briefly. Both Japanese were victims of shipwreck, rescued by American vessels during the period when the empire forbade visiting foreign countries. *California State Library*

35. Author, poet, and primitive public relations man for Sunny California, *Charles Lummis* was Los Angeles' most flamboyant personality of the nineteenth century. Head of the Public Library, editor of *Out West* and *Land of Sunshine* magazine, he trumpeted California's blessings so much that he must be held responsible, in part, for the smog, bulging freeways, and other inconveniences of modern Southern California. His living memorial is the institution he founded on the Arroyo Seco, still flourishing—the Southwest Museum. *The Southwest Museum*

36. *Lillie Hitchcock Coit* was the West's greatest fire buff, of either sex, and was early adopted by one of San Francisco's volunteer companies, Knickerbocker Engine Company No. 5. She was the city's outstanding female "character," for, although a lady, she was what would be called today anti-Establishment. This free spirit was also responsible for the Coit Tower on Telegraph Hill. *California Historical Society*

37. The ambitious *John C. Frémont* was an excellent explorer and naturalist, although hardly the Pathfinder he has been painted. In Northern California, particularly, he has had a mixed press, many *Norteños* having long memories and recalling his shameful treatment of Mariano Vallejo and John Sutter and, above all, his ordering Kit Carson to murder José de los Reyes Berryessa and the De Haro twins, Francisco and Ramón, near San Rafael in June of 1846. *Sutro Library*

38. The attack on the peace commissioners, under a flag of truce, was the beginning of the end for *Captain Jack* of the Modoc Indians. With the murder of General E. R. S. Canby (right) by Captain Jack, the latter's death warrant was signed. It took an army to run Jack out of the rugged Lava Beds, but he was, at last, run to earth and captured. On October 3, 1873, he "swung" for the treacherous action into which he had been goaded by some of his warriors. *Sutro Library*

39. *Captain Jack's* valiant fight against overwhelming odds in the Modoc War of 1872-73 not only made headlines, it captured the imagination of many Americans. One of the curious results was that editors of Midwest histories of the 1870s, for no good reason other than it would help sales, included a chapter on the faraway California war, complete with fanciful portraits of the chief, looking more like a Sac and Fox, perhaps, than a California Modoc. *Sutro Library*

40. *Dr. Ng Poon Chew,* pioneer Chinese newspaper publisher of both San Francisco and Los Angeles, was one of the first of his people to opt for integration and full participation in the California community at large. He also won a deserved reputation as a witty and enlightening speaker, sometimes being called "the Chinese Mark Twain." *California State Library*

more customers, deliberately spread the word in San Francisco. Soon the rush for riches was on.

Marshall entered into a mining partnership with Sutter and the only experienced gold miner in the area, Isaac Humphrey, who had mined in the Dahlonega and Auraria region of northern Georgia. And yet the partnership did not prosper. Sutter lost so much money in outfitting and supplying the prospecting expeditions that he pulled out. Shortly, the partnership fell apart. Even before wind of Governor Mason's decision reached Coloma, miners were digging on what Marshall claimed as his property. For a time, he was able to collect tithes, but, eventually, the squatters ignored his claims. The mill stopped work almost as soon as it started and became a flophouse for diggers. Jim Marshall wisely sold his interest in it. Like Sutter, he tried to protect the local Indians from the bigoted and murderous miners, but failed. At one point, he had to flee from Coloma to nearby Kelsey because his life was in danger as a result of his trying to defend the Indians.

Virtually forced off his own discovery site by the greedy and lawless Yankees, Marshall prospected elsewhere in the Sierra foothills but with little luck. Usually, he was trailed by miners who believed, seriously, that he had a God-granted gift for finding gold. He always drifted back from other diggings to his cabin at Coloma. According to Sutter, Marshall half believed the tales of his gold-finding gift himself, and disregarded modest bars and pockets in his unending search for the "fountainhead" of gold which existed in myth and in his mind. Sutter grubstaked him several times, more out of kindness than speculation, because he knew Marshall was obsessed with finding the lode of "big lumps" which did not exist. Ironically, Marshall was on the right track. Eventually he concluded, correctly, that California's future lay in quartz mining, not placer mining. But he was ahead of his time.

Once again, Marshall's life was threatened when he would not share his "divination" secret with others. Many miners, of course, paid court to him, flattering him as the discoverer of California gold. But, more and more, Marshall was becoming bitter because others claimed the glory of the first find. He complained to a friend, "They have robbed me of my land, and now they would filch from me the empty honor of the first gold discovery."

By 1851, the most famous (and unsuccessful) gold miner in the world was doing carpentry and joinery again to keep his belly full and the taxes on his modest cabin paid. He continued to roam the Sierra, guided by spirits or visions, but never found the El Dorado he sought. New legends began to cluster around him—that he was really fabulously wealthy; that he was insane. Both stories were untrue though widely held by both press and public. The Stockton *Argus* was only half correct when it reported that "Marshall, the first discoverer of gold in California, is hopelessly insane, a calamity brought upon him by inebriation." It was true that the millwright, like Sutter himself, was driven to drink more "Sacramento water" (as the local popskull was called) then was good for him. But he was never a lunatic, although a fanatic spiritualist and eccentric in other ways. (He treated his rheumatism by dousing himself with creosote until even the blue jays were driven from his immediate vicinity.)

Although Marshall dabbled in vineyards and orchards after the 1860's, he became Coloma's town character, if never quite the town's resident drunk. A soured and cantankerous old man before his time, Marshall liked to compare Australia's treatment of its gold discoverer, rewarded with five thousand pounds, with his own. He had been, of course, rewarded with nothing but robbery at the hands of late-comers. He acquired a persecution complex, too, when a mysterious fire destroyed his cabin and all his precious papers. He claimed that it was arson, and he may well have been right.

Eventually, the State of California took pity on Marshall, just as it did on Sutter. It gave him a pension of one hundred dollars a month, which he squandered on drinks for his shiftless friends in the saloons of Coloma and Kelsey. His pension was discontinued when word of his sprees reached the immaculate halls of the Capitol. Marshall returned to carpentry and blacksmithing.

The discoverer died quietly in bed, probably of a heart attack, on August 10, 1885. Even in death, Marshall was not spared. The rumor immediately spread that he had died of starvation. Once he was safely dead, society ennobled his reputation. He became something of a hero in California history and in 1890 a splendid monument to him and his discovery was dedicated at Coloma. Atop the great column is a statue of Jim pointing out the spot where he first found "color." The bronze lips are slightly parted, as if to loose the words which shook the world in 1848 and '49: "Boys, by God, I believe I have found a gold mine."

JOAQUIN MILLER

(*1837–1913*)

More poseur than poet, Joaquin Miller—born Cincinnatus Hiner Miller near Liberty, Indiana, on September 8, 1837—remains a major figure of California history and biography because of the grand style in which he assumed and played the role of wilderness poet. Although most of his poetry was turgid stuff, full of chanted redundancies and inappropriate rhymes, he still remains today "The Poet of the Sierras," as he was called a century ago.

A hundred years ago Miller's reputation as a liar was almost as great as that of a poet. He stretched a longer bow than either Jim Bridger or Baron Münchausen, and it is impossible to separate fiction from the (exaggerated) fact upon which many of his writings were supposedly based. His boast—"My cradle was a covered wagon, pointed west"—is patently false because he was fifteen when his family, succumbing to Oregon Fever, migrated westward. (Of course, Miller may only have been flourishing his poetic license; perhaps he was, indeed, reborn, as a poet, in 1852.) But the point is that Miller need not have fibbed so constantly about being a descendant of Pocahontas, a lieutenant of filibuster William Walker in Nicaragua, or a co-founder of an Indian Republic in California. His real-life career was genuinely adventurous and exciting. And here lies the tragedy of Miller's literary career—his roaming, restless life provided him with a surfeit of material for prose and poetry, but he was never able to rise to the challenge. He lived the frontier experience as few American writers have, and yet, instead of writing about it authentically, realistically, and powerfully, he imitated the polite poets of English drawing rooms and romanticized and sentimentalized his superb material into melodramatic doggerel and banal jingles. They hardly even possess identifiable Western locales. So colorful himself in manner and costume, he was utterly incapable of imparting regional color to his poetry and only to a handful of his prose paragraphs. It was not his trite ideas, his commonplace phrasing, weak poetical technique, or his semiliteracy (he rhymed Goethe with teeth!) which was Miller's undoing; it was his decision to falsify his experiences in order to make them more "poetic." Ambrose Bierce, with brutal insight, summed up Miller's output thus: "He rewrites his life from reading dime novels."

In 1854, young Nat Miller ran away to the gold mines of Siskiyou County's Humbug (!) Creek and later lived with the Indians of Squaw Valley on the McCloud River. He met an old scout, Mountain Joe (Joseph de Bloney), whose adventures he pocketed as his very own. The miners called him Crazy Miller; his Indian friends dubbed him Bobo—Spanish for "Fool." The young squawman may have participated in the Battle of Castle Crags. He always boasted of having been wounded in the fight. He certainly witnessed one of the shameful massacres of the Pit River Indians by settlers. Always torn between literature and adventure, he attended short-lived Columbia College in Eugene, Oregon, but his collegiate career was mainly in the university of hard knocks. In 1859, for example, he was arrested as a horse thief at Shasta but broke jail and escaped to Oregon after shooting and wounding a peace officer. He became a pony express rider between Idaho and Oregon, and edited pro-Confederate newspapers in Eugene until the Government shut them down as treasonable. Miller was not so much a Copperhead as he was a kind of pacifist and a friend of the underdog. He so saw the Confederacy, facing an aggressor North. (In this role, he resembled somewhat the antiwar "doves" of the Vietnamese 1960's in America.)

Miller married a local lady poet, Theresa Dyer, whose very Oregonian pen name was Minnie Myrtle, the Sweet Singer of the Coquille (River). They went to San Francisco but hardly took it by storm, although Miller was able to place a few items in the *Golden Era*. With San Francisco not quite ready for Hiner Miller, as he was then calling himself, the newlyweds returned to Oregon, where Miller practiced law at Canyon City, led militiamen against hostiles, served as a county judge, and impressed locals into involuntary audiences for his poems which he read aloud. At his own expense he brought out two slim volumes of poetry and, in 1870, tried San Francisco again. This time, he was welcomed by the literati but decided to push on to Britain in a literary hadj. He visited the tombs of Burns and Byron and laid a wreath of laurel, which he had picked in Sausalito, California, on the latter's memorial. In England he brought out two more volumes of poetry and, *mirabile visu!*, captivated literary London. By sheer luck, Miller had arrived at just the right time. The Pre-Raphaelites were fatigued with academic poets and enchanted with the feral poet of the Siskiyous.

Miller's *Songs of the Sierras* made his reputation overnight. He followed it with a semiautobiographical book, *Life Amongst the Modocs,* which the snobbish *Athenaeum* dismissed as "monstrously dull" but which was another great popular success and remains his most interesting and, probably, his best work. Since he was so busy being lionized by Rossetti and others, Miller let Prentice Mulford "help" him with *Modocs*. In fact, he later admitted, "Mulford did all the work." Its lasting interest, therefore, may be due more to the Mulford in it than to the Miller in it. Incredibly, the English were so infatuated with their bizarre poet from California and Oregon, dressed like a Mexican bandit, that they compared his tiresome rhymes to those of the poet he idolized and aped, Lord Byron. Now he was not only the Poet of the Sierras but the Byron of the Rockies. Eventually, of course, London came to its senses and grew bored with Miller and especially with his verse. America was less convinced of his genius from the start, and San Francisco least of all. Ambrose Bierce said of Miller, "He requires no fewer than 115 lines to relate the landing of a ship in fair weather with nothing to prevent it." Bayard Taylor labeled him "a vulgar fraud." At his worst—and Miller was frequently at his worst—he was a composer of versified clichés. A *Harper's* critic was painfully correct about the poetry of Joaquin. "Its fatal fault is that in its portraiture of American character it sacrifices truth to the poet's conceit."

As Bayard Taylor predicted, Joaquin Miller's star waned as fast as it had risen. The first verses of a sixteen-year-old Nat Miller, simple and crude as they are, ring far more honestly and appealingly than the pretentious stanzas of the "mature" poet who took the name Joaquin from the bandit Murrieta. Compare them:

(1854)   The day is dark and cloudy, too
             And the mist is edging 'round
             My toes. They ache, you bet they do,
             As I hear the chill winds sound.
             I guess when I'm as big as Dad

I'll leave this plaguey school
I'll make the teacher wish he had
Not made me mind his rule.

*

(1863) Divine Remembrance! Mother of the Muse!
Oh, lend me thine aid! my soul infuse
With the glowing flame of sweet poetic fire!
Awake my muse! Awake my silent lyre
And lade with notes of ecstasy the breeze!
Let float thy sweetest murmurs o'er the leas!
Vouchsafe to me your aid, oh, Sacred Nine!
Ne'er sweeter theme inspired a bard than mine.

Joaquin Miller was capable of good writing. When he was merely playful rather than ambitious or pretentious, he could even write humor. His series of letters (*Canyon City Pickles*) in *The Dalles Daily Mountaineer* were those of a pretty fair poor-man's-Twain. In describing the feverish business activity of Canyon City, for example, he wrote: "I saw three live merchants, all busy, of course. Bruner was lying on the counter, tickling his cat under the tail with a straw. McNamara was sitting at the breakfast table, picking his nose with a fork. Felsheimer had finished his breakfast and sat at the table quietly paring his toenails with the butter knife. A merchant sold a pair of shoestrings last week and went to his drawer for the change but the thing had rusted in its place from idleness, and he had to use a crowbar to open it."

Miller lived in the East for a time, then returned to California in 1886 to settle on a piece of land in the Oakland hills which he dubbed The Hights (his spelling). There he built four monuments. One honored Frémont, another Moses, and the third Browning, rather than Byron. The fourth was Joaquin's own funeral pyre. The poet's last efforts were in prose, and not bad. He contributed dispatches from the Alaska-Yukon gold rush of 1897, in which he lost two toes to frostbite and made one of the most atrocious puns of all California history, calling attention to his new status as a "no-toe-rious poet." Joaquin Miller died at The Hights on February 17, 1913.

Today, Joaquin Miller as a poet, per se, is something of a joke. But he is a Californian of considerable stature still, as a symbol of the wild days of the state and as a personality or character. Even before Buffalo Bill Cody, he symbolized the wild and woolly West to Europe. Although he was no family man and he callously ignored his ex-wives and his children much of the time, he was a friendly, gregarious, and convivial bohemian whose lies were never malicious, a man who was gracious even to the pests which are the bane of the writer's life. In short, the squawman and ladies' man, the poet of 1001 clichés, may have been less the artist than, say, Bret Harte, but he was more of a man. Miller had a kind of basic decency, too, underlying a seemingly selfish, hedonistic amorality. He sincerely sympathized with the Indians—and in writing—long before Helen Hunt Jackson. He forgave his first wife for the vicious public attacks she made on him. He regretted the anti-Mormon bias of his popular play, *The Danites in the Sierras,* as unfair.

Miller was certainly America's most picturesque poet whether one chooses to accept Tennyson's verdict on his poem *Columbus*—"a masterpiece"—or not. Curiously, Joaquin was one of the few to recognize Whitman's genius from the start. Although he imitated Byron in his verse and Bret Harte in such stories as *Fam'lies of the Sierras,* probably Owen Wister and the horse opera genre owe more to him and his account of the shootout in the Deadwood doggery (i.e., saloon) than to Harte's Mother Lode short stories. In his most interesting book,

Life Amongst the Modocs, Miller not only anticipated (in brief) the Western story, he also demonstrated—perhaps with Prentice Mulford's help—skill in narration and description and even some insight. For example: "It was late in the day when we passed, on one side of the dusty road we had been traveling but a short distance, a newly-erected gallows and a populous graveyard on the other. Certain evidence, under the present order of things, of the nearness of civilization and a city. . . . This cañon was as black as Erebus down there—a sea of sombre firs; and down, down as if the earth was cracked and cleft almost in two. Here and there lay little nests of clouds below us, tangled in the tree tops, no wind to drive them, nothing to fret and disturb. They lay above the dusks of the forest as if asleep. . . .

". . . There are men that exhaust me. There are men that, if they come into a room and talk to me or even approach closely, take my strength from me more speedily and as certainly as if I spent my force climbing a hill. There are men that I cannot endure; their presence is to me an actual physical pain. . . . They use me up; they absorb, exhaust me; they would kill me dead in less than a week."

Very likely, Joaquin Miller is the perfect prototype of the congress of California characters whose sketches fill this album. His work—like his life—was a mixture of good and bad. And although he was a poseur, he was completely unaware of it, like a demented actor whose personality has been entirely absorbed by the role he plays. He took himself and his most puerile poetry seriously, if not dead seriously. In Joaquin Miller are epitomized both major species of the Westerner. Like many other California pioneers, Miller was, unwittingly, a split personality, half hero and half humbug.

JOHN MUIR

(*1838–1914*)

John Muir's reputation as a writer is growing, which is only proper, but the fact remains that "John of the Mountains" taught us far more by personal example than by his written narratives. He should be remembered first as a naturalist, conservationist, and philosopher. Even had he never scribbled a line, his lifetime dedication to the outdoors inspired in millions of Americans a love and concern for the vanishing wilderness. Muir is memorialized much more appropriately than most of our pioneers, with the John Muir Trail along the Sierra's crest and Muir Woods, in the lee of Mount Tamalpais, for example. Too, his Victorian home and ranch in the Alhambra Valley near Martinez has now become a historical site administered by the National Park Service and, increasingly, a place of pilgrimage.

Muir was born in Dunbar, Scotland, on April 21, 1848, and came to America as a lad of eleven years. Like Thomas Edison and Luther Burbank, he was a natural-born inventor. Inventions helped him keep his sanity during a most unhappy childhood during which he was tyrannized by a fundamentalist father who preferred to whip his nonconforming son rather than try to understand him. (The "generation gap" in the Muir family resembled the Yosemite Valley in expanse, if not in beauty.) Later he would find himself equipped with a spirit which was a blend of that of the poet and the natural scientist, and he abandoned the inventing.

Life on the homestead near Buffalo, Wisconsin, would have been hard enough in the best of cases, but John's father drove him like a work ox and almost ruined his health. Worse were the psychological scars on the boy, some of which never healed. When his father grudgingly consented to his reading books, but only in the early morning when such a "waste of time" would not interfere with chores, John trained himself to awake every night at one o'clock so that he would have five glorious hours all to himself. The boy's inventiveness served him in one way—it brought the break between him and his father which had to come. He went to Madison to exhibit his contraptions—clocks, locks, latches, etc.—at the Wisconsin State Agricultural Fair in 1860 and next year entered the University of Wisconsin. Once set free, John Muir was destined to develop his unique, transcendental genius.

Somewhat at loose ends after leaving the university, Muir worked at odd jobs and nearly lost his sight in an accident. The shock caused him to reassess his life. He realized that he was destined to heed Thoreau's "different drummer" and, as he recuperated, he determined not to fritter away his life in the humdrum of a workaday existence. He would make his avocations—hiking, botanizing, the keeping of journals—into his life's vocation. As soon as he was well, he set out to walk from Louisville, Kentucky, to Florida. The subtropical peninsula was somewhat disappointing to him in that its most interesting areas were virtually impenetrable, so he switched his affections to California. But the thousand-mile walk convinced him that he had charted the proper course in life.

Henceforth, he would be on the side of nature against man or, at least, against so-called "civilization."

The young Scot arrived in San Francisco in March of 1868 and stayed exactly one day, little longer than the time it took to inquire the shortest way out of town. When he was asked where he wanted to go, Muir answered simply, "To any place that is wild." Luckily, he was steered toward the Sierra Nevada mountains, but since he had to eat he took work in a sheep camp in the lowlands. He caught his first glimpse of the most beautiful vale in the world—Yosemite Valley—at this time and also acquired an undying hatred for sheep. "Hooved locusts," he called them, as he saw them strip beautiful mountain meadows to the grass roots, setting in motion an almost incurable cycle of erosion.

Muir was still herding sheep during his first Sierra summer (1869), but he found time to reflect a good deal on the unity-within-diversity of nature and its "flow" of interrelationships and continuities. He began to fill voluminous notebooks which would be polished and published, long after (1911), in his most successful book, artistically speaking, *My First Summer in the Sierra*. Poor Muir—trapped in a sheep camp! He sympathized with the wild animals, not the tamed beasts "degraded" by man. The coyote was no skulking coward to him. To him, the azalea was a blessed shrub, not the "sheep-poison" of the local lexicon. Even the men, to Muir, were "tamed" and sheeplike. He asked Shepherd Billy to look at Yosemite, and the herder snorted his refusal, denouncing it as only a hole in the ground, full of dangerous rocks, and a damned good place to stay away from.

In 1870, John Muir was in Yosemite with the Le Conte geological expedition and by the following year, when Emerson visited him in the great valley of Ahwahnee, he was the area's resident naturalist. He argued with geologist Josiah D.

Whitney that Yosemite Valley was largely the product of glaciation, and he won. Since he already saw the threat posed to the mountain wilderness by encroaching civilization, via lumbering, herding, and tourism, he worked hard to get Yosemite made into a national park similar to Yellowstone. (Already, in 1866, Muir had been largely instrumental in getting the State of California to make a park of Yosemite Valley, proper, and the Mariposa Grove of redwoods.)

Muir took up the fight where Galen Clark left off. He was a mountain man on a much grander scale. He lectured, he wrote articles in West Coast newspapers and magazines, and, finally, in such journals as *Scribner's* and *Harper's,* realizing that all America had a stake in Yosemite. He founded the Sierra Club; he lobbied; he fought, he fought, he fought. And in 1890 the Yosemite Park bill was passed into law. Only then did Muir take the time to write his books, still maintaining his watchman's stance over Yosemite and the Sierra Nevada and so expanding his protective role that he finally personified the conservationist conscience of America.

Personally, John Muir was gregarious, although he loved freedom and disliked crowds. The common picture of him is an erroneous one of a gentle hermit. He was opinionated and, used to having his own way for so many years, could be a crusty curmudgeon at times. He managed to survive marriage, however, although it did limit his foot-loose wanderings. Surprisingly, he and his wife, Louie Strentzel Muir, ran a very productive and successful ranch, for Muir had a thumb almost as green as Luther Burbank's. Next to California, Muir loved Alaska—his natural glaciological laboratory—best, and he made five trips to the territory and wrote books about his experiences.

Much honored was America's apostle of nature when he died on the day before Christmas, 1914. He was a greater naturalist than Henry Thoreau, if not his equal as writer or philosopher. Earlier than almost anyone, Muir saw the need in man for an escape to nature, to reality, from the contrived existence most folk mistook for living in towns and cities. He urged Americans to climb the mountains in order to get their good tidings, and his advice is, increasingly, being heeded. John Muir was an unexcelled propagandist for preservation of our natural resources, although his one great defeat —the theft of the Hetch Hetchy Valley for a San Francisco waterworks—may actually have killed him and certainly hastened his death.

Perhaps, in the long run, John Muir's single major defeat has been a victory of sorts. The shock of the spoliation of the Hetch Hetchy Valley, second only to Yosemite Valley itself in grandeur, destroyed complacency and served as an early warning to all Americans that unending vigilance is necessary to protect even established parks and other scenic or historic areas from the cruelest symptom of mankind's nihilistic death wish.

WILLIAM MULHOLLAND

(*1855–1935*)

The never-failing tap in the kitchen sinks of hundreds of thousands of Southern California homes is the state's memorial to William Mulholland. For it was Mulholland, mightiest of dowsers, who sought, found, and brought life-giving water to the dry Los Angeles plain and the parched San Fernando Valley, enabling the city of the Angeles to metamorphose from cowtown to cosmopolis.

Yet, Mulholland's reputation remains under a cloud to this very day, long after his death, and not because he lacked the prescience to see that his delivery of water would mean overpopulation, traffic congestion, smog, and ghettos. No, the hatred toward Mulholland came from his (and the city's) ruthlessness in seeking water and because of an act of God—at least, in Mulholland's eyes—which virtually terminated his career and wrecked his reputation. The Irish-American was both hero and victim of a rags-to-riches tale which ended in obloquy and tragedy.

A poorly educated, Belfast-born lad of twenty-two years, Bill Mulholland dropped onto the rude planks of the San Pedro wharf for the first time in 1877, with just ten dollars in his pocket. He went to work as a ditch tender in the primitive water system bequeathed Los Angeles by its Hispanic founders, a network of open canals—*zanjas* or *acequias* ("zakies" to the Anglos)—fed by a *zanja madre,* or mother ditch, running from the off-again, on-again Los Angeles River. Before he retired in 1928 as chief engineer and general manager of the Los Angeles Department of Water and Power, Mulholland had succeeded in completely transforming Los Angeles via his water system. Most important to Southern California was the 225-mile-long Los Angeles Aqueduct, with its fifty-two miles of tunnels, bringing water across mountain and desert to the sea.

By 1886, Mulholland had risen through ability and hard work to the post of superintendent of the local water company. Observers described him in his early years as "a common laborer who could shovel more dirt and dig more ditch than any man on the job." When the city took over the water company in 1902, he became chief engineer and general manager of the new municipal department. Mulholland picked up the idea of tapping the Sierra Nevada for water, via the Owens River, from Fred Eaton, Los Angeles' city engineer. But it was Mulholland who planned the project and made it work, slaking the giant thirst of Southern California. "The Chief" carried out the project with the help of his department's chief legal counsel, W. B. Mathews, and shared the credit for the scheme by saying, "I did the work but Mathews kept me out of jail."

The self-taught engineer earned the hatred of settlers in the Owens River Valley east of the Sierra by draining off their water and turning the valley oasis into a desert. Many outsiders sympathized, too, with the rural folk robbed of their precious water by a bullying Los Angeles just as Yosemite had been despoiled of Hetch Hetchy Cañon by a thirsty San

Francisco in 1915. Already the pattern of urban domination of rural California was set, but there was little that the people could do other than denounce Mulholland's great siphon as "an obscene enterprise." So hard were the feelings of Inyo and Mono County folk against L.A. that masked night riders kidnaped and drove Los Angeleños from the valley, captured headgates, and sabotaged the project by dynamiting the aqueduct.

In volume, at least, the hatred of a handful of ranchers and farmers for Mulholland was more than counterbalanced by the gratitude of the citizenry of Los Angeles. But in 1928, Fate played a hand and destroyed Mulholland's reputation in the Los Angeles area itself. Hysterical victims of a disaster blamed on him cried, "Murder!" and at least one sign was painted which exhorted people to "Kill Mulholland!"

In San Francisquito Cañon, north of Los Angeles and at the head of the Santa Clara River Valley, Mulholland decided to build St. Francis Dam. As early as the 1890's, he had filed an application for a dam site on the waters of a tributary, Sespe Creek. Local settlers had formed an organization called the Santa Clara River Protective Association to save the Sespe, but they neglected the remote and seemingly inaccessible San Francisquito Cañon, far upstream. By 1920, the Los Angeles Bureau of Power and Light had planted two powerhouses in the cañon, a thousand feet below the course of the Los Angeles Aqueduct. A reservoir was next in Mulholland's plans. He gave it high priority because it would lie below the fault line and, should earthquakes rupture the great aqueduct, Los Angeles would have a year's supply of water close at hand.

Work started in 1924, although some of the laborers predicted that the streak of schist running through the sandstone of the dam site looked like a treacherous anchorage.

But when the Protective Association's engineers saw little danger and Mulholland agreed to a controlled flow of water to the local people, with the city using only the surplus water, opposition died down. When the water reached the fault line, leakage began around the dam. But Mulholland had complete confidence in the structure and, later, said, "Of all the dams I have built and of all the dams I have ever seen, it was the driest dam of its size I ever saw." While the reservoir was filling, saboteurs were dynamiting sections of the aqueduct from Owens Valley, so Mulholland was grateful for his close-in water reserve. On March 7, 1928, the high-water mark of 1832 feet was reached, and he ordered that no more water be stored.

There was more worried joking about Mulholland's leaky dam in that spring of '28, when new seepage occurred as when, on March 12, the damkeeper phoned Mulholland of a new, third, leak. The latter hurried to the St. Francis Dam but soon left after reassuring the fearful damkeeper.

Just short of midnight on March 12, 1928, the lights in Los Angeles flickered momentarily as voltage dropped. No one realized it, but these were the warning signals of disaster. Near the dam, the earth shook, and people thought that there had been either a landslide or an earthquake. But soon a wall of water as high as a ten-story building, cargoed with trees, animals, parts of houses, and ten-thousand-ton fragments of the ruptured dam, swept down the cañon. The deadly surge of water, moving at twenty-five miles an hour, obliterated Castaic Junction and threatened to do the same to Fillmore and Santa Paula. Luckily, the word was being spread and people fled to high ground. A California motorcycle highway patrolman was the hero of the moment, warning hundreds of the danger. When the water subsided, homes and cars were found to have been swept away; orange groves were flattened;

the whole valley was covered with slimy mud. Worst, the Ventura County Coroner listed 420 people as having been killed by the failure of Mulholland's dam. While relief measures continued, several investigations of the catastrophe began. (Tales flew that Mulholland used weak concrete, full of dirt, and that he substituted old bedsprings for steel reinforcing rods in his concrete structures!)

Mulholland himself, the builder of nineteen dams, suspected sabotage—dynamiting. But he did not push his belief in the face of his universal condemnation for faulty engineering. He had built a strong dam on rotten rock. Mulholland resigned and went into retirement, although he was kept on by the city as a consultant until his death in 1935. He was man enough to admit that he might have miscalculated and to accept full responsibility. At the Los Angeles Coroner's inquest he said, "Don't blame anybody else; you just fasten it on me. If there is an error of human judgment, I was the human."

NG POON CHEW

(*1866–1931*)

Most Chinese who came to California during the nineteenth century did not abandon their black pajama-like garb and so-called "pigtails" for Western dress and hair styles, nor did they accept the English language except for a pidgin sort of lingua franca used to transact business. This circumstance was not only due to the hundreds of years of powerful tradition pressing upon them but also because almost all of the immigrants from China did not intend to remain long in California. Like many others who rushed to El Dorado, most of them planned to be mere sojourners in *Gum Shan* ("Golden Mountains," as they so aptly termed California). They planned to return to Canton once they should make their fortunes.

An exception was Ng Poon Chew, born in Kwangtung Province on March 14, 1866. He came to stay. He was exceptional in many ways. Unlike most of the Orientals who jammed the sailing ships and steamers heading for San Francisco from Hong Kong, Ng was not a common laborer without education. When a small boy, he had been placed by his family in the care of a Taoist tutor. His grandmother had hoped that he might enter the priesthood. This career did not appeal to young Chew, but he acquired a taste for education and culture from his tutor. When his uncle returned to China from San Franicsco with eight sacks of Mexican dollars, each bag worth one hundred dollars, the boy immigrated to San Francisco in the company of a relative, intent on making a similar "pile."

Ng found the Gold Rush long past when he arrived in California in 1881, but he also discovered plenty of opportunities for profit in the state. He settled in San Jose and attended public school there at the same time that he worked as a servant in a San Jose home.

Ng's greatest asset was an open and receptive mind, something not at all common (yet) in immigrants from China. Most new arrivals were very conservative, culturally, unwilling to accept Occidental ideas. When Ng cut off his cue and began to wear American-style clothes, he was labeled a *fan kwei,* a "foreign devil" or Occidental. As he matured, Ng found his old hope of winning a fortune to be an insufficient goal in life, and he substituted a desire for learning and for the opportunity and ability to better the lives of his fellow-countrymen in America.

Step by step, Ng Poon Chew found himself integrating into the broader community. In 1882 he gave up Taoism and became a Christian convert. He entered the San Franciso Theological Seminary, later, and graduated in 1892. He became not only pastor of the Chinese Presbyterian Church but doubled (and tripled) as the church's organist and janitor.

With his strong practical bent and urge to be of service, Ng sought a wider field than the ministry in which to work. He decided to found a newspaper for the Asian community, although some of his friends laughed at the idea of Chinese reading a paper even if, through some miracle, he should be able to put one on the streets. Ng persevered and with the backing of more confident friends he was able to establish the weekly *Wah Mein Sun Po* in 1898 in Los Angeles. Two years later, he founded the first Chinese daily paper in America, San Francisco's *Chung Sai Yat Po* (Chinese Western Daily). He secured John Fryer, professor of Chinese literature at the University of California in Berkeley, as a member of his editorial staff. Managing Editor Ng himself soon won respect for his writing. He never missed publishing an issue except for the week following the earthquake and fire disaster of 1906, when he suspended publication temporarily. As early as 1905, Ng was considered an expert on the question of Chinese immigration and exclusion. That year, he and Patrick J. Healy wrote a book titled *Statement for Non-Inclusion,* but almost all copies were destroyed by the fire of April 1906, which swept the city.

Between 1906 and World War I, Ng served as an adviser to the Chinese Consul General. In 1913, he was appointed vice consul. Meanwhile, he had become president of the Chung Sai Yat Po Publishing Company and a director of the China Mail Steamship Company. He was active in the Commonwealth Club of California and the American Academy of Political and Social Science as well as other civic, religious, social, and scholarly organizations. He was a thirty-third-degree Mason, the first Shriner of Chinese descent. In that busy year of 1913, Ng won a high academic honor when the University of Pittsburgh awarded him a doctor of letters degree for his pioneering work in Chinese journalism. Pitt might just as well have given him the *honoris causa* degree for his long service as a bridge between the two cultures, in each of which he was uniquely at home.

Dr. Ng was even more effective on the boards than at the

editor's desk. As an earnest and witty speaker with a perfect command of English, he won the nickname of "the Chinese Mark Twain." He lectured on all kinds of subjects, from the loftiest to such lightweight matters as the changing mores of Chinese flappers, as young girls of very free conduct and speech were called during the Roaring Twenties.

By the time of Dr. Ng Poon Chew's death in 1931 he was the best-known, most respected, and most honored Chinese-American in the country. Small wonder that the dean of California historians, Dr. Rockwell Hunt of the University of the Pacific—dubbed "Mr. California" by the governor of the state—gave him a place in his *California's Stately Hall of Fame,* an ancestor of the volume in hand.

FRANK NORRIS

(1870–1902)

Jack London's chief rival for the honor of being the University of California's outstanding dropout of all time was Benjamin Franklin Norris, born March 5, 1870, on the South Side of the Windy City, just in time to enjoy the great Chicago Fire. His mother was an intellectually inclined actress, his father an all-business, no-nonsense jewelry salesman. The family being relatively well off, young Frank enjoyed a European tour before moving to California for the improvement of his father's health. About a year after his 1885 arrival in San Francisco, when he was sixteen, Frank began to write but was diverted from authorship by school, in which he did miserably, and by art study, which he enjoyed very much. Norris attended, first, the San Francisco Art Association, then the Atelier Julien in Paris. He learned more French than art but came home after two years with a frock coat, sideburns, and what used to be called "Old World manners."

Entering the University of California in Berkeley in 1890, Frank survived four years to Jack London's scant semester but did not graduate. He enjoyed only reading and writing and could not abide mathematics. The detached, reserved

Norris was liked—if hardly understood—by his classmates, and the "Fijis" (Phi Gamma Delta brothers) remained among his best friends for the rest of his life. He had long been enamored of the feudal period in Europe, and he got the passion out of his system by writing a Sir Walter Scott-like narrative poem. While still at Cal, he contributed material to the *Wave,* the *Argonaut,* and the *Overland Monthly,* as well as to campus magazines. He also began his magnum opus, the novel which he titled *McTeague,* but he had to take the still-unfinished manuscript East when he went to Harvard for a year in order to really learn how to write.

At this stage, Norris was almost equally influenced by Richard Harding Davis, Rudyard Kipling, and Emile Zola. Eventually, Zola would win and Norris would be called an American Zola. He was, indeed, a pioneer of the realistic or naturalistic novel in America but preferred to think of his work as a kind of blend of romanticism and realism. Since he was an incurable optimist, Norris *has* to be the most romantic of all naturalistic novelists, although his pet theme was the beast lurking beneath the veneer of civilized man and although his novel *Vandover and the Brute* was so cruelly realistic that it could not be published until twelve years after his death.

Norris always valued experience over knowledge. His credo was "Life is better than literature." He tried to live his stories before writing them, so, in order to gain experience, he went to South Africa as a correspondent for the San Francisco *Chronicle.* He was just in time to be in the thick of things in Johannesburg during the Jameson Raid fiasco. He was hustled out of the country by the Boers, almost dead from fever. (Later, he would see the shocking bloodiness of war as a correspondent in Cuba during the Spanish-American War.) Norris felt these adventures to be necessary; he felt it much more important to *feel* than merely to *know*.

Back in San Francisco, he joined the *Wave,* a Southern Pacific Railroad publicity sheet which plugged the pleasures of the S.P.'s posh Del Monte Hotel. But under the editorship of John O'Hara Cosgrave, the *Wave* got out of hand and became a literary rival of the *Argonaut, Wasp,* and *Overland Monthly.* Gelett Burgess, author of *The Purple Cow,* likened Frank Norris to a fine painter at this period and described his contributions to the *Wave* as "the studio sketches of a novelist."

During the spring of 1897, Frank Norris suffered from an enormous mental block; he felt written-out. Burgess had to take over his chores on the *Wave.* But it was a very brief lapse. He was soon back to work and his fame began to climb. Norris's adventure story (anticipating Jack London's yarns), *Moran of the Lady Letty,* was run as a serial in the *Wave.* It caught the attention of S. S. McClure in New York, and he published it as a book which the dean of American letters, William Dean Howells, praised publicly. Norris's autobiographical novel, *Blix,* based on his courtship of Jeannette Black, was a modest success, and, finally, his most powerful work, *McTeague,* was published although the general public, still on a diet of literary pabulum, was ill-prepared for its raw realism. Still, critics recognized it as a major American novel.

Norris began a trilogy, *The Epic of the Wheat.* The first novel of this series was *The Octopus.* It was quickly adopted by the muckrakers as an attack on the monopolistic Southern Pacific Railroad, which ran California. But this it was not, said Norris, who believed that polemic or propaganda in a novel would wreck it as a work of art. He was obdurate about this and said of *"The Squid,"* as he nicknamed the novel, that he was a detached storyteller, not an involved reformer. "Suffering must be for him [the writer] a matter of the mildest interest. . . . The working out of the *story,* its people, episodes, scenes, and pictures is for the moment the most interesting thing in all the world to him, exclusive of everything else."

With nationwide fame his now, Frank Norris spent more time in the East and in travel. He became a reader, or editor, for Doubleday, Page and discovered Theodore Dreiser and *Sister Carrie.* Meanwhile, Norris finished the second of his wheaten novels, *The Pit,* about the Chicago wheat exchange. Although it was a good book and sold very well, it was not as fine a novel as *McTeague* or *The Octopus.* He was struggling with the last of the three novels, tentatively titled *The Wolf,* when he was stricken with appendicitis and died, October 25, 1902, only thirty-two years of age.

Not only did Frank Norris die tragically young, in a sense he never grew up. He refused to abandon childhood and its magic, entirely, for the jaded, hemmed-in world of adults. This, he felt, was the secret of his gift for effective writing— that is, storytelling. "Within the heart of every mature human being . . . there is the withered remains of a little story-teller who died very young," he claimed. "But, sometimes, the little story-teller does not die but lives on and grows with the man . . . [who] shall find a joy in the mere rising of the sun, a wholesome, sane, delight in the sound of the wind at night, and a pleasure in the sight of the hills at evening, shall find God in a little child and a whole religion in a brooding bird."

Although he wrote about Chicago and Caney Hill and the Witwatersrand, Frank Norris was essentially a San Francisco writer. He identified completely with the city, saying "There are just three cities in the United States that are 'story cities' —New York, of course, New Orleans, and, best of all, San Francisco." The handsome, dark-skinned, and prematurely gray

Norris once asked in a *Wave* article, "Who shall be our Kipling? Where is the man that shall get at the heart of us, that shall go a-gunning for stories up and down our streets and into our houses and parlors and lodging houses and saloons and secretest chambers of our homes as well as our hearts?"

The answer, of course, was the questioner—Frank Norris. It was *he* who took dentist McTeague's ordinary residential-shopping street in San Francisco's Polk Gulch and, via the sorcery of his creativity, transformed it into as fascinating a milieu as any *arrondissement* of literary Paris.

EMPEROR NORTON

(*1819–80*)

Joshua Norton, self-proclaimed Emperor Norton I, has been adopted by Californians—or, at least, by San Franciscans —as a kind of historical mascot. He was only one of many eccentrics of the nineteenth-century scene, but was more interesting than the others and played his role with much more lunatic style than his peers.

He was born Joshua A. Norton in London on February 4, 1819. Before he reached California he put in some time at Algoa Bay, South Africa, near the Cape of Good Hope. The story that he was a member of the Cape Mounted Riflemen may be true because he was, briefly, a member of San Francisco's ante-bellum Highland militia unit (complete with kilts and pipes), the Wallace Guards.

Norton reached San Francisco via Rio de Janeiro in December of 1849 and entered into real estate speculation and import-commission plunging. He was a shrewd businessman, no doubt about it. By the end of 1853 he had run his initial nest egg of forty thousand dollars up to one of ostrich-like proportions, possibly a quarter of a million dollars. Apparently beset with the urge to become a millionaire, he decided to corner the entire California rice market. Soon, he held an enormous quantity of the thirty-six-cent-a-pound grain and was nearing his monetary goal. At that moment, not one but *two* sailing ships cargoed with rice entered the headlands. Prices fell below cost; the rice market crashed, taking related investments with it in domino fashion. Despite extensive litigation Norton was unable to collect major debts which might have saved him, and he had to sacrifice his real estate holdings. Almost overnight, he was ruined.

The shock of the financial disaster unbalanced Joshua Norton's mind. In his despondency, he disappeared for a time but re-emerged in 1857 with an entirely new personality. He was now as crazy as a Damariscotta loon. Obsessed with the idea that he had been Emperor of California and was now Emperor of the United States, Norton I began to issue handwritten imperial proclamations, an example of which may be seen in San Francisco's Sutro Library. By 1859, they were being printed. Friendly printers obliged His Majesty by running off money for him, too. Actually, it was script payable in 1880 "by the agents of our Private Estate, in case the Government of Norton the First does not hold firm." The City Directory now went along with the joke and listed the greed-crippled ex-merchant as "Norton, Joshua (Emperor), dwl. Metropolitan Hotel." When some wag suggested that Mexico was in bad shape and needed his attention, Emperor Norton extended his title to Protector of Mexico.

The mad Emperor anticipated the Civil War. One of his 1860 proclamations dissolved the Union. Early in the war he declared a blockade of the Rebel coast. (When the California Steam Navigation Company refused to humor Norton by providing free transportation to the Capital during the legislative session of 1866, he ordered the commander of the revenue cutter *Shubrick,* in San Francisco Bay, to blockade the Sacramento River, too, until the company should come to terms.)

Jokers probably invented some of the documents now attributed to Norton as well as those sent to him, such as the telegram from Confederate President Jeff Davis, asking for five hundred dollars so that he could buy a pair of trousers since he was down to one worn-out pair of pants. Another wire, supposedly from President Lincoln, instructed Emperor Norton to repair to Petaluma and to wait there for further orders.

In both his mad periods and his moments of lucidity, Emperor Norton got along tolerably well with everyone except Stellifer the King, a rival Guardian of Mexico, and the dangerous demagogue Denis Kearney. There were those who wished that the Emperor had ordered the sand-lot Caesar banished and that, for once, a Nortonian edict might have been carried out.

Emperor Norton's most famous gesture was his proclamation of August 18, 1869, commanding that bridges be built across San Fancisco Bay. "Preposterous!" said the wise men. Crazy as a fox, the Emperor wanted San Francisco tied to the overland railroad before Stanford and Huntington erected their Chinese Wall around the Oakland waterfront. His plan, of course, anticipated the San Francisco-Oakland Bay Bridge, although Norton would have run it from Hunter's Point to Alameda, rather than from Rincon Hill to Oakland via Yerba Buena Island.

The Emperor cut a rather striking appearance on Frisco's streets in his navy-blue uniform decorated with brass buttons and gilt epaulets. He first wore a military kepi similar to the "Sherman's bummer" of the Civil War but later replaced it with a splendid, tall beaver decorated with a rosette and a feather cockade. An admirer gave him a walking stick fashioned of an Oregon grapevine, and this became his twisted scepter. Like any good ex-Briton, he also carried a brolly during inclement weather, too. With his imperial mustache and beard, he resembled a shabby Napoleon III. He was forever gracing public gatherings, poking about schools and churches, bumming meals from one end of town to the other. Credit was seldom refused him, for his demands were not many. He did not drink but "commanded" free lunches at such popular saloons as Barry & Patten's and the Bank Exchange. Mostly, he strolled about his domain, surveying the city's unending street repairs and the hustle-bustle of the Embarcadero docks. Although he must have been something of a bore, Norton was wise enough never to pester his subjects; he did not make a nuisance of himself. For that reason he was not only tolerated but petted by the city.

Bummer and Lazarus are often described as Emperor Norton's retainers. They were not. They were free and independent; although they occasionally followed him in his rounds, they also attached themselves to other street characters or meandered on their own. Bummer was a dog of unknown ancestry but possessed of pride; Lazarus, of equally feeble genealogy, was a groveling cur under Bummer's protection. Local historians have made them into canine Sancho Panzas to the Quixotic imperialist, but they were not. They were merely acquaintances, hardly even friends. They eventually enjoyed obituaries (including one by Mark Twain), mock funerals, and stuffing by taxidermists.

The last practical joke played on Emperor Norton by San Francisco's scamps was to convince him that he should marry Queen Victoria in order to tie his empire to the next most powerful, that of Great Britain. Soon, Norton was receiving telegrams of congratulations purportedly from President Grant, Czar Alexander of Russia, Lord Beaconsfield, and Jules Grévy, President of France.

Norton died suddenly of apoplexy while standing on the corner of California Street and Grant Avenue on January 8, 1880. He was given a fine funeral at the Morgue and some ten thousand people paid their last respects. He was buried in Masonic Cemetery, which was later obliterated, but in 1934 a memorial stone was ceremoniously erected in Woodlawn Cemetery.

Norton was a pathetic figure, crippled (mentally) by his avarice when only thirty-five years old. Yet he maintained a kind of serene, if shabby, dignity which was his saving grace. It set him apart from the legions of derelicts and loonies in San Francisco. He was a gentle man who, when once taken into custody as a lunatic, was released with these words: "He has shed no blood, robbed no one, and despoiled no country."

JASPER O'FARRELL

(*1817–75*)

Atypical of Irish pioneers in the West was Jasper O'Farrell. For one thing, he was no peat-bogger driven to America by the Potato Famine of 1848. By that year, he was seven years in California and known, far and wide, as Gaspar O'Farrol among Mexican-Californians. He was not a so-called shanty Irishman but a lace-curtain Irishman. (By definition, these were folk who had flowers in the house even when nobody was dead.) Like J. Ross Browne, he was a Dubliner and "a gent." O'Farrell was also well educated in terms of *any* early arrival on the California scene, having been trained in civil engineering in the old country. He was so fluent in Spanish that not only gringos sought him out for accurate translations of Spanish documents but even General Vallejo himself asked his aid in handling legal documents in translation. While he did not eschew politics entirely, neither did he claw and scratch his way to prominence like David Broderick nor use the bluster and even fisticuffs which passed for statesmanship in Tammany-West 120 years ago. He was honest; he was an intellectual; he was an engineer. In a rural California short on skilled men, Don Gaspar was thrice-blessed.

Not ordinarily considered today to have been one of the stars of first magnitude in California's past, he was classed by H. H. Bancroft as one of the most prominent men to arrive in the state before '49. Since he was a professional man rather than a fortune-hunter or glory seeker, he has been somewhat neglected by antiquarians of Californiana as well as by their properly credentialed historiographical kin of academia. Yet many of the lines which he laid down on the land and on parchment and paper are matters of record, today, in California county courthouses. O'Farrell brought *some* order, at least, out of a chaos of property lines, conflicting claims, squatter's rights, and outright land frauds.

Jasper O'Farrell was born in 1817 in Wexford County, Ireland. There is a story that he was a cooper on a Yankee whaler who jumped ship in Sausalito, California, in 1843, but it appears that he was really a member of a British surveying expedition in South America in 1841 and sailed from Valparaíso to San Francisco or Sausalito via Mazatlán, arriving on October 20, 1843, aboard a U.S. coast survey vessel. By 1844 and 1845 his talents as surveyor and engineer made him essential to the government of California. He was distracted from his work by John Sutter's march to the relief of Governor Micheltorena in 1844. The bitterness of this taste of a military career—O'Farrell was quartermaster of Sutter's tight little army—was enough for the Irishman for all time. He served Sutter in various ways, including the laying out of the ditch from the American River to the fort, but decided to pick up the scattered pieces of his old career in 1846. When Colonel R. B. Mason, Military Governor of California appointed three official surveyors to adjust land disputes, O'Farrell was one of them, with an office on Portsmouth Square in San Francisco.

The Irishman made extensive maps of Sonoma County,

and, it is said, he was allowed one out of every twenty sections of land which he laid off. He found much unsurveyed and unclaimed land lying between the crudely drawn boundaries of the Mexican *diseños,* or sketch maps of record. These *sobrante* lands were often quite valuable. When Washington A. Bartlett was appointed first American alcalde of San Francisco (still called Yerba Buena in 1847) he employed Jasper and two associates to update and extend the original 1839 survey. O'Farrell quickly discovered that the streets did not intersect at right angles. He corrected the two-and-a-half-degree error by rerunning the east-west streets in what came to be called "O'Farrell's Swing." He extended the survey to Taylor Street and North Beach and laid out the South of Market district. The alcalde and his *Ayuntamiento,* or City Council, honored the surveyor by naming O'Farrell Street for him. In terms of more palpable rewards, the Irishman was slighted. Though he was promised an ounce of gold (sixteen dollars) for every fifty *varas* he surveyed, there was not enough money in the city treasury nor lots enough at Bartlett's disposal to sell in order to cancel the debt. It is believed that O'Farrell had to write off a considerable portion of his bill "to experience."

In June of 1847, Jasper O'Farrell was one of an eleven-man committee of prominent citizens who circulated a petition to the President of the United States protesting the appointment of John C. Frémont as governor. O'Farrell had been a witness to the shooting of unarmed José Beryessa and the De Haro twins, Ramón and Francisco. Don Gaspar never forgot and he never forgave Frémont, at whose orders the three Californians were murdered at San Rafael in 1846: "I feel degraded," he wrote, "in soiling paper with the name of the man whom, for that act, I must always look upon with contempt, and consider as a murderer and a coward."

When the military governor, Stephen Watts Kearny, granted, by decree, all beach and water lots between Rincon Point and Telegraph Hill to the city of San Francisco, the new alcalde, Edwin Bryant, ordered them surveyed and chose O'Farrell to do the job. In San Francisco today, O'Farrell is remembered with mixed emotions. He is cursed for laying Market Street out on a bias so that the streets to the south of it do not intersect with the old cross-streets to the north. This has played hob with traffic ever since. On the other hand, he ran Market from the Embarcadero's Ferry Building to Twin Peaks and made the thoroughfare so wide (broader than Manhattan's Broadway) that the street has been able to adjust to heavy horse-drawn traffic, four-abreast streetcars, fleets of buses, and massed automobiles. It would seem that O'Farrell had prescience and foresaw the colorful California custom of double-parking and even anticipated the need for room to burrow a Bart subway tunnel under Market Street in the 1960's. In short, O'Farrell was San Francisco's first (unrecognized) city planner, even if he had to flee a mob, indignant because he had wasted so much good Happy Valley property (in which they might have speculated) in his 120-foot-wide avenue. But O'Farrell had dreams of San Francisco's future and, as early as 1847, was referring to it as "the Empire City of the Pacific."

In 1846 O'Farrell married. He traded his Marin County property near San Rafael for the Cañada de Jonive Rancho near today's Sebastopol in 1848, added the adjacent Estero Americano Rancho near Dillon's Beach, and bought a nine-square-league ranch in Yolo County's Sacramento Valley. This huge Rancho del Capay transformed O'Farrell into a landed gentleman with sixty thousand acres to play with. He surveyed the sites of Vallejo, Martinez, and Benicia, too, but did not invest in that Carquinez Valley area. In 1848, with three partners, he carried on the first Yuba River gold mining and the quartet netted seventy-five thousand dollars in three months. But the miner's life was not a happy one for O'Farrell, and he returned to his Analy Ranch, at Freestone, named for the old Analy patrimony of the O'Farrells in Ireland, now Longford. He lived quietly at his home ranch for ten years, imitating his onetime employer, John Sutter, and was often strapped for cash with the house full of hungry visitors with no homes or incomes of their own.

O'Farrell allowed himself to be elected to the Legislature in 1858 as state senator from Sonoma and Mendocino counties and was a member of the State Board of Harbor Commissioners in San Francisco. He ran for lieutenant governor on the Breckenridge Democrat ticket in 1861 but lost out to Republican John F. Chellis as the Democrats fractured in the face of civil war tremors. (O'Farrell got 32,356 votes but ran third, trailing the Union Democrat candidate as well as the winner.) He retired from politics and lived quietly at Analy. In San Francisco on November 16, 1875, he died suddenly of a heart seizure.

If Jasper O'Farrell was an unusual Irish emigrant, perhaps he was the first typical Californian. Always torn between city and country, he resembles many commuting Californians of today. He made his reputation and acquired a considerable part of his wealth because of his urban surveys and his political offices, yet he ran the meets and bounds of rural lands, too, and was such a successful cattle rancher at Estero Americano that, to protect himself, he recorded his brand with authorities in Los Angeles, to which his rustled cattle were being driven more than four hundred miles away. O'Farrell died in the city but he lived in the country. Although he was a cultured gentleman with a reputation for kindness, geniality, and good humor, the merest glance at his photograph suggests a rugged dog lover, an outdoorsman completely at home with rifle, Colt, and bowie knife—no man to trifle with.

JAMES F. REED

(1800–74)

Gravelly Ford lies in Nevada's bleak Humboldt River Valley a half-dozen miles south of U.S. 40 between Elko and Winnemucca. Hardly a tourist attraction, it nevertheless pulls a small number of traveling history buffs to it, via Beowawe, in the mistaken belief that their detour has brought them to a historic site. Even the WPA Guide to Nevada suggests that the most fascinating subplot of the bizarre Donner Party story began here. Actually, the true site lies lost somewhere ahead on a mountain slope, probably near Golconda, east of Winnemucca.

James Frazier Reed, the protagonist of this story-within-a-story, was born in County Armagh, Northern Ireland, on November 14, 1800. He was from the start a major figure in the Donner Party. In fact, it was organized in Illinois as the Reed and Donner Emigrant Party. He was well to do and owned several wagons, including one huge, luxurious vehicle in which his ailing wife, Margaret, traveled with her aged mother until the latter died near the Big Blue River in Kansas. Although his diary reveals him to have been a poor speller,

Reed was no émigré bogtrotter but a real gentleman with aristocratic Polish blood (Reednowski) in his ancestry.

At least two days beyond Gravelly Ford, he began to play a major role in Act II of the unfolding drama. Act I had set the scene with the party's disastrous choice of Lansford Hasting's Cutoff across the Wasatch Mountains and Salt Desert —a "shortcut" which depleted their strength and provisions and threw them so far behind schedule that Reed knew they would feel the lash of wind-blown snow in their faces as they climbed the Sierra. Act III, of course, would become a nightmarish, Grand Guignol horror of cannibalism practiced upon those who died of starvation.

Had leadership passed from patriarchal but inept George Donner to Reed, California's classic tragedy might have been averted. But somewhere west of Gravelly Ford, Chance intervened to rule Reed out of any possibility of command at the same time that it sealed the fate of the Donner Party.

The strain was telling on the once-unified group by October 5, 1846, when the second section of the party, now split in more ways than one, reached a sandy hill covered with rocks at its top. It was no worse than many similar obstacles already overcome, and two double-teamed vehicles made it to the top without difficulty. But the driver of the third wagon, handsome young John Snyder, tried to make it without extra animals. Thinking that he was giving up, Reed's teamster, Milt Elliott, swung wide to pass him. Unfortunately, the lead yoke became entangled with Snyder's and soon, for little reason, the young man was in a fury, firing sharp words at Elliott and beating Reed's oxen violently over their heads with his whip.

When Reed rushed forward to protect his animals—upon which the very lives of his wife and children depended—and to pacify Snyder, he failed. When he suggested that they settle the argument atop the hill, the younger man retorted, "We will settle it now!" He then cursed Reed and offered to give him a hiding, too. Not about to accept a beating from anyone, James Reed drew his sheath knife to protect himself. Suddenly fearful, Snyder reversed his whip and struck the Irishman on the head with its heavy butt, cutting a long gash. When Mrs. Reed tried to intervene, Snyder struck her with the whipstock and then hit Reed twice more, knocking him to his knees. But not before Reed dodged and, blinded by blood, struck with his knife. It sank home in Snyder's chest. He staggered a few steps and said, "I am dead," as someone eased him to the ground.

Reed, covered with gore, was beside himself with remorse. He pulled away when his wife and daughter tried to treat his wounds, threw the knife away, and knelt beside the dying man. Some say Snyder forgave him, whispering, "I am to blame." Whatever the case, friends of the once merry and popular Snyder cried for revenge. Camp was immediately made and a tribunal formed. Only W. H. Eddy and Elliott stood by Reed, but the former won a compromise, disappointing Lewis Keseberg, who had propped up his wagon tongue on an ox yoke for a gibbet. (He hated Reed. The wife-beating German had robbed an Indian grave—thereby endangering the whole party—and Reed had caused his temporary exile as punishment.) Instead of being lynched, Reed was banished. He refused to comply until Eddy promised to look after his family and reminded him that he could speed relief measures to the main party, too, by going ahead.

The bandaged Reed rode off unarmed (but someone caught up with him and gave him a gun and ammunition) and soon passed the Donners in the forward section. One of his teamsters, Walter Herron, now accompanied him, alternately walking and riding his horse, Glaucus. Finally, the once-magnificent mount could not even be saddled and Herron wanted to kill the mare for food, but Reed would not hear of it. With all food gone, Reed spied a single bean on the trail and gave it to the delirious Herron. Eyes glued to the trail, he finally found four more jolted from some wagon and he split them with his partner. Exploring some abandoned wagons, he found a tar bucket and, to his delight, discovered that it had once been a tallow pot. He scraped up a ball of tarry tallow and gave it to Herron. When he tried a little himself, he gagged and was so sick that his friend thought he was going to die. Somehow, the two staggered over the summit of the Sierra and down into Bear Valley, where they ran into C. T. Stanton, whom Reed and the Donners had sent ahead for help from Sutter's Fort. So worn was Reed that his friend at first failed to recognize him.

Although he was in awful shape ("so much exhausted by fatigue and famine that he could scarcely walk," reported witness Edwin Bryant), he volunteered at the fort for the Mexican War force Bryant was forming. Elected captain, he declined but accepted the lieutenancy with the proviso that he would first aid the Donner Party—and his own family—now surely trapped in the Sierra. With supplies given him by the generous Sutter, Reed floundered to the head of Bear Valley, but when the pack horses failed him and he was sinking into powdery snow up to his neck, he had to give up. Sutter advised him to get help in Yerba Buena (San Francisco) from the U. S. Navy and to try again in February, when the storms would die down and the snow would pack hard enough for animals and men to travel on it. After serving as lieutenant in another force in the Battle of Santa Clara, Reed was finally able to raise $1300 in San Francisco to relieve the Donner Party.

Between Washington's Birthday and March 1, Reed's party

made the difficult mountain march to Starvation Camp at Donner Lake behind an earlier relief party, which he met on its way back out. Reed spent the last night of his march baking bread for the adults and sweetened "cakes" for the children. He wrote in his diary, "Here I met with Mrs. Reed and two children; two [were] still in the mountains. I cannot describe the deathlike look they all had. 'Bread, bread, bread, bread!,' was the begging of every child and grown person. . . ."

Bidding his wife and children, Virginia and Jimmy, goodby, Reed pushed on to rescue Patty and Tommy, who had been too weak to leave the "starvation cabins." Distraught with worry, he set a pace which even the mountain men with him could not equal, and he traveled by night (when the snow was firmer) as well as by day. He reached the grisly huts on March 1 and saw Patty sitting on a cabin roof. She tried to run to him but was too weak and fell in the snow. He found Tommy, looking like a skeleton, in the cabin. The boy did not know him and cried for Patty.

James Reed and his men hurriedly fed and washed the starving survivors and cleaned the filthy cabins. Then, afraid that the spell of good weather would break, he hurried out those who were able to walk—three adults and fourteen children. But he was caught in a vicious storm on the headwaters of the Yuba River. On March 6, 1847, Reed had a premonition of death and wrote in his diary, "I dread the coming night." Fatigue and cold finally won out, and the snowblinded Reed sank into a coma. The fire, atop green logs now deep in a hole melted in the snow, almost went out. But luckily for Reed and his charges, the Donner story has more heroes (Stanton, Eddy, McCutchen) than villains (Keseberg, Jean Baptiste), and McCutchen saved the fire and revived Reed.

Next day, with his sight restored, Reed took those who were able to move, sadly leaving the others in the hole with three days' supply of fuel. Cursing the soul of Passed Midshipman Selim Woodworth, who had promised to meet him with supplies and who failed him utterly, Reed set out. Patty rode on his back, warmed by his body heat. All the gruel was gone, and when McCutchen said to him, "Why, Reed, Patty is dying," he gave her the absurd "supply" of emergency rations he carried—a spoonful of crumbs in the thumb of his mitten. He had picked them from the seams of the empty food bags. The party slogged onward, their frozen and split feet leaving a bloody trail in the snow.

Eddy finally got the dillydallying midshipman to move, and Reed ran into the belated back-up party, at last, near Bear Valley. He had won. Other parties now could complete the rescue of the still-trapped survivors; the exile had more than done his part. Forty-two men, women, and children had died in the mountains and forty-seven had survived. (It was almost forty-three dead, for Reed had to stop Eddy from shooting the bestial Keseberg when the details of his cannibalism became known.) But all of Reed's family miraculously survived.

Like all of the Donner Party survivors, Reed was destined to a life of anticlimax after 1847. But he lived a long and rich life, prospering in the San Jose area before his death in 1874. He became no giant of commerce or politics; Reed's contribution to the story of California was his heroic example of courage, fortitude, family devotion, and compassion for others. This compassion extended even to the vile Keseberg, whom he forgave and washed and fed at Starvation Camp although the German was so ashamed that he begged for someone else to help him rather than the man whom he had wanted to hang near Gravelly Ford.

JEDEDIAH SMITH

(*1799–1831*)

Most of the fur-trapping gentry who ventured into California a century and more ago were a scruffy lot of illiterate squawmen, of the ilk of Caleb Greenwood or Jim Beckwourth. They were closer to Indian society than to Euro-American civilization. Possibly for this reason, a more literate, God-fearing, and relatively clean-cut mountain man has tended to be canonized by his partisans even more than John Sutter. Surely, no other mountain man has a fan club of the prestige of the Jedediah Smith Society, headquartered at the University of the Pacific, in Stockton, California.

Jed Smith is deserving of considerable praise. Not only was he a more respectable mountaineer than any other, he was a better businessman and organizer. Because of his intellect and interests, he was, too, the Pathfinder that John C. Frémont wishfully thought himself to be. Locally in California, he explored the Mojave Desert, Tehachapi Mountains, San Joaquin and Sacramento valleys, and was the first to explore the Sierra, the Redwood Coast ranges, the Trinity Mountains, and the Siskiyou Mountains of the Oregon-California border. More important, by his example he proved the feasibility of overland migration to California and, ten years after his death, the wagons began to roll westward from Missouri, bound for "Californy."

But Jedediah was not as perfect as his partisans would have you believe. He had one great weakness in his make-up. On the frontier, it was a cardinal sin. Jedediah Smith was careless. He tended to stretch his luck too far. For this, he paid in men and goods, heavily, on his California expeditions. Eventually, he paid with his own life.

Born in the Susquehanna Valley of New York on January 6, 1799, Smith was in command of such first-rank mountain men as Tom (Broken Hand) Fitzpatrick, William Sublette, and Jim Clyman by the time he was twenty-four years old. By the time he was twenty-seven, he was the senior partner in the fur-trading firm of Smith, Jackson and Sublette. Being of a more inquiring mind than most of his peers, Jed was not content with the profits of the fur business. He liked to see what lay over each consecutive western horizon. So, in 1826, he set out to lead a party from the Great Salt Lake to the even greater salt "lake" of Indian legend, the Pacific Ocean. En route, he hoped to fall in with the river which legend said was a rival of the Columbia. This was the fabled Buenaventura, about as real as the Strait of Anián.

Smith and his sixteen men crossed the deserts safely, although they lost thirty-two of their fifty horses. They reached the Colorado River on October 24, 1826, and passed into California, where, at Mission San Gabriel, Father José Bernardo Sánchez received them hospitably. However, the half-starved *yanquis* would have been thrown into prison by Governor José María Echeandía had not several American shipmasters in port interceded in Smith's behalf. The governor let the interloper pass through Alta California after he agreed to return to the United States via the route by which he had come. Jedediah Smith started to retrace his steps by going eastward through Cajon Pass. But he did not like the looks of the Mojave Desert any more than his men did, so he skirted it and swung back into California proper by crossing the Tehachapis and dropping into the San Joaquin Valley. He passed up the valley, then a tule-clogged swamp, looking for a break in the wall of mountains to the east. Early in the spring of 1827, he attempted a crossing but was turned back by snow. Taking two men, and leaving the rest at a camp on the Stanislaus River due east of San Francisco Bay, he again assaulted California's alps and after eight days of effort succeeded. He led his men across the basin and range country, the sandy desert, and the parching salt flats of Nevada and Utah and reached the Bear Lake rendezvous of the fur men, where he rejoined his partners, Bill Sublette and Dave Jackson.

The impatient Smith was unimpressed with his exploit and after only ten days of rest started back for California with eighteen men. He reached the Colorado River safely but found the Mojave Indians quite hostile. Incredibly, the veteran mountain man let the Mojaves catch his force while it was split in two by the river. On August 18, 1827, the Indians ambushed him and killed ten of his eighteen men with clubs and knives, not even needing their fearful poisoned arrows. After suffering greatly in the Mojave Desert, for the raiding Indians stole all of his stock, Smith led the other survivors into the Stanislaus camp.

Unwisely, he visited Mission San José and was locked up. But Governor Echeandía finally consented to his leaving after Smith signed a bond and promised to leave for Oregon, pronto. Selling most of his pelts to sea captains, Smith transformed his profits into a fine herd of about three hundred California mustangs, much in demand in the Rockies. Then

Smith tore himself away from the San Francisco Bay Area, which he found "fine, pleasingly varied by prairie and woodland . . . the soil excellent and the situation combining many advantages at the same time; most delightful and pleasant." He explored his way northward along the Sacramento River, which he pronounced the Buenaventura. At the head of the Sacramento Valley, he led his men across the Trinity Alps to the Redwood Coast. By Bastille Day of 1828, he was on the Umpqua River in southwest Oregon. Having apparently learned little from experience, he let his defensive posture lapse just as he had on the Colorado. While he was away, with two companions, a Kelawatsets war party wiped out fifteen of the sixteen men in his camp. Smith and the three other survivors of his South West Expedition (as it came to be called) headed for the safety of the Hudson's Bay Company post at Fort Vancouver. Dr. John McLoughlin, in charge there, treated him well and, soon, he was back in the Rockies and, in 1830, in St. Louis.

Doubtless, Jedediah intended to return to California. The gold discovery would have attracted him like a magnet even if fur trapping there was not as profitable as in the Rocky Mountain region. But in 1831, Jedediah Smith made the third careless blunder of his career. It was his last. Forgetting the consequences of such rash action, he ventured ahead of his party on the Santa Fe Trail when water became short. Alone on the hell-fired stretch of desert between the Arkansas and Cimarron rivers, he was ambushed by Comanches lying in wait at a water hole. The luck of Jedediah Smith, aged thirty-two, the first—and greatest—of all the pathfinders that California would see, ran out on May 27, 1831, with his life's blood, on the sandy plains of the upper Cimarron.

LELAND STANFORD

(1824–93)

Although engineer Theodore D. (Crazy) Judah liked to refer, paternalistically, to the Central Pacific as "my little road," the railway in reality was the baby of four others, foster parents who never gave the line's natural father his due but who transformed it into the Southern Pacific, themselves into multimillionaires, and the State of California into their political fief. These tycoons composed the legendary Big Four —Leland Stanford, Collis P. Huntington, Mark Hopkins, and Charles Crocker.

Few casual students of Western history have been able to sort out, biographically, this seemingly tightly knit foursome who all, at one time or another, claimed the primary responsibility for building the railroad over the Sierra to tie California to the U.S.A. It took Oscar Lewis and his brilliant book, *The Big Four,* to do the trick. A close study of Judah's successors reveals that two of them were really minor characters in the long-run drama of California railroading and the "Octopus," as the Southern Pacific came to be called.

Only Huntington was a true *giant* of California history. Crocker was a sort of superforeman who egged his coolies into great feats of construction. They laid a world's record of ten miles of track in one day, for example. As a man of action, however, Crocker faded once the actual building of the road was accomplished. The kindly, easygoing, "Uncle" Mark Hopkins lacked the drive of either Stanford or Huntington and phased himself out of power. But if Crocker was an uncouth blusterer and Hopkins an inoffensive duffer, what of Leland Stanford?

President Ray Lyman Wilbur of Stanford University, predictably, considered him a great man, an outstanding American pioneer. His partner and eventual enemy, Huntington, called him a damned fool who did nothing for the railroad between 1863, when he turned the first shovelful of earth, and 1869, when he drove the last spike. But, of course, anyone who disagreed with C.P. was a fool in the latter's book, and Stanford's political influence and public relations efforts were invaluable to the success of the great railroad project. Because of his pomposity and ponderous affability and vanity, Stanford has been written off by many biographers and historians as a mere figurehead for the railroad corporation. Certainly he lacked Huntington's ability as well as the latter's ruthlessness and business cunning. It is altogether possible that most of his leadership was mere role-playing. Oscar Lewis, for example, is convinced that Stanford spent thirty years in self-justification, content with seeming success rather than the real thing. One critic described him as possessing "the ambition of an emperor and the spite of a peanut vendor."

But Stanford had some good points; he was not just a huge 220-pound shell of a man. He tried, but failed, to convince his partners of the superiority of steam drills over pickaxes in digging the railroad's tunnels in the Sierra. (He was shortly proved to be right.) His devotion to his son was touching, and his choice of a memorial to the boy, dead of typhoid at fifteen years, was splendid. His services as California's Civil War governor were considerable. He personified the Central Pacific project. Although he was a dull and ponderous speaker and helpless without notes, Stanford's rare ad libs were sometimes revelatory of the reasoning human being behind the façade of vainglory. He once said, "It is pleasant to be rich. But the advantages of wealth are greatly exaggerated," and "If it rained $20 gold pieces until noon every day, at night there would be some men begging for their suppers." Another time, he told David Starr Jordan, president of Stanford University, "I learn every year more and more to love the landscape, and this the poorest man in California can enjoy as well as the richest."

The seemingly banal businessman-politician whose name nevertheless still looms large in California was born like so many Far Westerners (Jedediah Smith, Marcus Whitman, Jim Hume, William Fargo, and Mark Hopkins) in upstate New York. A farm near Watervliet was Stanford's birthplace, on March 9, 1824. He never used his first name, Amasa, making do with his middle name, Leland, all of his life. Although he attended Cazenovia Seminary, he did not excel as a student, nor did he graduate. But he managed to hang up his shingle as a Port Washington, Wisconsin, lawyer in his twenties. When his law office burned down, he took it as an omen and joined his five brothers, who were California mercantile men. Arriving on the Coast in 1852, poor as a parson, he was soon a prosperous grocer of the mining town of Michigan Bluff.

Unlike C. P. Huntington, who detested politics, Stanford became very active in the new Republican Party, running for state treasurer in 1857 and for governor in 1859 and being whipped on both occasions. He was again the gubernatorial candidate of Lincoln's party in 1861 and this time won over two Democratic rivals. Besides the split in the opposition, Stanford had personal popularity going for him. (His record of public service was nil except for a stint as justice of the peace in Michigan Bluff.)

To the considerable surprise of many, he performed fairly well in the governor's chair. During his term, agricultural and manufacturing ventures were subsidized by the Legislature; forest-conservation measures were enacted; savings and loan associations authorized. Stanford lent his support to bills aiding the building of a railroad eastward over the Sierra, of course, since he was the president of the Central Pacific. (In the Gilded Age and before, the concept of "conflict of interest" was as yet unborn.) Most important of all, he used the prestige of his office to hold California firmly in the Union. He was much more of a dedicated "Loyalist" than his predecessor, Governor Downey, and really meant what he said when he telegraphed President Lincoln over the newly completed line in October 1861: "Today California is but a second's distance from the national capital. Her patriotism with electric current throbs responsive to that of her sister states and holds civil liberty and union above all price." Despite floods, Indian raids, and Copperhead cabals, he kept California peaceful and loyal during the stormy Civil War years. This was, without a doubt, his greatest personal achievement.

When his two-year term ended, Stanford did not run as an incumbent but threw all of his energies into the struggle to get the railroad over the mountains and to a junction with the Union Pacific, which was building its way westward. He remained president and director of the Central Pacific from its founding until his death, returning to politics only as U.S. senator in 1885. While Huntington dug up money and equipment in the East, Stanford won support for the line as its spokesman in the West. It was Stanford who was chosen to drive the last spike into a special laurel tie at Promontory Point, Utah, when the rails of the two roads met on May 10, 1869. The ex-governor swung his silver sledge hammer but missed the golden spike. Telegraph keys flashed the official word of completion, nevertheless, and cannon boomed and fire bells clanged from coast to coast while T. C. Durant, vice president of the Union Pacific, drove the spike home.

Stanford shared in the phenomenal growth of the Central Pacific, the Southern Pacific, and its holding company. But, unlike Huntington, he had other interests than business. Not only did he and his wife travel, and entertain in their Nob Hill mansion; he bought a vineyard in the Sacramento Valley so that he might produce fine brandy; bred superior race horses on his Palo Alto farm; and even helped Eadweard Muybridge with his experiments in motion-picture photography.

With the death of his son, the millionaire and his wife devoted themselves to the boy's memorial, Stanford University. Founded in 1885, the campus opened in 1891 in the face of predictions that the professors at his "Circus" (as Huntington dubbed the university) would "lecture to empty benches in marble halls." Although the university overtaxed even Stanford's fortune and back pay had to be doled out to professors twenty dollars at a time, Stanford University succeeded and became one of the country's great institutions of higher learning.

The long-delayed break between Stanford and Huntington came in 1884, when the ex-governor ran for senator against C.P.'s friend, A. A. Sargent. The falling-out worsened in 1890, when Huntington criticized Stanford's political activities and managed to replace him as president of the Southern Pacific Company. Eventually, Stanford was no longer on speaking terms with his old partner and joined the long queue of Huntington-haters.

Stanford died on June 21, 1893, but his widow continued his building up of the university. If his intellectual capacity was as modest as his slow speech suggested, his concern for prestige lopsided, and his leadership as nominal as Huntington's was real, at least he had limitless energy at the right time for the right projects—the state, the railroad, the university. He never subscribed completely to the Huntingtonian philosophy of "The public be damned!" as his gift of Stanford University to the people demonstrates. An ordinary man, to be sure, Leland Stanford was shocked out of his philistinism by his son's tragic death and into a campaign of philanthropy which raised him far above his fellow "railrogues" in the esteem of Californians.

ROBERT LOUIS STEVENSON

(*1850–94*)

Although a Scotsman to the marrow, born in Edinburgh in 1850, Robert Louis Stevenson, the last of the great romantics, fell in love with California during a brief stay of eleven months in 1879 and 1880. It was the decisive year of his life; during the period he not only married, and most happily, but he also reached maturity as a literary artist. The notes which Stevenson scribbled so religiously in San Francisco, Monterey, and Napa County were seminal not only to his American-theme works, as *The Amateur Emigrant* and *The Silverado Squatters,* but also to such books as *The Wrecker* and *Treasure Island.*

Although racked by ill-health and poverty, the gaunt, tubercular writer made the journeys across the Atlantic and the vast American continent in order to join in Monterey the woman with whom he had fallen in love during a vacation in France in 1876. Fanny Van de Grift Osbourne was not yet freed from an unhappy marriage to Sam Osbourne, but the sickly Stevenson could not bear being separated from her. He set out, impetuously—against the advice of family and friends—on August 7, 1879, and endured a ten-day passage to New York. Then came the long and boring ride in crowded emigrant cars of the transcontinental railroad to the Coast. By the end of this sentimental and interesting but wearing journey, Stevenson was ill and exhausted. But the peaks of the Sierra Nevada and the dashing waters and the green grass of the mountain slopes acted like a restorative on his spirits. The oppressive heat of the sun vanished with the arid monotony of the Great Plains and the Basin and range country of Utah and Nevada. He joined the other dirty and tired emigrants who, with shining eyes, threw off weariness to throng the car's platform as the locomotive pulled them through Dutch Flat. But the Gold Rush town was only a preview of golden California; most impressive to the Scot was San Francisco and its great inland sea: "Day was breaking as we crossed the ferry; the fog was rising over the citied hills of San Francisco; the bay was perfect—not a ripple, scarce a stain, upon its blue expanse; everything was waiting, breathless, for the sun. A spot of cloudy gold lit first upon the head of [Mount] Tamalpais and then widened downward on its shapely shoulder; the air seemed to awaken and began to sparkle and, suddenly, . . . the city of San Francisco and the bay of gold and corn were lit from end to end with summer daylight."

Sick and hungry as he was during most of the time he spent in Monterey, trying to live on a single, two-bit midday meal, Stevenson found Fanny's home town a lovely place and not only because of her presence. The surrounding countryside seemed made for his long, lonely walks, while the town welcomed him to its simple society. In fact survival itself was made possible for the impoverished writer by the charity of the kindly restaurateur Jules Simoneau, and Crevole Bronson, editor of the weekly Monterey *Californian,* who paid Stevenson what he could—two dollars a week—for his literary contributions.

Although conservation in California was still in the process of invention by John Muir when Stevenson lived in Monterey, the latter saw, even then, the danger of deforestation of the state by man and fire. In his essay *The Old and New Pacific Capitals* he sounded an early warning: "California has been a land of promise in its time, like Palestine, but if the woods continue so swiftly to perish, it may become, like Palestine, a land of desolation." He then painted a frightening word picture of the effects of fire on the torch-like Monterey pines: "The fire passes through the underbrush at a run. Every here and there a tree flares up instantaneously from root to summit, scattering tufts of flame, and is quenched, it seems, as quickly. But this last is only a semblance. For after this first squib-like conflagration of the dry moss and twigs, there remains behind a deep-rooted and consuming fire in the very entrails of the tree. The resin of the pitch-pine is principally condensed at the base of the bole and in the spreading roots. Thus, after the light, showy, skirmishing flames, which are only as the match to the explosion, have already scampered down the wind into the distance, the true harm is but beginning for this giant of the woods. You may approach the tree from one side and see it, scorched indeed from top to bottom, but apparently survivor of the peril. Make the circuit and there, on the other side of the column, is a clear mass of living coal, spreading like an ulcer; while underground, to their most extended fibre, the roots are being eaten out by fire, and the smoke is rising through the fissures to the surface. A little while and, without a nod of warning, the huge pine tree snaps off short across the ground and falls prostrate with a crash. Meanwhile, the fire continues its silent business; the roots are reduced to a fine ash and, long afterward, if you pass by, you will find the earth pierced with radiating galleries, and preserving the design of all these subterranean spurs, as though it were the mould for a new tree instead of the print of an old one."

R.L.S. and Fanny married in San Francisco on May 19, 1880, and went on a honeymoon to Calistoga, chaperoned, as it were, by Fanny's little boy, Lloyd. When the rent of a cottage there proved overtaxing to their slender resources, the trio moved to an abandoned miners' bunkhouse at the ghost town of Silverado, on the shoulder of Mount St. Helena. There they lived an arcadian existence during the summer of 1880, an idyl which was the heart of Stevenson's book *The Silverado Squatters.*

R.L.S. was a born literary stylist. But his earliest works were marked by a self-conscious structuring and floridity. During his California stay, he not only gathered local color but added strength and discipline to his writing in general. His subsequent works were less affected, epigrammatic, and more powerful and moving.

Exactly a year to the day after he sailed for America, Robert Louis Stevenson, Fanny, and Lloyd were on board ship for Scotland. There would be later chapters in Stevenson's life, titled Hawaii and, finally, Samoa (where he died, world famous, on December 3, 1894), but he would never forget California as long as he lived, and Californians have never forgotten the gifted and charming R.L.S.

It is, perhaps, unfair to single out a particular work of Stevenson's to treat as a watershed between literary apprenticeship and maturity. But, if we dare to do so, surely that work is the seemingly modest *The Silverado Squatters,* with its true-striking characterizations, its marvelous evocation of setting, and its magnificent use of that imperfect tool, the English language. The entire book is a delight, but a high point among many is Stevenson's description of Northern California's sea fog. Professor James D. Hart has, rightly, likened this descriptive tour de force to a Japanese print by Hiroshige or Hokusai:

"Napa Valley was gone; gone were all the lower slopes and woody foothills of the range; and in their place, not a thousand feet below me, rolled a great level ocean. It was as though I had gone to bed, the night before, safe in a nook of inland mountains and had awakened in a bay upon the coast. . . . Far away were the hill-tops like little islands. Nearer, a smoky surf beat about the foot of precipices and poured into all the coves of these rough mountains. The colour of that fog-ocean was a thing never to be forgotten. For an instant, among the Hebrides and just about sundown, I have seen something like it on the sea itself. But the white was not so opaline; nor was there, what surprisingly increased its effect, that breathless, crystal stillness over all. Even in its gentlest moods the salt sea travails, moaning among the weeds or lisping on the sand; but that vast fog-ocean lay in a trance of silence. . . .

"Away in the extreme south, a little hill of fog arose against the sky above the general surface, and as it had already caught the sun, it shone on the horizon like the topsails of some giant ship. There were huge waves, stationary, as it seemed, like waves in a frozen sea; and yet, as I looked again, I was not sure but that they were moving, after all, with a slow and august advance. And while I was yet doubting, a promontory of the hills some four or five miles away, conspicuous by a bouquet of tall pines, was in a single instant overtaken and swallowed up. It appeared, in a little, with its pines, but this time an islet, and only to be swallowed up once more, and then for good. . . .

"Through the Toll House gap and over the near ridges on the other side, the deluge was immense. A spray of thin vapour was thrown high above it, rising and falling, and blown into fantastic shapes. The speed of its course was like a mountain torrent. Here and there a few tree-tops were discovered and then whelmed again; and for one second the bough of a dead pine beckoned out of the spray like the arm of a drowning man. . . .

"The wind veered while we were at dinner, and began to blow squally from the mountain summit; and by half-past one all that world of sea-fogs was utterly routed and flying here and there into the south in little rags of cloud. And instead of a lone sea beach, we found ourselves once more inhabiting a high mountainside, with the clear green country far below us, and the light smoke of Calistoga blowing in the air."

ADOLPH SUTRO

(1830–98)

Europe's loss was, very definitely, America's gain in 1848. Not only did the Potato Famine in Ireland start many Irishmen on their way to a new life in the United States, but the Revolution of 1848 and its political and economic aftermath sent to the New World such estimable emigrants as Carl Schurz of Germany, destined to become an Army general, U.S. senator, and Secretary of the Interior.

Another German self-exile who proved to be a particular human asset to the States of California and Nevada was Adolph Sutro. He migrated to the United States when his family's fortunes, tied to woolen mills, were ruined by the dislocations of the Revolution of 1848. Perhaps the violence of Europe shocked Sutro. Certainly, he tried to live a constructive and peaceful life after his move to America. He was largely successful in this goal. Sutro "warred" only in politics and economics, where he was a dogged fighter for what he considered to be right, often taking the side of the underdog when robber barons ruled the day. Although he was intellectually inclined, he liked to think of himself as merely one of the people, and prominent on his library bookplate was an engraving of his alter ego, "the honest miner."

Before his life was over, Sutro would be reckoned an engineering genius for his great Sutro Tunnel in Nevada; a philanthropist of vision because of his gifts to San Francisco and the State of California; and a maverick officeholder who found the existing political machines not to his taste. But Adolph Sutro is remembered on the Pacific Coast because he invested not only his wealth but his self in the future of San Francisco. He was, in short, a builder of the then-metropolis of the West, not a mere partaker of its riches.

The eventual mining man and mayor of San Francisco was born on April 29, 1830, in Aachen, Charlemagne's old Aix-la-Chapelle. Even as a child, Sutro was a bibliophile, compulsively spending lunch money and savings to secure volumes which he felt he needed to feed his voracious reading appetite. He was also interested in the machinery of the family's woolen factory in Aachen and the mill which he managed in Memel when he was nineteen years old. Ideally, Adolph Sutro should have been a student and, later, a scholar, but the untimely death of his father impelled him regretfully to leave school when he was but sixteen years of age.

When Adolph Sutro's mother decided to start life anew in America in 1850, the closely knit family did not argue her decision. The Sutros sailed to New York, and from there Adolph went to California, a land of even greater opportunity than "the States" back East, with a small stock of cloth and notions. He arrived in San Francisco on November 21, 1850, sold his goods, and set himself up as a commission merchant, sleeping in his store. Soon, he was a moderately successful businessman. Despite his disliking for violence, he took his stand with the vigilantes during the troubles of 1851. By 1855, he was a prosperous San Francisco tobacconist. That year, the violence which he abhorred touched him. A hothead named A. J. King cut his cousin's face with a knife after a misunderstanding. The same day, King attacked Adolph, mistakenly believing that the latter had called him a scoundrel. His knife made a gash on Sutro's face from ear to mouth. Ever after, Adolph Sutro wore full side whiskers to hide the scar.

One more time he would meet violence. He was an eyewitness when the survivors of Major William Ormsby's defeat by the Paiute Indians staggered into Virginia City in May 1860. The German-accented Sutro rose above his limitations as a speaker and writer of English in order to play the role of war correspondent for the San Francisco *Bulletin*. He sent two Paiute War dispatches to the paper and planned at least a third. But he never submitted it, and it is likely that Sutro was so sickened by the Indian war that he turned away from it and plunged into his mining interests in order to thrust it from his mind. His dispatches, for that day and age, were first-rate. In documenting the massacre of seven men at Williams Ranch by Paiutes, he suggested the evaporation of "courage" (really bravado) which was such a commonplace in the West's Indian wars: "Everybody seemed ready to go. Whether the darkness and bad news had any influence in getting up the spirits of so many individuals I really don't know; but, this morning, when it came to turning out, there were but precious few on hand, and the persons who said they didn't want any horse, either, if they couldn't get one— nor any weapons, if they were not handy—but would just go and slay so many thousands with their fists like Samson of old, were nowhere to be seen today." When the small army of 105 men led by Major Ormsby was defeated and cut up by the Paiutes, Sutro reported the debacle: "Only forty-eight have returned. A few stragglers will likely come in yet, but it is feared that all the others have been butchered by the savages. A gloom hangs over our young city. . . ."

Sutro was tempted from the mundane life of a businessman by the mineral wealth of the West. He was an unsuccessful Argonaut in the Fraser River excitement in Canada in 1858 but committed completely to the mining future of Nevada's Comstock Lode. By 1863, he had a stamp mill at Dayton, and when the deep mines under Virginia City began to be threatened by natural flooding, he came up with a four-mile-long tunnel to cure it. The Nevada Legislature gave him a franchise, but the Sutro Tunnel Company found the hard rock of Nevada's Washoe country to be like butter in comparison to the obstacle of the Bank of California. Financiers William Ralston and William Sharon did not wish to share their bonanza with the newcoming upstart. After seemingly supporting him, they tried to maneuver him out of the way in order to take over his grandiose project. They applied pressure on Nevada, California, and national legislatures, on banks and newspapers, until Sutro found himself a financial pariah. Hurt by the double-dealing of "friends" whose motto was Business Is Business, he fought back with all his will and ability but failed to sell his tunnel scheme to bankers in the East and in Europe. His venture seemed doomed when Fortune dealt him a strange face card in April 1869. The Yellow Jacket Mine caught fire, killing forty-five men. Sutro's tunnel would have saved them. The resentment of the miners toward the monopolists who controlled the Comstock became support for the loner who fought the latter. Sutro spoke to the miners at Piper's Opera House: "Miners and laboring men, what is the price of your health, your liberty, your independence . . . ? Who is there among you so avaricious as to refuse to give or donate outright a few paltry dollars per month to a cause . . . which will make you the power of this land, make powerless your oppressors, and break up your arch-enemy, the California Bank?" Demagoguery or not, Sutro's timing was perfect; the Miners Union voted him fifty thousand dollars to continue the hard-pressed tunnel. The Committee on Mines and Mining of Congress then recommended a two-million-dollar loan to the Sutro Tunnel Company and McCalmont Brothers—British bankers—invested heavily in Tunnel stock.

Since Sutro *was* the Sutro Tunnel Company, he was everywhere, and his personal interest and constant inspection made construction so safe that only twelve persons were killed in the entire operation, where the Hoosac Railroad Tunnel in Massachusetts, of similar magnitude, claimed 185 lives. When he completed the tunnel in 1879 and it began to drain the mines, Sutro turned to other worlds to conquer. With uncanny timing, he sold out just at the right time. The tunnel had come too late; the mines were past their peak. The lower levels ran to low-grade ore, unprofitable even with the easy access afforded by the Sutro Tunnel.

Now wealthy, Adolph Sutro invested in San Francisco real estate, planted trees, and bought thousands of books, all over the world, in order to make his Sutro Library one of the great collections of the Western Hemisphere. Soon, he was attacking C. P. Huntington and the Southern Pacific Railroad as the great Octopus of monopoly. He built a fine mansion overlooking Seal Rocks and the Pacific at Sutro Heights. He created Sutro Baths and a new Cliff House. To his mansion came a steady stream of distinguished visitors, like Kate Douglas Wiggin, the author; William Jennings Bryan, Andrew Carnegie, Oscar Wilde, and President Benjamin Harrison.

In 1894, Sutro was the choice of the People's Party for Mayor of San Francisco. He found himself to be the people's choice, too, over five other candidates. But Sutro, now sixty-

310

four, found his administration to be one long wrangle with the supervisors. In 1896 his mind began to fail and, as 1897 opened, he turned over the office to his successor, Mayor James D. Phelan. Sutro died on August 8, 1898, leaving a tradition of courage as a peaceable battler against odds; plus the tangible memorial of a great institution, the Sutro Library, now a San Francisco branch of the California State Library.

JOHN A. SUTTER

(1803-80)

The founder of American California, the George Washington of the Golden State, was a Swiss wanderer, John A. Sutter, whose first long journey began most inauspiciously. The date was mid-May 1834, the place, Burgdorf, Switzerland. The circumstances of his hasty departure? The Swiss, a bankrupt who was determined to see himself in hell rather than in a debtor's cell, fled like a chicken thief from the canton. Shortly, a warrant for his arrest, signed by the chief of police of Berne, gave him further momentum, and Sutter sailed from Le Havre for America and a new life.

In taking French leave, Sutter abandoned not only thousands of francs in bad debts but also five young children, a nagging wife, Annette, and a likewise nagging mother-in-law. These were all products of Sutter's passion and an unfortunate shotgun marriage; Sutter's oldest child was born only a day after the wedding ceremony. Doubtless, Sutter swore to his wife that he would send for her when the time was ripe. But time did not ripen to Sutter's satisfaction until sixteen years had passed. By then, the penniless debt dodger had made himself into the most powerful single man in all California and was, already, on a downhill run from the heights of power and prestige.

The secret of success is often easier to find than the secret of failure. The latter is most difficult to isolate in Sutter's case. Hard-working when he had to be, cunning enough to survive and flourish in a dog-eat-dog era and frontier environment, and blessed with great personal charm, he should have been the Croesus of California once his workers discovered gold in 1848. But he was doomed to failure, and usually at the eleventh hour. Fate toyed with Sutter, leading him on and on toward an illusory success, then dropping him into an abyss of misfortune.

The thirty-one-year old bankrupt shopkeeper who landed in New York in July 1834 had many weaknesses. He liked fine clothes, high society, good books and brandy, all of which were beyond his means. Yet he scattered money as if it were cigar ash. He was not particularly courageous; he was vain, conceited, and unethical in business dealings. He treated some of his friends shabbily. Yet, in the long run, these weaknesses were outweighed by three or four good qualities. His love of adventuring was not uncommon in the Far West, of course, but the other traits were rare to the point of extinction among the ambitious and ruthless men who flocked to California. In most vivid contrast to them, Sutter was generous, compassionate, and visionary.

Like so many young Europeans, Sutter was intrigued by the dream of an American frontier paradise even before it assumed a golden color. His mind fell prisoner of the myth of a Rousseauan wilderness of noble savages and of the subsequent dream of the American West being an Eden, an Arcady—literally the Garden of the World. From New York, he hurried to the German and Swiss colonies in Missouri, of which he had read in the writings of Gottfried Duden.

313

Sutter found the Missouri frontier far too tame for his taste, so he entered the Sante Fe trade during the 1835 and 1836 seasons. He was so low on cash that he had to outfit himself with trade goods from a St. Louis pawnshop. His profits were modest but he made many friends in Missouri and Santa Fe. Unfortunately, he also made enemies, for his associates turned on him when the second expedition incurred great losses of capital. Whether Sutter was blameworthy or not, he was deemed *persona non grata* in both St. Louis and St. Charles, so he made his way to Westport, now part of Kansas City. But there, again, disaster loomed in the shape of bankruptcy and the Swiss adventurer had to flee across the Missouri River to take refuge in the Delaware nation. It was not entirely a move of desperation; his course lay ever westward. Sutter's dream was still to found a colony of Swiss and Germans in California. He had met Charles Beaubien, the Alcalde of Taos, New Mexico, and when the French-Canadian spun fabulous yarns of California, which he had visited, the Swiss became a fellow-convert.

In the spring of 1838, Sutter found the solution of his problem. He bade his Indian friends adieu and attached himself to Captain Andrew Drips's American Fur Company party, en route to the penultimate annual rendezvous of the dying Rocky Mountain fur trade. From the Popo Agie River rendezvous, near Wind River, Sutter accompanied a Hudson's Bay Company party to Fort Hall and then made his own way to Fort Vancouver on the Columbia River. From there, he planned to drop directly south into California, to carve out an empire—or, at least, a duchy—for himself. Chief Factor James Douglas of the Hudson's Bay post warned him against both the wintry Siskiyou Mountains and the hostiles lurking in them, however, so Sutter took passage in the company bark, *Columbia,* to Honolulu. He was sure that he could transfer there to a California-bound vessel. But shipping was in the doldrums; although he stayed in Honolulu for months, there were no departures. The Swiss put his stay to good effect; he charmed the Hawaiian commercial community and won from them fine letters of recommendation to prominent officials in California. (These references joined equally enthusiastic letters given him by Chief Factor Douglas.) So winning were Sutter's ways that merchant William French chartered the brig *Clementine* for a tramp trading voyage and put Sutter in charge as supercargo. Sutter called at Sitka first, becoming fast friends with Alaska's Governor Kauprianov and eliciting more letters of recommendation from him. Thus, when he finally descended upon San Francisco and Monterey in July 1839, in what must have been surely the most roundabout route to California of any emigrant, he had a fistful of recommendations.

Governor Juan B. Alvarado was dazzled by the encomiums heaped upon his visitor in the letters which he bore. He immediately gave him permission to found a colony of New Helvetia (New Switzerland) on the Sacramento River, far beyond the last Mexican settlements of General Vallejo in the Valley of the Moon. Sutter set out to conquer this wilderness almost immediately—largely on credit. He did so with a permanent party of only three whites—a German, a Belgian, and the ubiquitous Irishman of history; a bulldog; and ten Kanakas from Hawaii, including two handsome wahines, one of whom, Manuiki, had more than a little to do with Sutter's postponing a reunion with his wife. A few beached sailors and other drifters signed on to get him established. They quickly left him out of fear of the Indians and the solitude of California's vast central valley.

The captain of the little fleet which took Sutter up the Sacramento River to find a site for New Helvetia, a half-

Hawaiian named William H. (Kanaka Bill) Davis, was as gifted with a pen as he was with a tiller or lead line. He described the leave-taking eloquently: "As the heavy report of the guns and the echoes died away, the camp of the little party was surrounded by hundreds of Indians, who were excited and astonished at the unusual sound. A large number of deer, elk and other animals on the plains were startled, running to and fro, stopping to listen, their heads raised, full of curiosity and wonder, seemingly attracted and fascinated to the spot, while from the interior of the adjacent wood the howl of wolves and coyotes filled the air and immense flocks of waterfowl flew wildly about. . . . This salute was the first echo of civilization in the primitive wilderness so soon to become populated and developed into a great agricultural and commercial center. We returned the salute with nine cheers from the schooners, the vessels flying the American colors. The cheers were heartily responded to by the little garrison and thus we parted company."

Sutter set his Hawaiians to making *hale pili* (grass shacks) for shelter and then began a highly successful career as an Indian diplomat. Alternately cajoling and threatening or bluffing, he pacified the hostile tribes although there were attempts by warriors to assassinate him. These assaults were frustrated by his watchdog. It was necessary to mount punitive expeditions against warlike Indian tribes, too, but, by and large, Sutter's paternalism won the redmen to his allegiance without undue bloodshed. Within five years, his Hawaiian huts were replaced by a powerful adobe fort, with bastions, and walls protected by more than a dozen cannon and garrisoned by a company of Indian grenadiers, outfitted in green Russian uniforms which Sutter had secured when he bought the Redwood Coast settlements of Fort Ross and Bodega from the Russians in 1841. Incredibly, the poor adventurer who had swatted mosquitoes while camped on a lonely hillock beside the American River in 1839 was the most powerful man in California by 1844.

Late in that year, Governor Manuel Micheltorena was threatened by a civil war. His Excellency immediately called on Sutter for help and the Swiss responded by leading a strong foreign legion out through the fort's gates on New Year's Day 1845. In the ranks were such doughty frontiersmen as Zeke Merritt, leader of the Bear Flag Revolt in just a year and a half; Michel Laframboise, veteran Hudson's Bay Company fur *bourgeois;* mountaineer Caleb Greenwood; and Kit Carson's brother, Moses. But Sutter made a grave mistake by impressing an enemy, Dr. John Marsh, into service. The latter spread doubt and dissension among Sutter's troopers. Worse, Micheltorena lost his will to win—if he had ever had it—and decided to abandon California after saving face by an engagement which would be little more than a sham battle. Unaware of Micheltorena's double-dealing, Sutter allowed himself to be trapped in an untenable position. His men abandoned him at the almost bloodless Battle of Cahuenga, near Los Angeles, Micheltorena hurriedly hoisted the white flag, and Sutter was captured.

Wild tales of Sutter's bloodthirsty American, Indian, and Hawaiian legionnaires had inflamed Southern California against him and the New Helvetian had good reason to fear for his life. But his captors released him from imprisonment, after he swore allegience to the new government, and allowed him to return to Fort Sutter. There he again established himself as liege lord of Northern California, but his days of supremacy were numbered. From the ranks of his own legion came men, like Ezekiel Merritt, who wanted no more of the *opéra bouffe* anarchy and chronic civil war of Mexican California. It would be a Yankee California, by God!, or it would be independent. With Captain John C. Frémont and his paramilitary force prowling the territory, the American filibusters decided to strike and to create a kind of bargain-basement Texas Republic in Northern California.

The brief Bear Flag Republic caught Sutter flat-footed. Although he was partial to the United States, he did not like the roughnecks who headed the "Sonoma Republic." Besides, he was still an officer of the Mexican Government. Now began a resumption of the erosion of his power which had begun at Cahuenga. Before long, Frémont threw his support behind the Bear Flaggers, and the Swiss became a virtual prisoner in his own fortress. His power continued to dwindle during the Mexican War, which followed. Although he made a partial comeback in 1847, all of his grandiose plans were trampled into the dust by the boots of the horde of miners who rushed to the Sierra for gold in 1848 and 1849.

Now a curious phenomenon took place. The once-cunning Sutter seemed numbed, paralyzed, by the decline in his fortunes. He was incapable of success in anything now, where no task had been too difficult to attack five or ten years earlier. Misfortune dogged Sutter. Speculators and swindling Yankee lawyers stripped away what property remained to him after the looting of it by miners and squatters. He sought solace and Dutch courage in the *aguardiente* bottle, but the brandy only made things worse. He became the butt of ridicule when he was in his cups, the befuddled, fallen giant. Although he was never reduced to poverty, as legend would have it, Sutter came close to oblivion and was never a political power after the Gold Rush, although the state, embarrassed by the pillage of his fortune, handed him such empty honors as the position of major general, commanding the State Militia.

Captain Sutter retreated from the shambles of New Helvetia to quiet Hock Farm on the Feather River. But even this retreat was not secure. The kindly pioneer, who had stripped his storeroom shelves to aid hundreds if not thousands of hungry and threadbare emigrants, like the Donner Party, was the victim of an American firebug. When the arsonist was through repaying Sutter for his handouts (and a well-earned thrashing for theft), Hock Farm lay in a smoldering ruins. Sutter turned his back on California forever.

Sutter made his way to Washington, D.C., to plead for compensation from Congress for his ruin at the hands of the very Americans whom he had helped so much. Although he haunted the Capitol, he had no success. Finally, in 1880, his will broke. He was found dead in his Mades' Hotel room of "natural causes" (heartbreak) just two days after Congress adjourned without taking action on his sixteenth claim.

As usual, in such cases, the country tried to make amends when it was too late. With Sutter dead, he was rehabilitated as a hero and his many weaknesses glossed over. His philanthropies and kindnesses to American emigrants all but made him a candidate for canonization. Later came the iconoclasts, to be sure, the debunkers with their destructive and inaccurate criticism, but the marmoreal myth of Sutter was too sturdy for their blunt chisels.

What kind of man *was* this slightly down-at-the-heels Founder of California? He was a mixture of good and bad, neither a Saint of the Sacramento nor a Scoundrel of the Sacramento, as hack historians would have him. He was compulsively generous; even his worst enemies admitted this. But his unique vision was not recognized for years. He saw the Gold Rush not as a triumph for California but as an interruption in its natural growth as an agricultural empire. Sutter was the first wheat king in the West; he experimented with cotton and irrigation; he started California's fisheries; dabbled in lumbering, mining, milling, distilling, and the manufacture of leather, hats, and blankets. Had the Gold Rush not crushed him and his plans, Sutter would surely have carried out his grand design of converting the Sacramento Valley into a great grain field, which would feed not only California and Oregon, but British Columbia, Alaska, Hawaii, and even far-off Tahiti and the Marquesas.

The secret of Sutter's failure was that he changed too much during his lifetime. In the 1830's, he was blessed (if that is the word) with what Maxwell Perkins, the editor, once called "qualities of competition"—selfishness, ambition, ruthlessness. In subsequent decades, these brutal traits were overcome by the gentler qualities which made him a better man than many of his peers but which handicapped him in a competitive situation so that he was swept aside by lesser men, stampeding for gold or land.

MARK TWAIN

(1835–1910)

One swallow—even one nested in the coarse-tiled eaves of Mission San Juan Capistrano—does not make a summer, and six or seven years of residence does not make a Californian. At least, it did not make a Californian of Mark Twain. But Twain, born Samuel Langhorne Clemens, has been adopted, like Robert Louis Stevenson, by literary historians of the West Coast and is considered to be one of the founding fathers of California letters.

California's claim to Twain is, indeed, tenuous, although the writer passed his entire apprenticeship out there, took his famous nom de plume while in Virginia City, Nevada, and won his first national—and even international—fame by means of a Western yarn, *The Celebrated Jumping Frog of Calaveras County*. But only three of his many books have roots in his "California period"—*The Innocents Abroad, Roughing It,* and the title just mentioned.

Twain, née Clemens, was of tough Tennessean stock, his antecedents having come to the Great Smokies state from Virginia via Kentucky. Ofttimes, alas, the Volunteer State's landscape is more impregnated with beauty than fertility, and so it was that John Clemens migrated to greener pastures in Missouri, where Sam was born (November 30, 1835) in the town of Florida. The family moved again, however, and thus it came to pass that Becky Thatcher, Huck Finn, and Tom Sawyer peopled Hannibal rather than Florida, Missouri.

Although Twain always said that he loathed traveling, except on foot, he spent much of his life occupied by that "loathsome" habit. He drifted from state to state and trade to trade as a young man, seeing in the process New York, Philadelphia, Washington, St. Louis, and Keokuk. When he heard of Lieutenant Herndon's Amazonian travels, he was determined (against the advice of his older brother, Orion) to go to the headwaters of the Amazon and to return home a rich planter. He took a boat from Cincinnati down the Ohio and Mississippi rivers to New Orleans, to catch a vessel to the port of Pará, in Brazil. Only one thing blocked his adventure, and he explained it in his autobiography: "When I got to New Orleans I enquired about ships leaving for Pará and discovered that there weren't any and learned that there probably wouldn't be any during that century." So Twain became a river pilot, and *Life on the Mississippi* was conceived.

The next stage of Twain's life was a rather inglorious military career. He served a full fortnight in the Confederate Army in Missouri before he tired of constant retreating, then decided to leave the war alone if it would let him alone. The young Missourian decided to accompany Orion to Nevada, his brother having been appointed secretary of the new territory. They left by stagecoach from St. Joe on July 26, 1861, and Twain made his home in the Far West for the next half-dozen years. During this time he skillfully mixed varying portions of observing, writing, and that avocation which he affected to despise—traveling. He wrote about what he saw and, to be sure, many things which he did not see but which he figured he might have seen, were Nature not so disorderly. His first literary efforts were modest, indeed, mere letters to the editor signed, "Josh." But, soon, the Virginia City *Territorial Enterprise* took him on as a regular correspondent. When the town's Number One local humorist, Dan DeQuille, went East for a vacation, Clemens filled in for him, took his now famous pen name of Mark Twain, and soon had the satisfaction of being not only the most popular writer in Nevada but the one most commonly reprinted in San Francisco papers.

Clemens visited San Francisco in 1863 and was welcomed as a contributor to the city's literary journal, the *Golden Era*. In May of 1864 he moved over the Sierra from Washoe to San Francisco and joined the staff of the *Morning Call*. The paper chose to misuse his talents entirely. Twain found the routine reporting to which he was assigned to be uninteresting for the most part, almost drudgery. He kept his sanity (and flexing wit) by continuing to send his more creative material to the *Golden Era* and the *Californian*. Luckily, he fell into the hands of a more polished and accomplished writer (at this stage of their respective careers), Bret Harte. The latter did him immense good with his advice and counsel. The rough-hewn Twain paid tribute to the more genteel—even dandyish—author by saying, "He trimmed and trained and schooled me patiently until he changed me from an awkward utterer of coarse grotesqueness to a writer of paragraphs and chapters that have found a certain favor." But the two never really became friends; they were poles apart in personality. Probably, Twain put it honestly when he described Harte later: "Bret Harte was one of the pleasantest men I have ever known; he was also one of the unpleasantest men I have ever known."

Mark began to broaden his scope when in San Francisco, shifting from writing merely good-natured jokes, hoaxes, and burlesques to the creation of the biting satire on man and his foibles which marked his later career. He sailed to Hawaii in 1866 in order to write a series of travel letters for the Sacramento *Union*. A tour of Europe and the Holy Land followed in 1867. This trip, and the example of a book title *Yusef*, by J. Ross Browne, led him to write *The Innocents Abroad*. He was already nationally and even internationally famous, because of his Angels Camp beshotted frog. Twain did not write much differently from Browne or John Franklin Swift, author of *Going to Jericho;* he just wrote much better. In fact, he would never be equaled at the fine art of Western humor with its alternations of understatement, incongruity, and wild overexaggeration. Too, he was not as limited, as regional, as Browne and Swift, or the earliest California humorist, John Phoenix. Perhaps this is why, once he left California, he did not return. He crossed the Atlantic possibly twenty times but never managed to find the time to pay a return visit to the city where he really got his start, San Francisco.

But *how* he could write! An example would be his description of a predecessor of the great 1906 earthquake. "It was just after noon, on a bright October day. I was coming down Third Street. The only objects in motion anywhere in sight on that thickly built and populous quarter were a man in a buggy behind me and a street car wending slowly up the cross street. Otherwise, all was solitude and Sabbath stillness. As I turned the corner around a frame house, there was a great rattle and jar and it occurred to me that here was an item—no doubt a fight in that house. Before I could turn and seek the door, there came a really terrific shock; the ground seemed to roll under me in waves, interrupted by a violent joggling up and down, and there was a heavy grinding noise as of brick houses rubbing together. I fell up against the frame house and hurt my elbow. I knew what it was, now, and from mere reportorial instinct, nothing else, took out my watch and noted the time of day. At that moment, a third and still severer shock came and as I reeled about on the pavement trying to keep my footing, I saw a sight! The entire front of a tall four-story brick building in Third Street sprung outward like a door and fell sprawling across the street, raising a dust like a great volume of smoke. And here came the buggy—overboard went the man and, in less time than I can tell it, the vehicle was distributed in small fragments along 300 yards of street. . . .

"Gentlemen and ladies who were sick, or were taking a siesta, or had dissipated till a late hour and were making up lost sleep, thronged into the public streets in all sorts of queer apparel and some without any at all. One woman, who had been washing a naked child, ran down the street holding it by the ankles as if it were a dressed turkey. Prominent citizens who were supposed to keep the Sabbath strictly, rushed out of saloons in their shirt sleeves with billiard cues in their hands. Dozens of men with necks swathed in napkins rushed from barber shops, lathered to the eyes or with one cheek clean-shaved and the other still bearing a hairy stubble. Horses broke from stables and a frightened dog rushed up a short attic ladder and out onto a roof and when his scare was over had not the nerve to go down again the way he had gone up. . . . A crack a hundred feet long gaped open six inches wide in the middle of one street and then shut together again with such force as to ridge up the meeting earth like a slender grave. A lady, sitting in her rocking and quaking parlor, saw a wall part at the ceiling and shut twice like a mouth and then drop the end of a brick on the floor, like a tooth. She was a woman easily disgusted with foolishness and she rose and went out of there. . . . The first shock brought down two or three huge pipe organs in one of the churches. The minister, with uplifted hands, was just closing the services. He glanced up, hesitated, and said, 'However, we will omit the benediction!,' and, the next instant, there was a vacancy in the atmosphere where he had stood. After the first shock, an Oakland minister said, 'Keep your seats. There is no better place to die than this. . . .' And added, after a third [shock], 'But outside is good enough!' He then skipped out the back door."

After a premature farewell in 1866, Mark Twain really said good-by to California in 1868. He lectured widely but never returned to the state after a very successful lecture on Venice in the Mercantile Library on July 2, 1868. Two days after the Glorious Fourth, Twain was on his way to New York and greater fame. Henceforth, Hartford, Connecticut, and the world, as well as San Francisco, would claim him as their own.

MARIANO VALLEJO

(1808–90)

Hardly "typical" of the settlers of Spanish and Mexican California was Don Mariano Guadalupe Vallejo. Like John Sutter he stood head and shoulders above most of the leaders of Arcadian California and, while he was never governor, he became one of the most powerful individuals in the entire province. And still the Yankee take-over of California was as disastrous for him as for Sutter or Vallejo's less impressive ranchero friends. What made Vallejo's case so distressing was that he had welcomed the Americans (and earned the name of "traitor" in some quarters, as a result) because he believed their rule would mean peace and order and growth instead of the directionless drifting of the Mexican period.

Vallejo and Sutter, rivals at first, became firm friends in mutual misfortune during the Bear Flag Revolt, Mexican War, and Gold Rush. Both were efficiently looted of their lands and other property by gringo squatters and shysters. Withal, Vallejo remained the most effective link between the two regimes and he accepted his disaster with more grace than the embittered Sutter. He lived out a useful life at his Sonoma estate, Lachryma Montis (Tears of the Mountain, so called for the hillside springs which watered his vines), a 280-acre remnant of his onetime feudal domain of tens of thousands of acres. Vallejo saw the urgent need of reconciliation between the two peoples; "Let the wound heal," he urged.

During his heyday, Vallejo's kindness and hospitality rivaled that of John Sutter, himself, and Reverend Walter Colton, U. S. Navy chaplain and Alcalde of Monterey, may have been thinking of him when he contrasted the native Californians with his fellow-Americans: "The shrewdness and sharpness of the Yankee . . . and the liberality of the Californian. . . . Give me the Californian!"

Whether Vallejo was, or was not, the most distinguished *Californio,* the "Noblest Roman of them all," as historian Rockwell D. Hunt used to insist, there is no challenging his importance to California in pre-Gold Rush days. He was born on July 7, 1808, in Monterey and profited more than most of his peers from the limited and haphazard education available from Alta California's few tutors. The young man was something of a protégé of Governor Pablo Solá, who appreciated the benefits of education, and Vallejo's talents were also recognized by Governor Luis Argüello, who appointed the young man his private secretary. Later, Vallejo imported the best library in California, although the clergy was outraged since many of the books were taboo because of the *Index Librorum Prohibitorum.* Mariano entered military service as a cadet at the age of fifteen, and by the time he was twenty-three he was in command of the San Francisco garrison and elected to the provincial legislature (illegally, since he was a soldier). In 1834, he was elected an alternate delegate to the Mexican Congress but was never called to Mexico City.

But Vallejo saw himself as a soldier, not a politician. He rose from ensign to colonel and even to *comandante general* of all California. He led punitive expeditions against hostile Indians and in 1829 won a considerable reputation when he whipped the rebel forces of renegade mission Indian Estanislao (or Stanislaus). However, his achievement was tarnished by his callousness in allowing his Indian allies to murder some of his prisoners. He supported the home-rule rebellion of 1832 by the Californians against the governor, Manuel Victoria, imposed upon them by Mexico City, and took part in the Isaac Graham affair, in which a number of Americans (suspected of being filibusters) were exiled. Later, however, Vallejo tried to remain more aloof from the chaotic rebellions and counterrebellions which dominated politics during the Mexican regime. He preferred to play a lone hand rather than galloping off at the drop of a sombrero to reinforce Juan B. Alvarado or José Castro in one of their power plays. Similarly, he was able to stay out of the sticky Micheltorena War of 1844, in which the governor was thrown out and Sutter was defeated and humiliated. (Vallejo had to go to the extreme of disbanding his military company—pretending that he could no longer afford to support it—but it worked.)

When Governor José Figueroa began to worry in 1833 about the presence of the Russians at Fort Ross and Bodega, he sent his most trusted officer, Vallejo, to reconnoiter the outpost of Russian Alaska and to make recommendations. The two men decided that a military post was necessary north of San Francisco Bay, as much to contain warlike Indians and potential Yankee filibusters as Russians, who seemed peaceable enough to Vallejo. Vallejo was not only named commander of the new post at Sonoma, he was given the title of Military Commandant and Director of Colonization of the Northern Frontier. In this new position, his power compared to that of Sutter and José Castro, *comandante general* of

California. By stabilizing Mexico's northwesternmost frontier Vallejo played his greatest role in California history. He whipped hostile Indians, won over others with just treatment, and made a powerful ally in Chief Sem Yeto (Mighty Army) of the Suisunes. He, several times, put a stop to the enslaving of Indian children by Mexicans and Indians alike, even by Chief Solano himself, none other than Sem Yeto after he became a Christian.

When the missions were secularized in 1833, Vallejo was named administrator of the Sonoma Mission, San Francisco de Solano. He was so efficient that he was accused of feathering his nest at the expense of the Indians and the ex-mission. But he took better care of the Indians than almost any other administrator; he increased the livestock while the herds of the other missions dwindled away. Small wonder the governor paid little heed to the complaints against Vallejo, most of them made by two discredited priests, so demoralized that they should have been defrocked long before. Later, Vallejo would protect the mission lands and herds (and the Indians) from the plans of the Hijar-Padrés Company to "colonize" the missions with newcomers from Mexico and elsewhere.

One reason why Vallejo cared little to meddle in governmental politics was that Governor Juan B. Alvarado, his nephew, was jealous of him and saw him as a rival. So he devoted himself to building up Sonoma and, in time, he became a sort of *cacique,* or chief, although his allegiance to Monterey was never in doubt, as was Sutter's. His domain, with his brother Salvador's, now stretched from Sonoma to Petaluma to Napa and all the way to Carquinez Strait. The Government paid no attention to his suggestions, reforms which might have delayed the American conquest. He repeatedly urged that the presidial companies not be allowed to waste away: "the only hope of salvation of the country, which needs positive and efficacious remedies before it is submerged in ruins." Unheeded, he built up his own extraofficial presidio at Sonoma, although he was forced to outfit and pay his troops from his own pocket most of the time. (In twenty-four years of military service to Mexico, Vallejo himself was apparently never paid so much as a plugged peso in salary.) At times, as when the governor wished to use his men in some ill-advised adventure, Vallejo could fall back on the fiction that they really constituted his private bodyguard. At another time he answered Alvarado's request for some of his men by saying, "My troops will always be ready to support the law, but not to abuse it."

The ambitious and ruthless John C. Frémont mistreated Vallejo just as he did Sutter, and, through the farce of the Bear Flag Revolt, captured and jailed Vallejo at New Helvetia. When Sutter protested the gross injustice of the act, Frémont threatened to hang the Swiss from his own oak tree. It took Commodore Robert Stockton himself to secure the release of Vallejo and his aides, on parole, from the little dictator, Frémont.

Belatedly, Vallejo was rewarded for his loyalty to the new government by being elected to the constitutional convention of 1849 in Monterey. There, he was largely responsible for naming the various counties of the state. He was also elected to the first State Senate, but his efforts to place the capitol in the town of Vallejo failed. After a brief itineracy, the capitol came to rest in Sacramento. When he heard of Marshall's discovery at Coloma, Vallejo wished his friend and erstwhile enemy the best: "As the water flows through Sutter's millrace, may the gold flow into Sutter's purse." Vallejo did virtually no gold mining himself. He devoted himself to his Sonoma estate, becoming a great vineyardist and vintner like his neighbor, Agoston Haraszthy, whose two sons married daughters of

Vallejo. Don Mariano also helped Bancroft write his history of California. On January 18, 1890, Vallejo died, and with him passed the last important tie with the Mexican period of California's history.

ISAAC VAN NUYS

(*1835–1912*)

Times change so markedly and swiftly in California that the heroes of yesterday, almost before they have moldered in the grave, are likely to become the villains of *mañana*. A good case in point is Isaac Newton Van Nuys, who had much to do with developing Los Angeles from a sparsely settled, semi-arid "cow county" into a booming megalopolis which is universally conceded to be a sneak preview of America's future cities, complete with strangulation from smog and traffic. Of course, it is unfair to blame Van Nuys for the willy-nilly growth of the Los Angeles Plain; the population explosion and the consequent migration fragmentation were not triggered by him. Van Nuy's reputation should be as unassailable today as it was when he died, on February 12, 1912.

The man has been honored by having a city named after him as well as a World War II liberty ship. It was fitting that a vessel should be named for him, since Van Nuys put the port of San Pedro on the map by shipping from it the first cargoes of Southern California wheat. In his lifetime, he was a miller, a shipper, a developer, an investor, and a firm and loving paterfamilias. But, above all, he was a farmer, virtually

333

from the day of his birth to Holland-Dutch parents on a farm near West Sparta, New York, on November 20, 1835. Like so many Easterners, Van Nuys was driven westward by ill health. While not a "lunger" (tubercular), he was the next thing to it—an asthmatic. In 1865 he sailed from New York to San Francisco. Arrived on the Coast, he settled at Monticello in the beautiful Berryessa Valley northeast of San Francisco, an area now under the spreading waters of Lake Berryessa. He did not farm the land but, instead, opened a one-man general merchandise store, with very modest living quarters in the back of the building. While running his general store, Van Nuys met land speculator Isaac Lankershim, who persuaded him to supervise his Northern California holdings.

It was in 1869 that the friendship of the two men set in motion one of the most grandiose land developments of all time. Lankershim became interested in the San Fernando Valley, a vast range for cattle and sheep since Spanish times. When he asked the ex-New Yorker's advice about buying much of the valley, Van Nuys urged him to go ahead. Not only was it good grazing land but Van Nuys was persuaded (by the height of the wild oats growing there) that the soil was perfect for wheat. Van Nuys accepted Lankershim's invitation to join him in his new syndicate, the San Fernando Farm Homestead Association, which bought the lower half of the old Mission Ranch (sixty thousand acres) from ex-Governor Pío Pico for $115,000. As yet, Van Nuys did not go to Southern California. He let his partner run their affairs in the South. Less prescient than Van Nuys, Lankershim was content to leave the great valley to its cattle and sheep. There were forty thousand of the latter alone.

In 1871, Van Nuys sold his Monticello store and joined Lankershim. He brought a knowledge and skill in farming to the Los Angeles area at just the right time. The drought of

1874–75 took his seed crop of wheat, to be sure, but it also wiped out the sheep business completely. Nothing daunted, Van Nuys replanted, and his 1876 crop resulted in two full cargoes of wheat shipped from San Pedro to Liverpool, the first wheat ever exported from Southern California.

So large was the old Pío Pico land grant that Van Nuys had to establish several ranches in order to properly manage the property. The Home Ranch was just west of the present city of Van Nuys; the West Ranch lay on the site of Reseda; the Workman Ranch where Cánoga Park is found today. (Lankershim established other ranches, which seeded such towns as North Hollywood and Tarzana, until there were a total of seven.) With Lankershim, Van Nuys built the first efficient wagon road through Sepulveda Cañon in 1874 and '75, on the route of the old Mission Trail of the Franciscan padres, in order to shorten the haul of his loaded wagons from ranch to wharf. Today, that wagon road is Sepulveda Boulevard. By 1878, wheat was so big a crop on his San Fernando Valley land that he and his partner had to build a mill in Los Angeles (population eleven thousand) to grind the grain into flour. When the grist mill began operation, Van Nuys moved from the Home Ranch into Los Angeles itself, living in the St. Charles Hotel.

The "Dutchman," convinced of the great future lying in store for Los Angeles (and it would hit a population of 102,479 by 1900), showed his foresight by investing his wheat profits in real estate. He bought himself a large house, too, and married his partner's daughter, Susanna, in 1880. After April 1882, when Lankershim died, the entire burden of management of the ranches and the Los Angeles Farming and Milling Company fell on the shoulders of the business-like, no-nonsense Van Nuys. He was never content with delegation of responsibility or loose supervision; one week of

335

every month saw him in his buckboard, making the rounds of the seven ranches, checking the progress of the seven "combines" (combined harvesters) which were never idle, by day, from May till November. Thanks to his unflagging supervision, the property produced bumper crops like that of 1888—510,000 bushels of wheat. That same year, Van Nuys sold twelve thousand of his more easterly acres near Toluca Lake to a syndicate which carved the area up into forty-acre farms, to sell at prices ranging from $5.00 to $150 an acre. Later, the community of North Hollywood grew up there.

Southern California's astonishing land and population boom of the 1880's brought headaches as well as profits to the developer. By 1890, 1200 squatters were on his land, driving off stock and trying to file claims. Some of Isaac's neighbors armed their cowboys and farm hands and had them dump the squatters and their goods, ceremoniously, in the middle of the county road. But Van Nuys was peaceable; violence was anathema to him. He preferred the long and costly (fifty-thousand-dollar) solution of a court case. The squatters appealed the decision against them all the way up to the Supreme Court, but Van Nuys finally won.

In his later years, the small, frail, and birdlike Van Nuys served as a director of banks and a brickyard as well as tending his own ranches and mill. He also continued to buy and sell land and to build downtown Los Angeles offices and other structures. In 1896, he erected the Van Nuys Hotel, for example, and in 1904 he sold the site of Huntington Park to streetcar magnate Henry E. Huntington. But failing health persuaded him to divest himself of his remaining forty-seven thousand acres in 1910 (for $2,500,000) to a syndicate, the Los Angeles Suburban Homes Company, whose principals included General Harrison Gray Otis and Harry Chandler.

Van Nuys went into retirement until his death, four years later.

One of the last great events in his life was the colossal auction of his ranch stock and equipment, the greatest such sale ever held in the state. It ran for four days, and each day he slaughtered six beeves to barbecue for the two thousand farmers and stockmen busily bidding. When the last lot was knocked down, Van Nuys had sold off two thousand horses and mules, ten harvesters, six threshing machines, four blacksmith shops, four harness shops, and hundreds of farm wagons, harrows, mowers, and gang plows.

Robert J. Burdette's sketch of Isaac Van Nuys in his mug book *American Biography and Genealogy* is unabashed eulogy but not too far from the truth: "He coveted success but scorned to gain the same except through industry and honest means. He acquired wealth without fraud or deceit. . . . He was ever mindful of his stewardship as a man among men. Few have made more distinct and valuable contributions to the industrial development of Southern California. . . . He was a loyal citizen of Los Angeles. Every dollar he made he expended here." Most remarkable (if true) was his biographer's claim: "He left not a single enemy behind him."

TIBURCIO VÁSQUEZ

(1835–75)

Ever since the *Epistles,* it has been commonly said that art is but an imitation of nature. Sometimes, however, the positions are reversed and nature seems to imitate art. Joaquín Murrieta—if he existed as a single individual at all, rather than as a composite of perhaps five Mexican bandits—had his career so invested with romanticism by writers that he came to be much more a part of California myth, folklore, and legend than of its history. But twenty years after his supposed death, a dead ringer for Joaquín struck dread into the hearts of travelers and settlers alike in the Coast Range country.

Tiburcio Vásquez did not wait for twenty years to begin a career in crime; it simply reached its apex then. He began his apprenticeship as a *bandido,* in fact, during the very year (1853) of Harry Love's battle with Murrieta at Cantua Creek. With two other men, the eighteen-year-old son of a respectable Monterey family was involved in the killing of Constable William Hardmount at a fandango. Brave and elusive like Joaquín, Tiburcio was also his equal as a horseman and devilishly hard to track down in the mazes of chaparral brush which clothed the foothills of the Coast Range mountains. Vásquez, like Joaquín, also subscribed to the idea of guerrilla warfare telling the editor of the Los Angeles *Express* after his capture of his idea to retake the state from the *yanquis:* "Given $60,000, I would be able to recruit enough arms and men to revolutionize Southern California." Ironically, the bandit and murderer felt a real concern for the plight of the native (Mexican) Californians, largely law-abiding to the point of meekness. "I believed we were unjustly and wrongly deprived of the social rights that belonged to us."

Vásquez was handsome though short and slight in build, about five feet six and 130 pounds. He wore a neat mustache and short beard, dressed well—even elegantly, at times—and could read and write well in both Spanish and English, an accomplishment not to be sneered at in the California of a century ago. No sadist, he was, in fact, much less bloodthirsty than reports painted him, and uniformly preferred to tie up his victims rather than blast the life out of them with pistol balls.

After the murder of Constable Hardmount, to which Tiburcio Vásquez was apparently an accessory, he palled about with older criminals for a time. By 1857, he was on his own, with a following of a few friends. That year, he rustled a herd of horses from a Santa Clara River ranch in Los Angeles County and was arrested when he tried to sell the stock. Vásquez was sentenced to five years in San Quentin, and although he escaped in the big break of June 25, 1859, he was recaptured and had to finish out his sentence. After his release in '63, Tiburcio went straight—almost. He became a professional gambler at the quicksilver settlement of New Almadén, near San Jose. But his greed got the best of him again and he became involved in the robbery and murder of an Italian at the Enriqueta Mine. By one of those flukes of chance, Sheriff J. H. Adams hired Vásquez, almost certainly one of the guilty men, to be his interpreter as he investigated the case. There was insufficient legal evidence to arrest anyone, and although Vásquez fled, there was no pursuit.

During the next two years, Vásquez was an associate of such desperate bandits as Procopio and Juan Soto, but when things got too hot for him in the Santa Clara Valley, Vásquez took an extended vacation in Sonoma County to the north of San Francisco. Unfortunately, he wandered into the cattle-thieving trade again. As a small businessman of this sort, Tiburcio was doomed to failure. He was sent to San Quentin for a third time. Discharged in June of 1870, he returned to his old Monterey County haunts but changed his *modus operandi* to a successful one, the robbing of stagecoaches, stage stations, and whole towns. His career was almost nipped in the bud at this stage when he let his "Casanovism" lead him astray. He ran off with a married woman who happened to be the wife of one of his confederates. Mrs. Salazar was willing enough, but her husband did not like playing the fool and cuckold to an erstwhile friend. He went after Vásquez with a gun, and in one of the rare street duels of Western history (which are such a commonplace of fiction) he shot Vásquez in the neck. Friends intervened and broke up the gunfight on San Juan Bautista's dusty back street, but Salazar was not content. He swore out a warrant for Vásquez's arrest for attempted murder. The grand jury, delighted at last to have something concrete to hang on an obvious outlaw, found it a true bill. But Vásquez gave the law the slip, vanishing into the Panoche Mountains of the Coast Range.

When Vásquez appeared again, it was with a vengeance. In the fall of 1871 he and two companions robbed the Visalia stage at Soap Lake, near Hollister. All passengers were relieved of their wealth, laid out in a row on the ground, and tied up. The same day, Vásquez robbed a traveler who had informed on him to Sheriff Harry Morse of Alameda County, but he did not harm his victim. Tiburcio did not move fast enough and Sheriff Tom Wasson of Monterey County surprised his camp in the hills near San Juan Bautista. Vásquez managed to escape during the gun battle but was again overtaken near Santa Cruz by Marshal L. F. Roberts. The latter shot him through the body, the bullet hitting him below the nipple of his right breast but, luckily, ranging sideways instead of plowing deep. It came out under his right shoulder, sparing his lungs. Vásquez wounded the marshal, in turn, and then rode for sixty miles, weak with shock and bleeding, to his favorite hideout—none other than the Cantua Creek of Joaquín Murrieta's last stand.

Recovered from his wound, Vásquez led a newly recruited gang in the first of a series of raids which terrorized Central California. He struck first at Firebaugh's Ferry, a little town on the San Joaquin River, because he had heard that cattle baron Henry Miller had left a thirty-thousand-dollar payroll for his cowboys in a strongbox there. The information was false, but Vásquez made do by robbing the store and its dozen customers. After this raid, Vásquez did not really go into hiding, merely loafing about the Cantua Creek ranch of one of his men, Abdon Leiva, or in the town of New Idria. Apparently, the superintendent of the New Idria quicksilver mine had an arrangement with him, a kind of a truce in which neither man bothered the other. Many Mexican-Californians were afraid of Vásquez, of course, and others proud of his fiery independence. They protected him with a conspiracy of silence as to his movements. When a raid in the summer of 1873 on a Southern Pacific Railroad train fell apart, Vásquez raided the Twenty-one Mile House, instead. This inn lay between San Jose and Gilroy. The bandit got only $155 and a few watches from the house and its four occupants, but it was just a warm-up. On August 26, he pulled off his most notorious raid. He sent some of his men ahead into the town of Tres Pinos (now Paicines; the current Tres Pinos is a more modern settlement), near Hollister, then followed himself. They took over the store and the stage when it arrived from New Idria. Clerk and customers made no resistance, but a Portuguese shepherd chose to stroll by just at the wrong time. The sheepherder did not understand Vásquez's order to halt and one of his men shot the fellow through the head. Next, a little boy bolted out of the back door of the store but was laid low by a clubbed pistol. Finally, George Redfield drove up in a wagon. The teamster did not obey Vásquez's orders but, bewildered and panicky, ran for it. Vásquez shot him dead. (Only later did he learn that Redfield was deaf and had not understood his command.) The proprietor of the hotel in town now, unwisely, chose to try to bolt his door against the bandits. Vásquez shot him dead with his Henry rifle. When the bandit and his gang rode out of town, it was with $1200 in cash and jewelry and other valuables loaded on eight stolen horses. But behind him lay three dead men; something the state would not forget. Bad luck and miscues turned his raid into a bloody affair which earned him, too, the wrath of ordinary citizens.

Vigilantes formed themselves up; posses under Sheriffs Adams and Wasson beat the brush country and trailed the raiders all the way to the sloughs of the San Joaquin Valley, where they lost the trail. But the peace officers did not give up. Captain Adams, the Santa Clara County sheriff, finally ran Vásquez down in the Tehachapi Mountains near Tejon Pass, with the help of Sheriff William Rowland of Los Angeles County. Vásquez and his sole companion held off the posse with their fifteen-shot Henry repeaters, and although they lost most of their horses to the lawmen, both escaped into the dense chaparral covering the mountain sides.

Vásquez made another big mistake when he took advantage of friendship again for a little adulterous romancing. This time it was with Abdon Leiva's wife. Leiva tried to gun him down, à la Salazar, but friends broke up the fight, so he surrendered to the Undersheriff of Los Angeles and turned state's evidence against Vásquez. (For his part, the dashing and handsome Vásquez cruelly abandoned Señora Leiva in the mountains, pregnant and doomed to a miscarriage.) Vásquez tried, but failed, to hire a man to poison Leiva in his San Jose cell, then came out of hiding on the day after Christmas 1873. He and his men sacked the town of Kingston in (then) Tulare County, near modern Hanford. With nine or ten men, he robbed two stores and the hotel, tied up or knocked out thirty-six (!) men cowed by his Colt and Henry rifle, but killed no one. Finally, one of the townspeople who had not been captured showed some gumption. He took on the whole gang and when he was through, J. W. Sutherland had wounded two of Vásquez's lieutenants and captured a third. (It was lucky for Vásquez that he did not often run into men of Sutherland's mettle.) Still, the bandit got away with $2500 and the two wounded men as well as the healthy members of his band.

After the Kingston raid, the Bakersfield *Southern Californian* opined: "Vásquez seems determined to excel the daredevil exploits of the famous brigand chief, Joaquín Murieta." Monterey and Santa Clara counties had already offered rewards for Vásquez; now the state joined them. Governor Newton Booth offered three thousand dollars for the bandit alive, and two thousand dollars, dead. This did not scare Vásquez. Just a month later, in February of 1874, with only one man to help him, he held up the Coyote Holes stage station near Walker Pass on the road over the Sierra to Inyo. His

343

reputation was enough to buffalo twenty men, who made no resistance. However, "Tex," a drunk who belligerently demanded, "What the hell is up?" was repaid by Vásquez for his insolence with a rifle ball in the leg. The bandit took the Wells, Fargo treasure box, but it proved to be empty of cash, containing only drafts and stock certificates worthless to Vásquez. He departed, with curses, taking all the horses in order to slow pursuit.

Now, the governor decided to imitate his predecessor's action in hiring Harry Love and his California Rangers. Booth hired a far better man than Love in Sheriff Harry Morse of Alameda County, who chose seven men. Four of them were fellow peace officers and a fifth was his son. All were of a superior caliber to Love's roughnecks of twenty-one years earlier. Although Morse was tenacious, intelligent, and capable of using disguise skillfully to move freely in pursuit of his quarry and to gain information, he could not catch Vásquez, even when he carried out the greatest man hunt in California history, a sixty-one-day, 2720-mile expedition. Though technically a failure which led the governor, in desperation, to up the reward to eight thousand dollars and six thousand dollars, Morse actually turned up the clue, or, better, tip, on his hunt which proved to be Vásquez's undoing. Wisely, he offered good money for good information. At Fort Tejon someone leaked to him a tip on the bandit's whereabouts, an adobe on the La Brea Rancho of Greek George Allen in the Cahuenga Mountains near Los Angeles. Morse passed the word to Los Angeles and a disbelieving sheriff finally, after a ten-day delay, dispatched a small posse commanded by the undersheriff, Albert J. Johnston. On May 14, 1874, Johnston got close to the hideout by commandeering a wagon and its drivers and hiding himself and five men in the wagon bed. None of the bandits paid any attention to the familiar wagon until the lawmen jumped out, pistols cocked. Vásquez made a flying leap through a back window of the adobe but right into the sights of George Beers, a San Francisco *Chronicle* reporter who was a member of the posse. Beers's bullet caught him in the shoulder and it was followed by a charge of buckshot from another posseman's weapon. A pained Vásquez was cool. He joked with Beers, "You dress my wounds and nurse me careful, you boys get $8,000! If you let me die, you only get six. You get $2,000 for being kind."

In the Los Angeles jail, fascinated females sent Vásquez food, wine, bouquets of flowers, and letters of sympathy. He was still an *homme fatal*. By a change of venue, he ended up in the San Jose jail and there, again, was the source of much attention from fluttering females. A genuine celebrity, worthy of the attention of a Barnum or a Disney, the murderer posed for photographs which he inscribed and then sold as souvenirs! But he did not sway the jury. They reminded the public that Vásquez was a killer with their verdict—guilty. Judge Belden sentenced him to death by hanging, and Governor Pacheco turned down an appeal for clemency. To keep the crowds down, Sheriff Adams had to print and issue invitations to Vásquez's hanging and, to prevent "scalping," had to mark them "Not Transferable."

Vásquez had nerve. When a devout Christian tried to comfort him with assurances of the immortality of his soul, the bandit answered, "I hope your belief is correct for, in that case, I shall see my old sweethearts tomorrow." When the noose was adjusted in place around his neck, Vásquez had just one word for his hangman, Undersheriff Winchell: *"Pronto!"*

STEPHEN M. WHITE

(1853–1901)

If a statewide poll of Californians were to be taken today in order to select the *typical* Los Angeleno, the winner might be a personage like Sam Goldwyn or Aimee Semple MacPherson, but it would hardly be Stephen Mallory White, although thousands of L.A. citizens pass his statue daily in Civic Center near the County Law Library.

For one thing, White was born in San Francisco (January 19, 1853) and although he moved to Los Angeles in 1874 to be admitted to the bar, hang up his shingle, and start on a lucrative law practice, he remained more a San Franciscan than a Los Angeleno in his manners, his life style. He had attended St. Ignatius College (now University of San Francisco) and Santa Clara College after a boyhood spent in Santa Cruz County's bucolic Pájaro Valley. (His Irish father had fled to California from British oppression.) For another thing, White was neither flashy nor bizarre even when most successful as a politician. He was more solid than flamboyant, whether considered as a true Southern Californian or as a Northern émigré. But he demonstrated a political integrity which impressed most Californians and which won him the support of Southern Californians, urban and rural, as well as the small farmers—particularly of the San Joaquin Valley—who were being victimized by the Southern Pacific Railroad and other agents of monopoly.

Although White had blind spots (e.g., his support of Chinese exclusion) and he compromised often with politicos, out of what he saw to be necessity, his work paved the way for Hiram Johnson and the more thorough-going reforms of the Progressives. Too, like James Phelan, he demonstrated that a man of some taste and intelligence could survive in the jungle of politics. Basically, he was antitrust, anticorruption, and anti-imperialism. He opposed the annexation of Hawaii and American intervention in Cuba. In 1898 he demonstrated his gift for oratory (and integrity) when he vainly opposed our making war on Spain. He reminded his senatorial colleagues that Spain was already yielding to American demands and that war was absolutely unnecessary. But the warhawks had their way. Privately, he was convinced that the reason for their jingoism was not so much patriotism as pressure from sugar interests playing a "grab game" in Hawaii as well as in Cuba.

White never confused mere wealth with monopoly and as an Independent, first, and later as a Democrat, he declared his chief enemy to be "incorporated greed." Although opposed, from time to time, by many powerful Democrats, including Judge Stephen J. Field, George Hearst and Chris ("Christ Almighty") Buckley, the Blind Boss of San Francisco, he was a master-politician himself, and enjoyed a brilliant career in politics. He was elected district attorney of Los Angeles County (1883), presiding officer of the Democratic National Convention (1886), state senator (1887), and U.S. senator (1893). He was a member of San Francisco's Bohemian Club and of the Los Angeles Chamber of Commerce, a trustee of Los Angeles State Normal School (now UCLA) and a regent of the University of California.

Stephen White was born at just the right time. Whether one accepts the traditional or the revisionist view of Reconstruction, there was a turning-point in American history about the time of President Rutherford B. Hayes's inauguration (1877), a turning away from the echoes of the Civil War in order to face up to the need for controls on the social and economic abuses of the Industrial Revolution which had grown up, virtually unchecked, since the War. Rockefeller and Carnegie had organized combinations in oil and steel which had hardened into monopolies which were models for other big-businessmen. Corporations bloomed everywhere, and not only in heavy industry. By the time Stephen White came along, there was even a Whiskey Trust! Business, to protect its interests, hired political bosses in both major parties to battle against profit-cutting social and economic reforms. The ex-San Franciscan entered the fight which Hiram Johnson, Bob LaFollette and Teddy Roosevelt would also join. Nowhere, perhaps, was the struggle more difficult than in California. Gold Rush and vigilante violence had bred a disdain for law in many people, an appetite for violence and a tolerance of venal legislatures, and the acceptance of ruthlessly rugged individualism on the part of business. The battles seesawed back and forth but White and his comrades saw some victories —civil service reform, the Australian ballot, the Corrupt Practices Act, and the Sherman Anti-Trust Act.

Los Angeles was not yet a big city when White moved there and he was so poor that he had to move in with a friend, borrowing money for a little furniture. He proved himself to be an excellent attorney and soon won fame in local land cases in which he put to good use his knowledge of Spanish. He worked hard to patch up the dissension-torn Democratic

Party behind antimonopolist George Stoneman when the latter defeated George Hearst for governor in 1880. For a time, at least, it looked as if the S.P. might, at least, be forced to pay its taxes. But the Democrats were not as strong as they seemed. Stoneman lost supporters and White had to play politics and patronage in order to hold the state's Demos together. He had to support his rival, George Hearst, at times and the party boss he despised particularly, Chris Buckley. White even worked for the S.P. as an attorney and managed, somehow, to emerge untarnished. Finally, I. W. Hellman in 1886 persuaded White to *really* enter politics and he did so, evolving a philosophy of compromise in order to be effective. He would not let crusading get in the way of political solidarity. White chose, always, to work through the Democratic Party structure rather than going it alone out of reforming zeal. Hence, he often had to hold his fire against Buckley and his "lambs" (spoilsmen) although he was disgusted by them and their machinations. He did not like the dirt in politics but he accepted it. Thus he wrote a friend, sarcastically, when a number of candidates for the office of Sacramento postmaster appeared, that he was currently comparing the criminal records of the various possibilities.

White's willingness to accept the "system" guaranteed him political success but it lessened him as a man. Still, because of his great fight against the Southern Pacific in what came to be called the Los Angeles Harbor Contest, he emerges as a bona fide hero of California's political history. During the boom of the 1880's it became evident that Los Angeles would develop into a major port and would have to have a harbor worthy of a metropolis. The Army Engineers reported the best location to be behind a breakwater to be built at San Pedro. But the Southern Pacific Railroad, building a pier at Santa Monica, advocated the location of the new breakwater and port there. A second board of government engineers again recommended San Pedro over Santa Monica, unanimously. According to the *Congressional Record,* the S.P. was buying up seaside land to prevent any other railroads reaching the Pacific. The Los Angeles *Times* predicted that the railroad monopoly would try to secure government funds for its own benefit (again) and, sure enough, Collis P. Huntington appeared at a Congressional hearing to ask for four million dollars for Santa Monica. Although the *Times's* normal press opposition was, for once, in agreement, and although non-partisan support for a free harbor at San Pedro (versus an S.P. controlled port at Santa Monica) was widespread, the Senate Committee on Commerce was in favor of the S.P.'s site and Stephen White had his work cut out for him. He had taken his time to make up his mind but when he compared the two possibilities, he, too, opted for San Pedro. Now, White's plain political skill showed its worth. He successfully worked for a postponement of a vote in the Committee until the session closed, and two of the anti-San Pedro men left the Senate. Then he worked to replace them with non-S.P. and non-Santa Monica men. His allies, like the *Times,* hurt him by trying to hurry him, demanding immediate appropriations for San Pedro. Representative Cannon, a hybrid Democrat-Populist, actually claimed that White had been bullied and frightened by Huntington. Actually, the Government was strapped and White knew the time was not ripe to push a request for three million dollars for San Pedro Harbor. But, as a member of the Steering Committee, he got pro-San Pedro Democrats appointed to the critical Commerce Committee and then got an initial $400,000 for the inner harbor included in the session's Rivers and Harbors Bill. Huntington tried to insert an appropriation for Santa Monica, too, but White got the amendment stricken when he showed the Rivers and Harbors Committee that the S.P. tycoon and his engineers had attended a hearing of which they had kept the California delegation in deliberate ignorance. But now, White almost lost the battle when two of the Commerce Committeemen upon whom he had counted failed him and lined up in a nine-to-six vote for a three-million-dollar appropriation for Santa Monica. It appeared that C. P. Huntington's enormous influence in Congress had won again. Grudgingly, White said of him, "He is really a remarkable individual. He has a large number of rooms at his hotel, has an army of lobbyists [in them] and attends to more work than any of them, himself." He added, "H. told me the other day that it was said that I was the most obstinate man in California, and I said that that was true—when *he* was absent."

The chips were down when White debated with Senator William P. Frye, whose amendment would give Santa Monica (and the S.P.) three million dollars. White offered an amendment to provide the money not for Santa Monica *or* San Pedro but for a place to be designated by a commission. Skillfully, he argued that public money must not be used for individual advantage. Making no demands for San Pedro, he rested his case on the solution of having a disinterested commission decide which site was the best. He won. The Senate supported his plan as being eminently fair. The S.P. did not get its three millions. Huntington did not quit but tried to control the board of experts and White had to compromise. But the vote of the committee was for San Pedro, although Huntington's man dissented. The railroad magnate called in all kinds of delaying actions but victory was White's and on July 21, 1898, Huntington's hopes for a coup were buried when the contract was let for work on the harbor—at San Pedro. It was the most important victory of Stephen White's career, which ended on February 21, 1901 when he died in Los Angeles, survived by his wife and four children.

BENJAMIN D. WILSON

(*1811–78*)

Don Benito Wilson, as the colorful Los Angeleño was called in Mexican-Californian days, was Southern California's Sutter, although their personalities were as different as their careers. Where Sutter fled California almost penniless, Wilson prospered mightily. Today, he is remembered, if at all, because Mount Wilson—of the famed observatory—is named for him. Don Benito built the first trail to the summit when he carried on lumbering operations on the mountain's flanks. It would do him greater justice to recall him as a pre-Gold Rush pioneer (1841) of the Pacific Coast and as an Indian campaigner and grizzly bear hunter of awesome prowess. The name Big Bear Lake was given the body of water in the San Bernardino Mountains because Wilson and some of his *compadres* lassoed twenty-two bears there during a punitive expedition of 1845 which he led at Governor Pío Pico's request against Indians who were raiding the ranchos.

Wilson has never had a full-scale biographer, where Sutter has had a half-dozen. But John Caughey of UCLA, who studied the ex-Tennesseean as much as anyone, held that he was an average man in unusual times rather than an exceptional individual. Maybe so. But when only fifteen years of age, Ben Wilson kept a trading post to the Choctaws and Chickasaws near Vicksburg, Mississippi, and although he had to move west because of his declining health, he was still tough enough to survive being shot with a poisoned arrow by California Indian marauders.

Before he went to California, Wilson stopped off in New Mexico. He arrived at Sante Fe in 1833 and trapped the Gila River for the Rocky Mountain Fur Company. After eight years in New Mexico as a mountain man, during which time he was captured by murderous Apaches but managed to escape with the help of Chief Mangas Coloradas, who took a liking to him, Wilson decided to head for California via the Old Spanish Trail. He marched with the John Rowland-William Workman party of 1841 from Abiquiú, near Taos, to Los Angeles, driving a herd of sheep through the rugged and arid Southwest. His final destination was not California but China. However, failing to find a ship bound for the Orient, Wilson made the best of California.

Ben Wilson settled down, married Ramona Yorba, daughter of ranchero Don Bernardo Yorba and turned rancher, himself, at Jurupa, near today's Riverside and San Bernardino. Unlike Sutter, Bidwell, and other pioneers, Wilson never got a land grant. The Nashvillian refused to apply for Mexican citizenship and preferred to buy his land. He secured several other ranches, including a half-interest in San José de Buenos Aires (site of UCLA) and Hugo Reid's ranch, which he renamed Lake Vineyard, near the site of the modern Huntington Library. Before he was through, Don Benito Wilson owned large portions of Los Angeles, San Bernardino, San Pedro, Pasadena, South Pasadena, San Marino, Alhambra and San Gabriel. He never really missed China. He finally wrote, "After many unsuccessful attempts to leave California and receiving so much kindness from the native Californians, I arrived at the conclusion that there was no place in the world where I could enjoy more true happiness and true friendship than among them. There were no courts, no juries, no lawyers, nor any need for them. The people were honest and hospitable, and their word was as good as their bond."

Benito Wilson took part in the defeat of Governor Micheltorena and John Sutter at Cahuenga in 1845. He was, briefly, held prisoner by the native Californians during the Mexican War because he tried to remain neutral, like Sutter, in the conflict. Finally, he helped conciliate the opposing forces. Wilson played no real role in the Gold Rush, preferring to tend his cattle and vines. He allowed himself to be elected Mayor of Los Angeles but it was just a sleepy, dusty, cowtown, then, alongside a very intermittent Los Angeles River.

One of the strongest characteristics of the man was his understanding of, and compassion for, the Indians. He was aware that his ideas were ahead of their time and suggested to historian Hubert H. Bancroft that whatever credit he deserved should come because of his work in behalf of the Indians. As Indian Sub-agent for California's Southern District —about the size of New England!—he searched for and found reservation sites, held councils, and supervised the supplying of the reservation Indians with rations. His friend, Benjamin Hayes, explained the choice of Wilson for the post: "Before his appointment, their chiefs, visiting the City, habitually came to see and talk with him about their business, as much as if he were their Agent. Notoriously, he is a favorite with them—no stranger. His good sense, kindness of heart, knowledge of mountain life, familiarity with all the tribes and reputation for integrity of purpose are difficult to combine in anyone else."

Before he resigned, because of disagreements with his

superiors, Wilson submitted an important report on *The Indians of Southern California in 1852*. Probably, Benjamin Hayes helped him by polishing up his phraseology and cleaning up his orthography, but the ideas were his own. He saw that the Indians needed protection from the whites, not vice versa, just as J. Ross Browne argued. Raids by any of the former, he stated, were followed by the bloodier counter-raids of the latter on *any* Indians, guilty or innocent, who happened to be handy and, finally, by the generous filing of preposterous war claims against the Federal or State government. He strongly supported the reservation system of the original Indian Commissioners and Superintendent of Indian Affairs Edward F. Beale but after the removal of the latter, for political reasons, he saw the system so corrupted that he had to agree with J. Ross Browne that a California Indian reservation was a place "where a very large amount of money was annually expended in feeding white men and starving Indians."

As a major landholder on the coast, Wilson ran cattle and sheep and drove them as far as Sacramento, to feed the mining towns. He raised oranges, lemons, wheat, barley, alfalfa, pears and walnuts, experimented with sugar cane, mulberry trees (for silk) and planted grapes and made fine wines. Eventually, his vintages were sold in New York, Boston, Philadelphia and across the Pacific in Japan. A life-long Democrat, Wilson was stubbornly pro-Confederate although he donated the land for Drum Barracks, chief post in Southern California of the Union Army. He managed to weather the storm of the Civil War, whose waves broke even on Southern California's political shores. Besides silk and sugar, he guessed wrong only on oil in his investments. He gave up when he found only water, gas, and dry holes. Wilson dabbled in early telegraph and railroad projects but really made his mark in water

355

and real estate development of Southern California. Thrice —1855, 1869, and 1870—he was a state senator. Besides being Mayor of Los Angeles, he had been alcalde, or justice of the peace, of his district in Mexican times.

As perhaps the most prominent agriculturist and public figure south of the Tehachapi Mountains, it was only natural that Don Benito Wilson should be the recipient of hundreds of letters from Americans in the East who were curious about California. He became an enthusiastic booster, anticipating Charles Lummis as a sort of one-man chamber of commerce. His booming of the area had much to do with the several land rushes to California after the Civil War. As he aged in the '70's, he kept up his promotion of Southern California but had to turn much of the actual letter-writing over to his son-in-law, J. DeBarth Shorb. As a politician, Wilson was less impressive than William Gwin, Phineas Banning or Benjamin Hayes. But, with Abel Stearns, he typified the Yankee turned Mexican *patrón* and gentleman-farmer.

INDEX OF NAMES

357

358

Stanford, Leland, 47, 52, 108, 116, 156, 158, 182–86, 294–99
Stanislaus, 329
Stanton, Charles T., 238, 287, 288
Stearns, Abel, 19, 356
Steffens, Lincoln, 178
Steinbeck, John, 5
Stellifer the King, 276
Sterling, George, 8, 53–55
Stevenson, Robert Louis, 87, 300–5, 321
Stewart, George R., 43, 88
Stockton, Robert F., 99, 208, 331
Stoddard, Charles Warren, 228
Sublette, Bill, 39, 40, 291, 292
Sutherland, J. W., 343
Sutro, Adolph, 10, 24, 155, 306–11
Sutter, John, 17, 40, 43–46, 57, 94, 97, 98, 206–8, 242–47, 280, 287, 290, 312–20, 327–31, 352, 354
Swift, John Franklin, 324
Sykes, Bill, 154

Taft, William Howard, 177
Taylor, Bayard, 174, 251
Taylor, Edward Robeson, 187
Taylor, Zachary, 40
Thacker, Jonathan, 30, 152
Thoreau, Henry, 79, 259
Thorn, Ben K., 29
Three Fingered Jack, 222
Tojetti, Amelio, 146
Tora, 143
Tovey, Mike, 154
Troy, Thomas, 143, 144
Twain, Mark, 11–12, 54, 63, 90, 129–31, 277, 321–26

Ung Hung, 74

Vallejo, Mariano, 279, 315, 327–32
Van Nuys, Issac, 333–37
Vásquez, Luis, 40
Vásquez, Tiburcio, 194, 338–45

Waldo, William, 92
Walker, Franklin, 129
Walker, Robert J., 60–61
Walker, William, 248
Wallace, David R., 33
Wasson, Tom, 341, 342
Waterman, T. T., 160, 161, 164
Webber, J. B., 160
Wheaton, Frank, 169
White, Stephen M., 25, 134, 346–51
White, Stewart Edward, 172, 217
Whitfield, W. H., 142
Whitman, Walt, 141, 253
Whitney, Josiah D., 257–58
Whittier, John Greenleaf, 97, 100
Wilbur, Ray Lyman, 295
Wild Yankee, the, 2
Williams, Virgil, 146
"Wilmington, Duke of," 22
Wilson, Benjamin D., 23, 352–56
Winchell (undersheriff), 345
Wister, Owen, 90, 253
Woodward, R. B., 111–12
Woodworth, Selim, 289
Wright, Ben, 167
Wueste, R. C., 136
Wyatt, 209

Yelland, Raymond, 146
Yellow Bird, 112, 223
Yorba, Ramona, 353
Young, Brigham, 10, 56–58, 97
Young, John Russell, 118